International Intervention in Ethnic Conflict

International Intervention in Ethnic Conflict

A Comparison of the European Union and the United Nations

Etain Tannam

Assistant Professor in International Peace Studies, Trinity College Dublin, Ireland

First published 2014 by
PALGRAVE MACMILLAN

Palgrave Macmillan in the UK is an imprint of Macmillan Publishers Limited, registered in England, company number 785998, of Houndmills, Basingstoke, Hampshire RG21 6XS.

Palgrave Macmillan in the US is a division of St Martin's Press LLC, 175 Fifth Avenue, New York, NY 10010.

Palgrave Macmillan is the global academic imprint of the above companies and has companies and representatives throughout the world.

Palgrave® and Macmillan® are registered trademarks in the United States, the United Kingdom, Europe and other countries.

ISBN 978–0–230–27335–1

This book is printed on paper suitable for recycling and made from fully managed and sustained forest sources. Logging, pulping and manufacturing processes are expected to conform to the environmental regulations of the country of origin.

A catalogue record for this book is available from the British Library.

A catalog record for this book is available from the Library of Congress.

For Matthew and Michael
and
In memory of Professor Dónal Hollywood
(1959–2013)

Contents

Tables

Acknowledgements

I would like to thank the Start-Up Fund, Trinity College Dublin, for funding this research, as well as all the officials I interviewed in the EU, the UN and Irish Department of Foreign Affairs and Trade, Sam Daws and Thomas Weiss. I would also like to thank all my colleagues at the Irish School of Ecumenics Trinity College Dublin, and all the students who have undertaken MPhil in International Peace Studies for creating such a supportive and stimulating environment: Carlo Aldrovandi, Iain Atack, Christine Houlahan, Jude Fernando Lal, Andrew Pierce, Mary Priestman, Geraldine Smyth, Aideen Woods and Gillian Wylie. I am also grateful to my former colleagues in the Dublin European Institute, University College Dublin (UCD), especially Dolores Burke, and Ben Tonra; to John Coakley, School of Politics and International Relations, UCD; James Ker-Lindsay, European Institute, London School of Economics and Political Science; Neophytos Loizides, University of Kent and Stefan Wolff, Department of Political Science and International Studies, University of Birmingham. Thanks also to former colleagues in the Department of Political Science, Trinity College Dublin, especially Michael Gallagher and to my PO4700 political science students. Special thanks, as always, to Robert Elgie and to my late mother Rosaleen Tannam and to Des Tannam.

Abbreviations

ACABQ	Advisory Committee on Administrative and Budgetary Questions
AIA	Anglo-Irish Agreement
AKEL	Progressive Party of Working People
CAP	Common Agricultural Policy
CFSP	Common Foreign and Security Policy
COREPER	11 Committee of Permanent Representatives
CPC	Committee for Programme and Coordination
CSCE	Conference in Security and Cooperation in Europe
DFA	Department of Foreign Affairs and Trade
DG	Directorate General
DG	RELEX Directorate-General for the External Relations
DPKO	Department of Peacekeeping Operations
DPA	Department of Political Affairs
DRC	Democratic Republic of Congo
ECJ	European Court of Justice
ECSC	European Coal and Steel Community
EDC	European Defence Community
EEAS	European External Action Service
EEC	European Economic Community
ENP	European Neighbourhood Policy
EOKA	*Ethniki Organosis Kyprion Agoniston* (National Organization of Cypriot Fighters)
EP	European Parliament
EPC	European Political Cooperation
ESC	Economic and Social Council
ESDP	European Security and Defence Policy
EUFOR	European Union Force
EULEX	European Union Rule of Law Mission in Kosovo
FMLN	Farabundo Marti National Liberation Front

FOD	Field Operations Division
GFA	Good Friday Agreement
HLP	High Level Panel on Threats Challenges and Change
ICISS	International Commission in Intervention and State Sovereignty
ICJ	International Court of Justice
ICTY	International Criminal Tribunal for Former Yugoslavia
IIC	Independent Inquiry Committee into the Oil-for-Food Programme
JFD	Joint Framework Document
KLA	Kosovo Liberation Army
KVM	Kosovo Verification Mission
LDK	Democratic League of Kosovo
MEP	Member of the European Parliament
MINUSAL	United Nations Mission in El Salvador
NATO	North Atlantic Treaty Organization
NGO	Non-governmental organization
NSMC	North South Ministerial Council
OEEC	Organisation for European Economic Co-operation
OFOESA	Office of Field Operational and External Support Activities
ONUMOZ	The United Nations Operation in Mozambique
ONUSAL	United Nations Observer Mission in El Salvador
ORCI	Office for Research and Collection of Information
OSPA	Office of Special Political Affairs
P-5	Permanent Five
PISG	Provisional Institutions of Self-Government
PLO	Palestinian Liberation Organisation
R2P	Responsibility to Protect
RCC	Baltic Regional Cooperation Council
SAMCOMM	Missions Communication System in Brussels
SCA	Special Agriculture Committee
SDLP	Social Democratic and Labour Party

SEA	Single European Act
SEM	Single European Market
SEUPB	Special EU Programmes Body
SPU	Strategic Planning Unit
SRSG	Special Representative of the Secretary-General
TRNC	Turkish Republic of Northern Cyprus
UDI	Unilateral Declaration of Independence
UNAMIR	United Nations Assistance Mission for Rwanda
UNEF1	UN Emergency Force
UNFICYP	United Nations Peacekeeping Force in Cyprus
UNHCR	United Nations High Commission for Refugees
UNIFIL	United Nations Interim Force in Lebanon
UNMIK	United Nations Mission in Kosovo
UNOSOM	United Nations Operation in Somalia
UNPROFOR	United Nations Protection Force in the Balkans
UNSC	United Nations Security Council
UNSOEK	United Nations Special Envoy's Office for Kosovo
UNTAC	United Nations Transitional Authority for Cambodia

1
International Intervention, Ethnic Conflict and Theory

Since the early 1990s, international intervention in ethnic conflict has gained increasing attention. The dramatic failures of the international community to respond effectively to genocide and violence in the Balkans, Rwanda and many other cases have led to criticisms of international actors for poor management and for failing to prevent conflict (Tonra, 2007). However, detailed accounts of international organizations' policy-making processes in conflict resolution are relatively rare. This book focuses on the role of bureaucracies in two international organizations, the European Union (EU) and the United Nations (UN), in dealing with conflict and compares these organizations' policy-making processes to determine how far they differ and why they differ from each other.

This chapter explains the aims of the book and the rationale for setting out these aims. In the first section, definitions of ethnic conflict, international intervention and international organizations are provided, followed by an overview of International Relations perspectives on international intervention. In the final section, an overview of methodology is presented.

Aims and definitions

The main argument of this book is that the UN Secretariat and the European Commission have autonomy under certain conditions and that reducing explanations of EU and UN's policy outcomes to 'political will', or to the preferences of member states, is inaccurate. Autonomy is defined as 'the capacity to act independently' (Verhoest et al., 2004, p. 9), and it refers to 'the extent of decision-making competencies and the constraints exercised over performance of those competencies' (Verhoest et al., 2004, p. 9). International intervention is defined in this book as comprising economic, diplomatic or military actions by the EU and UN to bring about cooperation in conflict or post-conflict zones. Conflict is defined as 'a situation in which two or more actors pursue incompatible, yet from their individual perspectives entirely just goals' (Cordell and Wolff, 2011, p. 4). Ethnic conflict is defined as a conflict where the goals of at least one party in the conflict are defined in (exclusively) ethnic terms and in which the primary fault line of confrontation is one of ethnic distinctions' (Cordell and Wolff, 2011, p. 4). The EU and UN are both defined as international institutions': 'sets of rules meant to govern international behaviour' (Simmons and Martin, 2001, p. 194). This approach avoids any 'qualifying criteria about the social construction of rules, nor about whether rules are explicit, or implicit', and informal rules may be defined as norms (Simmons and Martin, 2001, p. 194).

The definition of international intervention adopted in this book reflects the fact that whereas classical approaches to intervention viewed military intervention as inevitable and as the best way of achieving peace, contemporary definitions emphasize multifaceted approaches, including diplomacy and the engagement of grass-roots actors (Ramsbotham et al., 2009, p. 25). External intervention comprises non-coercive intervention, coercive intervention and mediation. Non-coercive intervention refers to international actors that either provide incentives for cooperation, for example, EU membership, or inflict punishments for actors who do not cooperate, for example, the use of sanctions (Lake and Rothchild, 1996, p. 65). Coercive power refers to military intervention, or humanitarian intervention. Thus a range of tools is available for the EU and UN in intervening in conflict.

EU and UN interventions are examined in three cases in this book: Northern Ireland, 1988–98; Cyprus, 2002–04; and Kosovo/Serbia (the Kosovo–Serbia relationship), 2006–08. In Northern Ireland, it is assumed that the conflict has been resolved, although tensions still exist, and in Kosovo and Cyprus the conflicts are frozen. The Council Secretariat is also examined in the Kosovo/Serbia case study, but overall, the Commission is the main focus of this study.

It must be noted that the aim of this book is not to evaluate the EU and UN's success in resolving conflict in the three cases, but to examine and compare their policy-making processes with particular emphasis on the role of bureaucracy. The underlying assumption is that even though some policies may be unsuccessful, it is possible to discover ways of improving policy outcomes by understanding the policy-making process more deeply. The theoretical rationale for examining the role of bureaucracy is derived from comparative politics literature, where bureaucracies are shown to have significant autonomy because of their policy expertise and capacity to implement policies, especially where policies are vague (Huber and Shipan, 2002, p. 12). However, as this chapter shows, the rationale for this book is also drawn from debates in International Relations theory and from empirical gaps in that debate.

Empirical and theoretical rationale

The task of comparing the role of the UN Secretariat with the European Commission and Council Secretariat's role is a complicated one that begs many questions. Firstly, many observers would comment that the EU and the UN are not comparable. For example, as the next paragraphs show, their bureaucracies have different roles and powers, and both the UN and the EU have markedly different institutional frameworks. The underlying assumption of this book is that although the two organizations have different structures, rules and membership, their status as international organizations, their post-war birth, their common aims of conflict resolution and the EU's increased activities in conflict resolution make a comparison necessary and possible. Thus, the core rationale is that there is a need to establish 'systematic comparisons across time, across states, or across international institutions...to explain the world around us' (Martin and Simmons, 2013, p. 344). Moreover, the very existence of differences between the EU and the UN justifies a comparison to highlight the specific features of each organization, which may contribute to certain outcomes.

Clearly, the functions of EU and UN's bureaucracies vary, as discussed in Chapter 2. For example, unlike a classical bureaucracy, under the Rome Treaty, the Commission has formal policy initiation and implementation powers in designated policy areas, whereas the

UN Secretariat does not have initiation powers formally. The hybrid nature of the Commission may lead to the criticism that it obviously has a degree of autonomy from EU member states and that it will have more autonomy than the UN Secretariat. However, as this chapter shows, in fact there is an ongoing academic debate about the Commission's role vis-à-vis the member states' role': does it simply reflect the preferences of France, Germany and the UK, or is it a supranational entrepreneur? The Commission has no formal initiating power in EU foreign policy, so it might not be expected to display autonomy in conflict resolution issues. Similarly, there is a debate about the role of the UN Secretariat: are its rules and standard operating procedures responsible for policy failures in the UN, or is the Secretariat simply beholden to the instructions of the UN Security Council (UNSC)? Thus, the different formal powers of the Commission and the UN Secretariat do not imply that they should not be compared, but rather these differences actually beg a question about whether these formal powers influence their levels of autonomy in practice. In other words, the differences between the Commission and the UN Secretariat point to the need for more systematic empirical comparison of their relationship with EU and UN member states.

Another possible criticism of the decision to compare the EU and UN's bureaucracies is that both bureaucracies use different tools in resolving conflict. The UN Secretariat's key role in conflict resolution is its mediation role, implying its use of diplomacy and envoys to resolve conflicts, bolstered by aid, at times. Thus the Cyprus and Kosovo/Serbia case studies focus on the role of the Secretariat's small mediating team who were sanctioned by the UNSC to negotiate a political agreement. In contrast, the Commission's involvement was through EU enlargement policy to entice agreement in Cyprus and in Kosovo/Serbia. In Northern Ireland the Commission aimed to bolster the peace process through economic aid packages to Northern Ireland to bolster the peace process in the 1990s. Thus, the role and functions of the bureaucracies differ.

Again, this difference between the Commission and the UN Secretariat is not problematic but actually reveals the potential for theoretical and empirical richness in comparing both institutions. Specifically, does the EU's emphasis on enlargement policy as a tool of conflict resolution imply that the Commission has more autonomy from member states in conflict resolution by using a functional policy area, or does the Secretariat's power to mediate in a conflict (an explicitly political role) provide equal or more autonomy to its officials? This question is at the heart of a larger and enduring debate between International Relations theorists, as this chapter will show. Overall, the aim of this book is to determine whether EU and UN bureaucracies, dealing with similar conflict problems, but often using different tools, display autonomy from EU and UN member states, and if so, what are the underlying conditions that allow this autonomy to exist. Rather than posing a methodological and intellectual obstacle, the differences between the Commission and the UN Secretariat form a justification for this study. These differences are not obstacles to the study, but rather, they justify it. In the next section, the theoretical justification for this book is elaborated.

International Relations perspectives

A core debate in International Relations has been 'do international institutions really matter?', and 'missing from this debate is sustained inquiry into how these institutions actually work' (Koremenos et al., 2001, p. 761). In this section, key theoretical approaches to international cooperation are examined and their relevance to EU and UN intervention is explored, exposing the theoretical gap in the literature about how the EU and UN make policies with respect to ethnic conflict.

As a grand theory, neo-realism has much to say about international intervention in conflict, by arguing that if intervention occurs, it does so because of state preferences. Drawing from realism, international law is argued to reflect power politics and is 'divorced altogether from ethics.... It is an expression of the will of the state and it is used by those who control the state as an instrument of coercion against those who oppose their power' (Carr, 1981, p. 176). Fundamental to both realism and neo-realism is an assumption that individuals and states are prey to constant and innate insecurity and fear. Five additional assumptions can be identified: (1) the international system is anarchic, comprising separate states with no government; (2) states possess offensive military capacity giving them the potential to inflict hurt and destruction; (3) states can never be certain about the intentions of others; (4) the basic motivation for state behaviour is survival; and (5) states are concerned with their relative gains, not their absolute gains as they wish to maintain the exiting balance of power (Mearsheimer, 1994, p. 10). Therefore, international institutions do not cause cooperation; they reflect state preferences and calculations (Mearsheimer, 1994, p. 13).

It is argued that these assumptions underlie both EU and UN intervention in conflict. The interests and preferences of states will determine whether both organizations intervene in ethnic conflict, as well as how they intervene. The development of EU foreign policy, involving increased intervention in conflict zones, is explained by state preferences and the demise of the Soviet Union. Post-war European cooperation is also explained by state preferences, not by the EU as an institution (Paul, 2005, p. 57). The EU's key states seek to provide a balance to the US, in the absence the Soviet Union (Paul, 2005, p. 57). However, while applications of neo-realism to the EU exist, 'neo-realists like Waltz have not been much interested in European integration processes' (Stone, 1994, p. 457), and theoretical explanations for EU intervention in ethnic conflict have not been well developed by neo-realists. In contrast, many explanations for UN intervention make neo-realist assumptions, although not always in a rigorous manner.

For neo-realists, the dominant role of UNSC, the use of veto on the UNSC and the enshrinement of sovereignty as an underlying principle in the UN Charter imply that state preferences will dominate, particularly those of the permanent five (P-5) on the UNSC. According to neo-realists, there are countless examples of this domination. UN military intervention in Syria in 2012 was impeded by a Russian and Chinese veto. UN recognition of Kosovo as an independent state was impeded by Russia and China on the UNSC (Ker-Lindsay, 2009). In addition, development of the doctrine of Responsibility to Protect (R2P) has provoked a stronger debate about whether state preferences are the sole force behind UN intervention.

The International Commission on Intervention and State Sovereignty (ICIS) chaired by Gareth Evans, former Australian foreign minister, developed the R2P doctrine to circumvent limitations of just war theory (based on state sovereignty) by setting out conditions that justify international intervention in conflict, even though a sovereign state does not consent to intervention. Although intervention is often assumed to be defined solely in military terms, the

R2P doctrine has placed great emphasis on mediation, early warning and conflict prevention (Evans, 2011). The key conditions for military intervention are whether or not there is a case of large-scale human rights violations and whether a 'last resort' threshold has been reached and whether multiple criteria, including moral legitimacy and international legal authority, good advocacy mechanisms, good arguments and good leadership exist (Evans, 2011).

Critics of R2P point to empirical evidence whereby humanitarian crises have not met with an effective response. For example, Western strategic interests have been blamed for the failure to implement R2P in Darfur (Bellamy, 2005, p. 52). Similarly, in explaining UK's policies on Afghanistan and Kosovo, it has been observed that even if there are ethical dimensions to explaining international intervention, 'ethical humanitarianism is part of, not the only justification' (Bulley, 2010, p. 448). However, these criticisms and the neo-realist perspective do not examine international institutions in any depth. In contrast, rationalist approaches since the 1950s have examined the independent impact of institutions on international cooperation, and by implication its findings are relevant to comparing the EU and UN's approaches to international intervention.

Rationalists

In contrast to neo-realists, neo-functionalists, rational institutionalists and intergovernmental institutionalists have devoted more attention to the development of international cooperation and institutions and to the evolution of EU. Neo-functionalism was the first 'school' that provided a theoretical account of the role of international institutions, specifically the role of the European Commission (Koremenos et al., 2001). The expansion of the welfare state and severe economic problems in the post-war period meant that economic policy necessitated political coordination by a centralized institution – the European Commission. Once formed, the supranational institution would provide an underlying dynamism for the integration process by upgrading common interests. In other words, state preferences would gradually change as the Commission persuaded them of the merits of an increased number of common policies. The Commission's status under the Rome Treaty is that of a guardian of the Treaty, its formal powers to initiate policy and its technical expertise all empowered it to 'upgrade' interests.

This upgrading was more effective than other bargaining processes – a compromise – satisfies no state completely and lowest common denominator agreements were so diluted to be meaningless. However, upgrading interests implied that significant policy integration would occur, but with member state support – a non-zero-sum outcome. The central institution's interaction with national agents was also to be used as a measure of integration. The neo-functionalist view assumed that Commission officials themselves would subsume the aims of the European project and adopt Europhile preferences. The EU would also be characterized by a growing number of networks of EU and national actors whose interests and activities intermeshed-*engrenage*.

In more recent accounts of European integration, many of the above neo-functionalist assumptions are retained (Niemann and Schmitter, 2009). However, more recent studies criticize the classical debate between intergovernmentalists and neo-functionalists for focusing solely on whether integration occurs, or whether national sovereignty dominates in a zero-sum manner, rather than examining the EU as a complex political multi-layered system (Rosamund, 2013, p. 89). Supranational governance theorists argue that the role of the autonomous supranational Commission is central to understanding the evolution of EU (Stone-Sweet and Sandholtz, 1998, p. 6). The EU moves on a continuum between intergovernmentalism and supranationalism, and the presence and intensity of rules, organizations and transnational society determines how supranational is the EU in a given policy area (Stone-Sweet and Sandholtz, 1998, p. 9). The transactionalist approach explains why integration across policy sectors varies and also rectifies the myopia caused by focusing only on grand bargains in EU history, which by their nature are intergovernmental (Stone-Sweet and Sandholtz 1998, p. 14). Institutionalization is a crucial component in garnering transnational demands and creating a supranationalist dynamic:

> Rules define roles and the EU's supranational institutions gradually shape what actors define as their interest. Notably, where there is no Treaty basis for growth of supranational activity, in the midst of increased cross-border activity, the relevant actors will create one.
>
> (Stone-Sweet and Sandholtz, 1998, p. 19)

Over time, rules evolve in unpredictable ways and national actors become locked into those rules through a process of path-dependence (Stone-Sweet and Sandholtz, 1998, p. 19). This process of path-dependence has been illustrated by the growth of specific directorate generals in the EU from 1960 to 1993. Fligstein and McNichol showed that almost all expansion of competences occurred after major treaty revisions in order to achieve the EU's original purposes – for example, the single market. However, 'this "frame" has been used skilfully to make agreements that have substantially expanded the policy domains of the EU' (Fligstein and McNichol, 1998, p. 74). Path-dependence helps explain this development. As the number of decisions made by policy actors increases (issue density), supranational autonomy increases, because national actors cannot firmly control policy developments (Pierson, 1998, p. 39). Issue density creates overloaded problems and also leads to a process of spillover. The short-term horizon of politicians implies that these developments have unintended consequences to which they are locked in. These institutional dynamics empower EU supranational institutions over time.

A similar approach to examining international institutions is adopted by principal–agent theorists (Pollack, 2003). The key arguments are that states (the principals) set up institutions (the agents) to serve their aims, but agents have an independent influence on policy outcomes. The agents may have a monopoly of information and expertise that makes it difficult for the principal to regulate its behaviour (Pollack, 2003, p. 36). The principal may delegate agenda-setting to the agent (Pollack, 2003, p. 36). These functions and the influence of the agent become locked in, as the transaction costs of changing arrangements is too large (Pollack, 2003, p. 37). Comparing the EU and UN policy-making processes with respect to their rules and to the extent to which they are locked into their rules with unintended consequences is an important aspect of examining EU and UN policy-making towards conflict zones.

In contrast to the above accounts, rational institutionalists counter the supranational underpinnings of neo-functionalism and do not focus on European integration in much depth, but agree that international institutions explain international cooperation under certain conditions (Keohane and Martin, 2001, p. 41), not simply state preferences. Early institutionalist work examined the conditions under which institutions were created (Keohane and Martin, 2001, p. 46). However, later work examined the impact of institutions on political outcomes 'to demonstrate that institutions are sometimes significant for political outcomes and to determine the conditions under which this is the case' (Keohane and Martin, 2001, p. 47). For example, rather than relative gains always determining state behaviour, one study showed that in issues involving oil pollution, 'whether states complied with institutional regulation depended on the nature of the rules' and that rules had an independent causal effect on behaviour (Keohane and Martin, 2001, p. 48).

The above rational institutionalist accounts tended to ignore the EU. However, in contrast, intergovernmental institutionalists addressed the EU and institutionalism by explaining how EU outcomes reflected key states' interests, moulded by the Commission, but not determined by the Commission (Moravcsik, 1999). Moravcsik investigated whether there was a new statecraft 'grounded in international networks managed by supranational entrepreneurs' (Moravcsik, 1999, p. 267). Moravcsik summarized that the main source of supranational power is the manipulation of ideas and information (Moravcsik, 1999, p. 271). However, he argued that in asserting supranational influence, researchers must identify informational asymmetries that impede effective negotiation and describe how and why international officials are in a unique position to overcome resultant bargaining bottlenecks (Moravcsik, 1999, p. 272). Instead of anecdotal causal explanations, Moravcsik argued that supranational actors influence outcomes only where:

> [r]apid economic or political change lead to new social interests, where transnational coordination is required and where cross-issue package deals among highly heterogeneous issues (from the perspective of domestic bureaucracy) are necessary to achieve a bargain.
>
> (Moravcsik, 1999, pp. 284–85)

However, EU enlargement is argued to provide an example of a policy area that does allow for more supranational entrepreneurship (Moravcsik, 2009, p. 410). The EU's institutional framework may be necessary to manage enlargement successfully.

The above accounts focus on the benefits of institutions in inter-state bargaining and on whether they are the sum of their parts (member state preferences) or have added value to policy outcomes. Other rationalist literature examines the specific designs of institutions and is helpful in identifying dimensions of comparison between the EU and UN. In examining why differences exist between various institutions, it is assumed by rationalists that states design institutions to further their own goals (Koremenos et al., 2001, p. 762). For that reason, states pay attention to their design. While states design institutions, these institutions also evolve, as new problems arise and members learn from past experience (Koremenos et al., 2001, p. 767). Of specific relevance to comparing the EU and UN, institutions may vary according to five key dimensions (Koremenos et al., 2001, p. 763): membership rules; scope of issues covered; flexibility of arrangements; centralization of tasks; and rules for controlling the institution. Membership may be universal or restricted. Scope may be narrow, or it may include issues that seem unrelated. Where unrelated issues are included, these issues may be manipulated to allow side-payments to occur and therefore facilitate agreement (Koremonos et al., 2001, p. 770). Centralization of authority in an international institution is viewed as a threat to sovereignty, but the EU is an example of such centralization, albeit uniquely so (Korememos et al., 2001, p. 771). However, other institutions also have some centralized powers; for example, information gathering, bargaining and dispute resolution (Korememos et al., 2001, p. 771). Control relates to questions such as how decisions are made; what are the rules for electing officials; and do all members have equal votes? As regards flexibility, the core question is how rules and procedures shall accommodate new circumstances (Koremenos et al., 2001, p. 773). The type of institution designed is a response to various factors, according to this logic: uncertainty about each state's behaviour and their preferences, uncertainty about 'the state of the world' and enforcement problems in a given issue area as well as the number of relevant actors in a given issue area (Koremenos et al., 2001, p. 778). These reasons determine institutional design. In turn, there are various conjectures about how these variables interact; for example, flexibility will increase with uncertainty (Koremenos et al., 2001, p. 793). All the above-mentioned rational institutionalist accounts assume that interests are at the heart of behaviour. Another, but increasingly complementary, starting point to understanding EU and UN governance is provided by constructivists.

Constructivists

For constructivists, ideas and norms provide the clearest understanding of social behaviour, hence of international relations: 'Constructivism is centrally concerned with the role of ideas in constructing social life' (Fearon and Wendt, 2002, p. 57). For example, the concept of normative power in Europe (Manners, 2006) implies that the EU can use the prospect of EU membership to entice states to adopt EU norms. Although norms may matter for rational institutionalists also, a key distinction can be drawn between the use of norms in both constructivism and rational institutionalism: do actors respond in a certain way because they feel it is their role, or because they have calculated the benefits of doing so (the logic of appropriateness vs. the logic of consequences) (Jupille et al., 2003, p. 14). Secondly, do they adopt norms because it is useful (a rational institutionalist and a neo-realist approach), or because they think it is right or legitimate to do so (a constructivist approach) (Fearon and Wendt, 2002, p. 61)? For constructivists, norms become internalized, that is, they become preferences in themselves (Fearon and Wendt, 2002, p. 61). Indeed, as the next section shows, in contrast to neo-realism, 'one branch of research associated with sociological theories focuses on the role of IOs [international organizations] as international bureaucracies with agency in their own right' (Martin and Simmons, 2013, p. 335).

Rather than treating institutions as mere arenas or mechanisms through which other actors pursue interests, some constructivist approaches explore the social content of organizations – culture, legitimacy concerns and dominant norms (Barnett and Finnemore, 1999, p. 706). For example, the decision of who is a refugee is not only legal but also discursive (Barnett and Finnemore, 1999, p. 711). Bureaucracies are empowered and legitimized by their rules – 'just doing my job' (Barnett and Finnemore, 1999, p. 708). Bureaucracies are also powerful because they have specialized technical expertise that is not available to other actors (Barnett and Finnemore, 1999, p. 708). Bureaucracies present themselves as depoliticized and neutral (Barnett and Finnemore, 1999, p. 708). However, bureaucracies 'always serve some social purpose, or set of cultural values' (Barnett and Finnemore, 1999, p. 708). In addition, bureaucracies behave in a certain manner because of their concern to appear to be rational (Barnett and Finnemore, 1999, p. 708). International organizations' bureaucracies are 'prone to dysfunctional behaviours'

(Barnett and Finnemore, 1999, p. 715), and 'rules and routines may come to obscure overall mission and larger social goals' (Barnett and Finnemore, 1999, p. 718). In addition, specialization and compartmentalization may limit bureaucrats' field of vision and lead to sub-optimal outcomes (Barnett and Finnemore, 1999, p. 719). Different segments may also develop different world views and experience different local stimuli from their environment (Barnett and Finnemore, 1999, p. 724). There are also variations in the degree to which information received is processed and fed back about performance (Barnett and Finnemore, 1999, p. 722).

Drawing from Barnett and Finnemore, the UN's failure to respond effectively to genocide in Rwanda is studied by examining the UN's Secretariat from a sociological institutional perspective. The argument made is that bureaucratic inflexibility and irrationality impeded the UN in Rwanda (Piiparinen, 2008, p. 699). Rather than UN intervention, or non-intervention being reduced to the political will of states, 'bureaucracies wield considerable powers by classifying and organizing information, fixing meanings and defining the norms of proper behaviour' (Piiparinen, 2008, p. 699). In the case of the UN, the Secretariat's expertise was enhanced in the early 1990s (Piiparinen, 2008, p. 701). However, the rules and norms of the Secretariat led to 'concerns about Rwanda' being 'replaced by heartless bureaucratic logic' (Barnett, 2003, pp. 174–91). In particular, there was a primary concern to appear non-partisan which impeded a swift reaction, or prevention of genocide. Also there was a preoccupation with maintaining a peace-keeping approach, necessitating that all parties to a conflict consented to the deployment of UN troops (Piiparinen, 2008, p. 707). Specifically, a faxed warning that genocide was being planned was not delivered to the UNSC because its sender was the Force Commander of UNAMIR (United Nations Assistance Mission for Rwanda) and technically did not have responsibility for political matters (Piiparinen, 2008, p. 709). Early warning 'was trammelled by the rigidity of bureaucratic categories' (Piiparinen, 2008, p. 711). The detailed focus on international institutions discussed above leads to various questions that help compare the EU and UN's policy-making approaches: what rules, defined as formal and informal rules, govern EU and UN committees; how compartmentalized are EU and UN divisions that are responsible for ethnic conflict issues; and how much communication occurs between units.

Checkel also has examined international institutions more deeply, by examining the role of the EU in socializing actors into supranational norms. Socialization is defined as 'a process of inducting actors into the norms and rules of a given community' (Checkel, 2005, p. 804). The core question is when do actors switch from consequences to appropriateness (Checkel, 2005, p. 805)? Rationality plays a part in that strategic calculation, which occurs in switching as well as normative persuasion and role-playing (Checkel, 2005, p. 805): what starts as rational calculation may be followed by internalization 'because of various cognitive and institutional lock-in effects' (Checkel, 2005, p. 809).

While rational calculation occurs, actors are limited by bounded rationality. Therefore, simplifying short cuts and buffers can lead to particular role conceptions and role-playing (Checkel, 2005, p. 810). Role-playing becomes deeply internalized under certain conditions: where contact between actors is long and sustained and where contacts are intense (Checkel, 2005, p. 811). The effect of these factors depends on whether actors have had previous extensive experience in international policy-making settings, or whether they have been involved in domestic networks more than international ones (Checkel, 2005, p. 811).

Similarly, a study of how far Commission officials have become Europeanized finds that Commission, while shaping of its members' preferences, is modest over time (Hooghe, 2005, p. 876). However, it is stronger for those who joined the Commission in their twenties (Hooghe, 2005, p. 876). Mobility hinders members being socialized into a particular unit (Hooghe, 2005, p. 879). In fact, national socialization is far stronger than supranational socialization (Hooghe, 2005, p. 879). A later study also found that a majority of Commission staff had no real preference for a federal Europe and national factors were stronger determinants of their preferences. Although these constructivist studies resonate with themes of bureaucratic behaviour, constructivism is not central to the aims of this book, as the next section explains (Hooghe, 2013).

There are two main reasons why a constructivist analysis in itself is not central to the aims of this book. Firstly, the role of standard operating procedures, highlighted in Piiparinen's account of the UN's failure in Rwanda, fits equally well with an institutionalist account, but institutionalism avoids the sterile debate about whether a norm or a value is an interest. The definitions of institutions include rules and norms, and in later accounts, rules are assumed to have a normative dimension (see above). Therefore, it is unclear why the account of Rwanda is necessarily constructivist, as opposed to institutionalist. The reliance on bureaucratic rules, regardless of the crisis at hand, fits equally well with concepts of bounded rationality, 'muddling through' standard operating procedures emphasized by institutionalists and public choice theorists. Similarly, role perception among UN Secretariat and Commission members may be linked to standard operating procedures and 'careerist' self-interest and also to values. In other words, 'the boundaries between schools have come down' (Martins and Simmons, 2013, p. 341). Overall, it is assumed in this book that the distinction between rational institutionalist accounts and sociological ones is very fine and is not relevant to the aim of this book. Therefore, for the purposes of this book, it is fruitless to attempt to determine how far norms underpin behaviour as opposed to interests -and rules they are assumed to be intertwined.

The second reason why a constructivist approach is not seen as appropriate in this book is that the core aim is to examine how much autonomy the UN Secretariat and Commission have; that is, how much freedom they have from member states to influence policy processes. The question whether their behaviour reflects interests, or values, is not being examined. In other words, the starting point in the case studies is 'what were their negotiating strategies in each conflict zone and how far could secretariats pursue them in an unfettered manner?' Attention is paid to the question of how far their preferences simply emulate member state preferences, because if bureaucracies are found to adopt state preferences, then their autonomy is highly questionable; but again the issue whether the reasons for emulation are normative or rational is not central to the argument.

Therefore, applying a constructivist approach is not central to the aims of this book. The main aim is to determine the validity of the neo-realist argument that international organizations' policy outcomes reflect member state preferences. The counter to this argument is that international bureaucracies can have autonomy and that international organizations' policy outcomes are not simply the sum of the parts of key member states but of the preferences and decisions made by bureaucrats. The key is to identify whether these decisions are determined by member state control or by the bureaucrats themselves, and the role of norms is less relevant to this core aim. If bureaucrats' behaviour was found to differ from member state preferences, a further study could examine why they differed and how far norms mattered, but that is beyond the scope of this book. In the following section, the methodology used in determining bureaucratic autonomy in the light of International Relations theory is presented.

Methodology

Drawing from the above theoretical overview, Table 1.1 lists the indicators of relevance in comparing the Commission and UN Secretariat.

The case study chapters (Chapters 4–6) provide a thick description of the role of bureaucrats, based on interviews with 35 EU, UN and national officials, from 2010 to 2013, as well as drawing from newspaper archives and secondary literature. The aim was to identify the main features of decision-making in the EU and the UN in each case study, with particular emphasis on addressing the above indicators. A background section in each chapter provides an overview of state preferences in the EU and UN about key issues in each case study.

The choice of case studies and time periods was made for a number of reasons. All three cases are European and therefore of key relevance to both the EU and the UN. The UK and, therefore, Northern Ireland have been EU members since 1973, Cyprus[1] became an EU member in 2004 and Kosovo and Serbia are seeking EU membership. Thus the EU was a very immediate context for all three cases, and therefore

Table 1.1 Comparing the EU and UN: Indicators

Flexibility of rules and formality/informality of procedures; for example, communication and feedback channels to headquarters
Density of institutionalization
Concentration of power in EU and UN bureaucracies specifically and in EU and UN generally
Role conceptions: do they differ between EU and UN staff engaged in conflict intervention
Policy priorities: elite driven or grass roots
Issue uncertainties in EU and UN committees
Intensity of preferences of representatives on each committee
Autonomy of bureaucrats to shape agenda and implement policy

---

the role of EU enlargement policy in EU conflict resolution can be determined. Secondly, the UN and the EU have been deeply involved in Cyprus and in the Balkans. Therefore, a comparison of their approaches, as well as whether their policy processes were interlinked in any way, is very pertinent. However, the choice of Northern Ireland in this regard requires further justification, as the next paragraph explains.

In Cyprus and Kosovo, both the EU and UN have been deeply involved, whereas in Northern Ireland only the EU was involved. Northern Ireland was chosen because it was the first conflict case where the EU became involved. It is both a landmark and a benchmark which is crucial not only to assess the evolution of EU involvement in conflict resolution and peace building but also to assess the evolution of the EU–UN relationship. Specifically is there a difference between EU processes to conflict when the UN is not involved and EU policy processes when both the EU and UN are involved? Northern Ireland was heralded as the first successful peace project in the EU, and it highlights the EU's approach to conflict resolution before the end of the Cold War and its relative isolation from the UN in conflict resolution in the late 1980s and early 1990s. A final reason to examine these cases is that all these cases have a relatively long history of EU and/or UN involvement, compared to more recent conflict cases that allow for a fuller examination with the benefit of hindsight.

The periods examined in this book precede the creation of the European External Action Service (EEAS) in the EU, devised to take responsibility for foreign policy and conflict resolution issues. As Chapter 2 shows, the EEAS was provided for under the Lisbon Treaty and subsumed DG RELEX, the Commission's unit dedicated to crisis management. The EEAS also represents the European Council, the intergovernmental arm of the EU. The decision to choose an earlier period of EU history was determined by the inability to assess the role of the EEAS thoroughly, as it only became fully functional in latter half of 2011. Similarly, it was not feasible to choose more recent case studies, as it would hinder a balanced analysis – the benefit of hindsight and access to key protagonists would be less possible. The choice of these earlier periods was also governed by the fact that during these periods both the EU and the UN were closely involved and had potentially overlapping responsibilities.

The core methodological problem in this study is a typical endogeneity problem: if international bureaucrats appear to display autonomous behaviour, is it because their decisions reflect state preferences and hidden lobbying in the first place? The methodological conundrum is evident in the above analysis of the UN Secretariat's response to warnings of genocide in Rwanda. While the rigid compartmentalization of functions impeded delivery of the warning, it was also evident that France did not want intervention in Rwanda and had called for the dismissal of the army officer.

The identification of key states' preferences in each case study chapter and the extensive use of primary resources and secondary literature seek to clarify the distinction between state preferences, UN Secretariat preferences and Commission and/or Council Secretariat preferences. The sources used reveal a distinction between macro-level 'grand' decisions made by the P-5 and key EU states and micro-level implementation decisions that have policy implications but are not directly connected to specific state preferences – they operate on a different level. While this multi-level approach was developed in EU studies (see, for example, Peterson and Shackleton, 2002), it has not been always applied systematically to EU foreign policy or to the UN.

By separating out these different levels and types of decisions, the core finding in this book is that the existence of a UNSC mandate, or of an EU policy aim, creates the rationale for the Commission and UN Secretariat's involvement. In that sense, member states determine bureaucratic behaviour. However, the macro-level of mandates and policy initiatives is different from the micro-level of implementation. In order to achieve member-states' aims while implementing policies, member states often did not have a preference on specific issues or were not in a position to formulate a preference. The case studies in this book highlight the range of smaller 'coalface' decisions where state preferences were not evident, as opposed to EU and UN's 'grand' decisions in a crisis. The indicators listed above provide criteria that help compare the EU and UN's bureaucracies and help identify, not only levels of autonomy, but also institutional determinants of autonomy.

Conclusion

This chapter has a core set of aims: to set out the aims of the book, to justify those aims and to lay out the research design. This chapter has

shown the synergies between rational institutionalism and constructivism in examining international institutions rather than favouring
one approach over the other. In other words, the merits of theoretical
pluralism (Checkel, 2013, p. 227) are particularly stark in comparing
the EU and UN's institutional processes. Clearly, this book does not
constitute a comprehensive analysis of decision-making in all cases,
but it does identify and compare some policy-making characteristics
of each institution and also identifies whether bureaucratic staff have
been free from state control in specific decisions. It does not make
causal connections between bureaucratic autonomy and policy outcomes. In this way, this book is a initial attempt to understand and
explain bureaucratic behaviour in the EU and UN, and further studies
of the impact of international bureaucratic behaviour will be needed.
In the next chapter, an overview of the historical evolution of the
EU and UN's institutional framework and of its bureaucracies will be
provided before discussing EU and UN intervention in conflict zones.

2
The EU and UN: Institutional Frameworks and Conflict Resolution

This chapter focuses on the key institutions and institutional processes that govern foreign policy in the EU as well as security and conflict in the UN. The chapter begins with a historical overview of the origin of the EU and UN so as to highlight how various factors led to different institutional outcomes in the EU and UN. The second part of the chapter examines the EU's institutional framework, followed by an overview of the UN's framework. In conclusion, a comparison of both systems is provided.

The EU and UN's foundation

The origins of the EU and UN share not only some key similarities but also some differences, as the next paragraphs show. One similarity between both organizations is that they were created ostensibly with the aim of achieving peace and/or international stability. Another similarity is that the US strongly influenced the formation of the UN and was also a significant influence on the establishment of the European Economic Community (EEC) in 1958.

As regards the UN, the US Department of State spearheaded the preparatory work before the signing of the UN Charter. Many private organizations and non-governmental organizations (NGOs) presented proposals and ideas to the Department of State (Le-Roy Bennett and Oliver, 2001, p. 34). In 1939, the Commission to Study the Organization of Peace was established, comprising academic experts in the field of international organization (Le-Roy Bennett and Oliver, 2001, p. 34). In addition, various religious groups presented proposals (Le-Roy Bennett and Oliver, 2001, p. 34). A key role was also played by 'an elaborate system of sub-committees', established by the Department of State, particularly the Division of Special Research played an increasingly active role (Le Roy Bennett, p. 36). The high degree of public interest was recognized by the US administration. The Department of State distributed approximately 1,900,000 copies of the Dumbarton Oaks proposals, provoking an enormous public response (Stephenson, 2000, p. 274). Moreover, 100 organizations were invited to participate in a briefing and discussion of the proposals for the UN at the Dumbarton Oaks Conference in 1944 (LeRoy Bennett, p. 35). The US delegation to San Francisco included representatives of 42 NGOs, representing labour, law, agriculture, business and education, women, churches and civic groups (Stephenson, 2000, p. 274). Indeed, the first director of the Division of Human Rights at the UN, John P. Humphrey, commented that human rights would have received 'only a passing reference...but for the efforts of a few deeply committed delegates and the representatives of forty two private organisations brought in as consultants' (Farer and Gaer, 1993, p. 245).

However, intergovernmental politics was the strongest feature of the Dumbarton Oaks negotiations and the San Francisco Conference that led to the ratification of the UN Charter. Indeed, human rights while receiving more than a passing reference was still subordinated to other purposes (Farer and Gaer, 1993, p. 245). For example, the UN's founders stopped short of allowing armed intervention to protect human rights. The main protagonists in the negotiations were the US, the UK and the Soviet Union. A series of meetings were held between the Allied Powers, culminating in summits at Dumbarton Oaks and San Francisco. In San Francisco, 50 states were represented by 282 official delegates and 1,400 advisers and staff (LeRoy Bennett and Oliver, 2001, p. 41). While the larger states determined the broad shape of the Charter, small states succeeded in amending some articles of the final Charter. Thus, Chapter XI of the Charter contained principles that obliged colonial powers to advance inhabitants' economic, social and educational welfare (LeRoy Bennett, p. 43). Small states also lobbied successfully for the inclusion of recognition of the right for collective self-defence in the event of Security Council's immobilization (LeRoy Bennett and Oliver, 2001, p. 43). Clearly, while predominantly influenced by the Allied Powers, particularly the US, the UN was also 'based on ideas and experience from a vast variety of sources' (LeRoy Bennett and Oliver, 2001, p. 45). However, the UN Charter enshrined state sovereignty explicitly and laid out rules to maintain security and peace in the post-war world. The enshrinement of sovereignty in the UN system was exemplified by the rules governing the Security Council under the UN Charter. Each of the five permanent members (P-5) had the power of veto, but the ten non-permanent members did not have a veto. Under Article 25, the Security Council's will is binding on all members, and under Article 41, if a threat to peace exists, it can call on all members to impose economic sanctions and/or to cease communication. The Security Council nominates the UN secretary-general (UNSG) and judges on the International Court of Justice. It also has the power to investigate disputes and can decide whether an act of aggression has occurred.

Chapter VI of the Charter lays out the ways in which the Security Council can promote peaceful resolution. Chapter VII specifies actions the Security Council can take in response to threats to peace or breaches of peace and acts of aggression. Under Article 42 of the Charter, the Security Council can call on members to take such action 'by air, sea, or land forces' as may be necessary to maintain or restore international security. Under Article 109, the Charter may be reviewed by a General Conference of the UN (Luck, 2008, p. 654). However, the major powers, particularly the Soviet Union 'insisted on keeping the hurdles to amending the Charter at high level. None of them was eager for the lesser powers to tamper with the handiwork they produced at Dumbarton Oaks' (Luck, 2008, p. 654). As the next section shows, the EU's foundation was also strongly determined by the post-war environment, but its institutional framework and underpinning principles differed markedly from those of the UN.

Like the UN, the origin of the EU is linked to 'negative assessments of the pre-war political situation and economic practices' (Urwin, 1995, p. 7). Like the UN, the US and the Cold War played a key role in stimulating the EEC's foundation (Urwin, 2013, p. 12). Politically, the establishment of the North Atlantic Treaty Organization (NATO) provided a military shield for Europe and enabled its governments to establish the EEC (Urwin, 1995, p. 25). Economically, the drive for European integration was encouraged by the US, insisting that Marshall aid to help reconstruct Europe would be dependent on the Allies establishing an organization to distribute the aid (Dinan, 2004, p. 19), and in 1948, the Organisation for European Economic

Co-operation (OEEC) was established to do so. Thus, US hegemony was a key factor in the background to the EEC's foundation.

The OEEC spawned the European Coal and Steel Community (ECSC), first proposed by Robert Schuman, the French foreign minister in 1950. The real aim of the ECSC was to manage the supply of scarce coal and steel. Politically, the ECSC included the High Authority, the embryonic European Commission and for Schuman and Jean Monnet. This High Authority would become an engine to promote European economic and political integration. The failure of the European Defence Community in 1952 led to a 'mood of despondency' (Urwin, 1995, p. 71). However, the expansion of trade in the post-war era and the determination of key actors such as the French Foreign Minister Robert Schuman and the Belgian Prime Minister Paul-Henri Spaak (Dinan, 2004, p. 37) led to the Messina Conference in 1955 to discuss the creation of a common market (Urwin, 2013, pp. 17–18). The Messina Conference was attended by heads of government from the Benelux, France, Germany and Italy. It precipitated the Spaak Report in 1956. The Spaak Committee 'was charged with drafting the appropriate treaties' (Urwin, 1992, p. 75), and in 1957, meetings between foreign ministers and their advisers culminated in the Rome Treaty 'to establish a common market and progressively approximate the economic policies of member states' (Urwin, 1992, p. 79). As a result, the EEC was established and held its first meeting in March 1958.

The period from 1954 to 1958 was marked by a strong lobbying by key European figures and also by a high degree of secrecy. Thus, the Schuman Plan Conference that preceded the ECSC was relatively closed: 'We were not prepared to negotiate with private interest groups about a venture of such great public importance' (Monnet, 1978, p. 318). However, the French foreign ministry announced that various relevant interest groups would be consulted: leaders of employers and employee unions and of coal and steel unions (Monnet, 1978, p. 322). Moreover, in 1955, preceding the foundation of the EEC, Monnet himself travelled throughout the Benelux, France, Italy and West Germany to recruit political and trade union leaders (Monnet, 1978, p. 410). However, unlike the UN's foundation, broader NGO consultation did not occur, partly because the subject matter was narrower than broad questions of peace and security, which are discussed in the UN Conferences.

This secrecy extended even to key actors and their governments. Thus, Jean Monnet kept plans for the ECSC from the then French Foreign Minister Bidault until he was sure of receiving support from the rest of the Cabinet (Yondorf, quoted in Lindberg and Scheingold, 1970, p. 15).[1] The plan was made public only after French support was assured. Moreover, the plan was announced without notifying the UK government (Urwin, 1995). Thus,

> [t]he birth of the European Community was...largely the work of political and technical elites....The supranational system that has materialised continues to evidence [sic] this elitist bias....The business of the European Community tends to be largely economic, and consequently rather obscure.
>
> (Lindberg and Scheingold, 1970, p. 22)

The negotiations that led to the formation of the EU and the UN also differed in their aims. The UN Charter was firmly based on the concept of sovereignty and discussions did not entail plans to establish a 'world political union'. The EU's negotiations contained various strands. Some key actors such as Monnet, Schumann and Spaak favoured a political union. Others, for example, the French administration were less keen. Thus, 'some political parties were prepared to vote for radical maximalist schemes. Others would not have accepted even the most artfully designed compromise' (Lindberg and Scheingold, 1970, p. 17). As the next section shows, these differences had implications for the procedures and processes of the UN and EU.

The evolution of the EU foreign policy-making process: The role of the Commission and Council

The EU's institutional framework did not provide for a common foreign policy, as the fate of European Defence Community in 1953 showed that states would not share, or relinquish sovereignty in such a politically sensitive area. However, it will be shown in this section that the Commission increased its influence in EU foreign policy gradually and that international bureaucrats on various EU committees can wield significant influence.

The Rome Treaty provided for a European Commission to initiate policy in specific economic areas where states shared common interests, such as customs and agriculture that is low politics. The Council of Ministers, comprising ministers for a given policy area was the sole institution to legislate for common policy issues. A European Assembly initially was purely consultative and unelected, but over time its powers increased to being an elected European Parliament (EP) with co-decision over specific policy areas. The European Court of Justice (ECJ) was to make judgements on violations of EU legislation and various advisory institutions (the Economic and Social Council (ESC) and the Special Agriculture Committee (SCA)) played consultative roles. In 1974, the European Council was established in response to the EU's failure to respond to the oil crisis but was not formally part of the EU's institutional framework until 1986, under the Single European Act (SEA). The consultative Committee of the Regions was established under the Maastricht Treaty, 1992 to represent regional representatives in the EU. The 1998 Amsterdam Treaty also contained foreign policy institutional change and was a landmark in the EU's foreign policy evolution, as the next section shows.

The Amsterdam Treaty provided for a new European Security and Defence Policy (ESDP) and the creation of the post of High Representative of the Common Foreign and Security Policy (CFSP) and a new Policy Unit 'to assist the Council and the Presidency in formulation, preparation and implementation of policy decisions' (Keukeleire and McNaughton, 2008, p. 54). The Amsterdam Treaty also 'gave EU access to the WEU's (Western European Union) EU's operational capability for humanitarian and rescue tasks, peacekeeping tasks and combat forces' task in crisis management (the 'St Petersburg tasks') (Keukeleire and McNaughton, 2008, p. 55). Of all these changes, the ESDP was the most significant and the creation of a Policy Planning and Early Warning Unit (PPEWU) with Commission representation (Marsh and Mackenstein, 2005, p. 68).

The 1998 Franco-British St. Malo Declaration agreed that the EU must have the capacity for autonomous action and the declaration was adopted at the Cologne Council in 1999 (Marsh and Mackenstein, 2005, p. 68). The St. Malo Declaration was a direct response to 'joint-Franco-British concern about the lack of EU military capacity in the event of a crisis such as Kosovo' (Howorth, 2007, p. 207). In 2000, the EU agreed under the ESDP to deploy military forces (the Helsinki Headline Goal) and to create a standing PSC, a

Military Committee and Military Staff (Keukeleire and McNaughton, 2008, pp. 56–57). It also agreed to develop civilian crisis management through rule of law and police missions (Keukeleire and McNaughton, 2008, p. 57). In 2002, under the Berlin-Plus Agreement, the EU agreed a system of access to NATO's military assets and command structure and military and civilian operations followed in Macedonia, Balkans, Africa, the Middle East and...Asia (Keukeleire and McNaughton, 2008, p. 57). The Amsterdam Treaty, by creating the PSC, deepened the role of committees in the EU foreign policy-making and also deepened the Commission's role.

Indeed, overall, 'one of the most important characteristics of this system is its considerable dispersal of political power' (Nugent, 2002, p. 202). This dispersal implies that

> [t]he Commission has not been subject to the same degree of political direction as national administrative agencies. This has presented opportunities for the Commission to exercise not just the advisory and administrative roles that are the normal business of national civil servants and international secretariats, but also leadership roles in relation to the shaping and management of political and policy agendas.
>
> (Nugent, 2002, p. 203)

The Commission has been heavily criticized over the years. Its unelected status and agenda-setting and initiation powers made it the focus of Eurosceptic opinion that viewed it as undermining national sovereignty and being inherently undemocratic (Nugent, 2002, pp. 202–03). Criticism reached a head when Denmark rejected the Maastricht Treaty in 1993 (Nugent, 2002, p. 46). This rejection was followed by a series of scandals where Commission officials were accused of corruption. In particular, in 1999, the Santer-Commission was forced to resign (Nugent, 2002, p. 53), following the EU's Court of Auditors report that there was evidence of 'missing funds' in the Commission and its strong criticism of the Commission's management practices (Nugent, 2002, p. 54). It was argued, particularly by the EP, that 'there was too much complacency and incompetence' (Nugent, 2002, p. 54) in the Commission. The wave of allegations was a catalyst for Commission reform in 2000.

In 1999, Romano Prodi, the new president of the Commission, commissioned a report by 'three wisemen' for reform. However, it met with deep opposition from the European Council, encapsulated by the then Spanish Prime Minister Jose Maria Aznar's response to Prodi: 'We don't need your wise men. We *are* your wise men' (Peterson and Shackleton, 2002, p. 12). The subsequent 2000 White Paper on Commission reform was a more modest document, which provided for greater transparency and communication to the European public (Commission, 2000). It also provided for 'an over-haul of staffing policy, more efficient and performance-related work-ing methods and a new system of financial management' (Nugent, 2002, p. 57). However, the Commission's growing informal involve-ment in EU foreign policy was an increasing cause of concern, not least among other EU institutions, particularly the Council.

The Commission and EU foreign policy

Formally, under the Rome Treaty, the Commission was not involved in foreign policy, which remained a purely intergovernmental policy sector. Successive reforms in the Treaty and institutional changes did not alter this situation formally. However, a significant caveat is that the Commission's DG1A (the Enlargement Directorate-General) has significant powers over EU enlargement policy, designated as a sepa-rate policy from EU foreign policy and DG1A plays a significant role in EU's foreign policy committee system, as the next section shows.

EU foreign policy machinery has altered significantly since the early 1990s. The key reason for institutional change was the chal-lenge of ethnic conflict after the fall of Communism. The failure of the EU to respond adequately to various crises and to prevent them (see Chapter 1) preceded various institutional changes in the EU. In 1998, the Amsterdam Treaty established the High Representa-tive of the CFSP in order to strengthen coherence and effectiveness (Smith, 2008, p. 5). Under the 2000 Helsinki Agreement, it was agreed not only to set up rapid reaction missions but also to develop civilian policing missions, the rule of law and support for civilian adminis-tration and peace-building (Merlingen and Ostrauskaite, 2006). DG RELEX was created in the Commission with responsibility for the management of civilian aspects of crises. Similarly, under the 2001 Göteborg Summit, targets were set for civilian protection (Merlingen and Ostrauskaite, 2006). In 2004, these aims were updated so as to strengthen the EU's peace-building vocation. A policy early warning unit was also established, in response to the EU's weakness in the face of ethnic conflict in the Balkans (Smith, 2008, p. 41).

Largely because of its role in enlargement policy and because of DG RELEX, it was argued that the Commission played an increasingly important role in EU foreign policy committees (Trondal, 2010, p. 259).While constituting separate 'pillars' of the EU, enlargement policy and foreign policy became increasingly interlinked. This inter-linkage was particularly evident when the EU was dealing with new fragile democracies seeking to join the EU, but engaging in ethnic conflict, or in a fragile post-conflict situation. Enlargement policy developed as a significant foreign policy tool where the Commission stipulated that if a state was to join the EU, it must meet certain democratic and economic conditions, as Chapter 1 showed. There-fore, the offer of EU membership was a fundamental diplomatic instrument and it was cross-pillar, not purely intergovernmental (Smith, 2008, p. 67). The long duration of the enlargement process implied that the Commission could reap significant changes in a given state. Table 2.1 lists the stages of enlargement negotiations with a given state.

The Council authorizes the Commission to open negotiations with third countries (Smith, 2008, p. 37). The Commission con-ducts negotiations and the Council concludes the agreement (Smith, 2008, p. 37). The main element of enlargement policy is the accep-tance of a new member states on condition that certain conditions laid out in the Commission's guidelines have been met. As regards the Balkans, for example, the Commission's enlargement strategy requires that social inclusion, strengthening the rule of law, freedom of expression, reconciliation, regional cooperation and bilateral

Table 2.1   Phases of enlargement process

Feasibility Study: written and proposed by the Commission
SAA negotiations
SAA agreement
Application for membership
Commission's avis
Candidate status granted
Membership talks: Council, Commission, state
Accession Treaty: approval needed from EP and Council
Accession

Source: Simplified List of stages, European Commission, interview with the author, March 2, 2010.

issues in the Balkans are all addressed by the applicant state with Commission help (Commission, 2010, pp. 6–11). The provision of regional aid is also subject to conditionality: rules that must be accepted if aid is to be received. The Commission became, according to Smith, a formal entrepreneur by launching aid to in part for political reasons to states such as Cyprus and Portugal and attaching political conditionality to rules to whether aid was received (Smith, 1998, p. 327).

Thus, gradually the Commission became an active member of EU foreign policy's committee system (Smith, 1998, p. 320): 'the rigid distinction between the European Council/EPC and the Council of Ministers/EC began to disappear as Foreign Ministers considered how EC resources or procedures could give more weight to EPC actions' (Smith, 1998, p. 320). Overall, 'the Council of Ministers and the Commission must ensure the coherence of the Union's external policies, thus giving these bodies – one an intergovernmental forum, the other a supranational organization – a joint role in this responsibility' (Smith, 2001, p. 175). Therefore, 'segments of sectoral organization and supranational dynamics coexist within this intergovernmental body (Smith, 2001, p. 175), causing a "consensus" reflex' (Smith, 1998, p. 320).

The EU's committee system

The evolution of EU foreign policy has been accompanied by the evolution of a highly influential committee system involving member states and Commission representatives: 'the methods by which foreign policy decisions are made reflects very much submerged below the water line ... a much larger body of administrative interaction, which to a significant degree involves the work of committees' (Christiansen and Larsson, 2007, p. 1). Before the creation of the EEAS (and therefore for the period covered in case studies chapters), the main committees were the Political and Security Committee (PSC), comprising a representative from DG RELEX in the European Commission, a Council Secretariat representative and national representatives, the Committee for Civilian Aspects of Crisis Management (Civcom), the EU Military Committee, EU Military Staff and the Joint Situation Centre (Smith, 2008, p. 42).

In addition, COREPER, representing national permanent representatives deals with various sensitive political matters, including foreign policy. In practice, as the EU's workload has increased, many of these delicate matters are also decided by the PSC, but as Chapter 5 shows, COREPER 11, not the PSC was the key committee in the policy process towards Cyprus in 2004.The committee system has evolved in response to external challenges. For example, Civcom was established in 2008 in response to the proliferation of EU missions in conflict zones: by 2010 there were 13 EU missions causing problems of coordination and complication.

The role of the PSC is particularly significant in understanding the Commission's role. The PSC provides guidance and strategy to the Council, the Military Committee and a military staff (Smith, 2008, p. 42). However, despite the PSC's high significance, it has been 'under-appreciated' in academic literature (Duke, 2007, p. 120). Under the Nice Treaty, the PSC was empowered to take political and strategic decisions in crisis management, 'a function normally reserved for the Council' (Duke, 2007, p. 136). The justification for this empowerment was that the EU should 'develop a consistent approach to crisis management and ensure a synergy between the civilian and crisis management aspects of crisis management' (Duke, 2007, p. 136). Thus, the PSC is 'the lynchpin' of the CFSP (Duke, 2007, p. 136) and its Chair is closely involved in coordinating CFSP and overlapping EU policies (Duke, 2007, p. 137).

Precise membership of the PSC varies depending on the agenda, but on average there are four to five members of the Council Secretariat, a Commission representative, and at least three national representatives (Irish Department of Foreign Affairs, interview with author, March 3, 2011). The agenda for the PSC is set by the Secretariat and the Presidency and according to observers, the Secretariat's agenda-setting role has been immensely powerful (Irish Department of Foreign Affairs, interview with author, March 3, 2011). The agenda-setting stage of policy in the EU has been particularly influenced by Commission–Council committee interactions. The Commission gathers information and provides information at this stage. It is also highly important in implementing policy. Observers have noted 'Brusselsization' of foreign policy, whereby the role of member states has diminished and decisions are discussed and decided by EU institutional committees (Smith, 2008, p. 38).

'Comitology', a term coined in the 1960s, became increasingly evident in the EU's foreign policy framework. Participants noticed how

Council committees dealing with the Balkans and other accession states, increasingly relied on information provided by the Commission representatives on its committees and informally between meetings (Irish Department of Foreign Affairs, interview with author, March 3, 2011). Thus, while the Council appears to be intergovernmental, the Council Secretariat and the Commission have exhibited consensus-building EU attributes, rather than simply reflecting individual state preferences. Indeed, it has been observed that 'the Council is the chameleon of EU institutions because it equals more than the sum of its parts (member states)' (Lewis, 2013, p. 145).COREPER 'illustrates how the Council does not only defend national interests, but is also a collective decision-making process' (Lewis, 2013, p. 148).

Moreover, the Council Secretariat has also played an increasingly important role. Beach argues that the role of the Council Secretariat has 'been all but discounted in the literature', but that it is crucial in its 'behind the scenes facilitating leadership role, oiling the wheels of compromise, ensuring that more "integrative" decisions are reached in the Council than would otherwise have been the case' (Beach, 2008, p. 220). The reason for the Secretariat's importance was precisely because of the intergovernmental nature of the Council, whereby high transaction costs can easily lead to negotiation failure (Beach, 2008, p. 220). The Council Secretariat has a monopoly of information in certain policy sectors and usually defines its interests in terms of finding workable solutions that avoid lowest common denominators (Beach, 2008, pp. 225–26). The Council has a 'bureau-shaping' dynamism that seeks to strengthen the EU, but not necessarily to reflect what all governments want (Beach, 2008, pp. 225–26). The Secretariat under the High Representative for the CFSP, Javier Solana was a trusted actor by member states and succeeded in hammering deals that otherwise would have been highly unlikely, for example reforming the CFSP finance system in 2005 (Beach, 2008, pp. 225–26).

Within the complex committee system, the Commission also plays a key role and the Commission-Council Secretariat axis is vital in ensuring smooth flow of up-to-date information. For example, prior to the Lisbon Treaty, the Commission's DG RELEX was a political unit with its own budgetary powers. The CFSP and ESDP had no autonomous budget and the Commission was the key budget holder, for example, the Commission financed election monitoring, police reform from the EU budget (Irish Department of Foreign Affairs, interview with the author, January 23, 2010).

As such the Commission's DG RELEX unit was at the heart of Council conflict prevention activities, but as a Commission unit, less subject to Council controls. Partly in response to growing Commission influence within the EU's blurred system, the creation of the EEAS under the Lisbon Treaty attempted to alter aspects of the overall foreign policy-making process and limit the Commission's involvement. The EEAS subsumed DG RELEX, so the Commission no longer had a separate representative from DG RELEX on the PSC. The Head of the EEAS (Catherine Ashton) became the permanent Chair of the PSC. Before 2011, the Chair was held by the Presidency and therefore rotated, empowering the Commission and the Council Secretariat to a greater degree in agenda-setting and brokering (Irish Department of Foreign Affairs, interview with the author, January 23, 2010). Therefore, the EEAS is present on all key committees and holds the Chair of the PSC. The aim was to blend Commission and Council elements in policy and provide greater coordination (Smith, 2008, p. 42). These changes have not diminished the Commission's role as much as might be expected however. In particular, DG1A has remained a separate Commission unit and its operation has not altered under the Lisbon Treaty, or its aftermath.

An obvious question is why the DG1A was not also subsumed under the EEAS, if it so closely overlapped with its work? A key reason for retaining DG1A's status was that legally and practically it was difficult to divide its units dealing with post-conflict, or conflict zones from its units dealing with stable non-EU states (Irish Permanent Representation, Brussels, interview with the author, March 3, 2011).

Secondly, the task of DG1A was to ensure that new EU states meet the range of conditions necessary to adopt the *acquis* (Irish Permanent Representation, Brussels, interview with the author, March 3, 2011). The range of legal, democratic and technical issues related to conditionality and the *acquis* made it infeasible for the EEAS to subsume enlargement tasks. Thus, the Commission's status in foreign policy 'changed from that of invited guest to that of an active participant' (Smith, 1998, p. 326).

Overall, the evolution of the committee system in EU foreign policy and the changes made to that system reflect a maxim of form following function and also reflect intra-institutional rivalry and competition. Institutional changes to the committee system were made in response to new challenges and events. Stimulants for change included enlargement, ethnic conflict following the end of the Cold War and the Commission's entrepreneurship (Smith, 1998, p. 332). Practitioners have observed that the EU's experience of peace-building highlighted the need for greater coherence between Commission and Council (Merlingen and Ostrauskaite, 2006, p. 137). However, other factors also caused institutional change in the EU. Criticisms of the EU's democratic deficit and particularly of the Commission's lack of transparency and accountability led to reform in 2000. An underlying and constant factor in the institutional evolution is the presence of turf battles between the EU's institutions, where each institution vies for power. This intra-institutional competition occurs within Commission and Council Secretariat, as well as between institutions. These forces for change in the EU's institutional system have also been evident in the UN, although there are also obvious differences, as the next section shows.

The UN's institutional framework

The foreign policy challenges of the 1990s that precipitated institutional reform in the EU also affected the UN dramatically. For example, changes in the UN's policy agenda after the Cold War had strong implications for the Security Council's operation (Mingst and Karns, 2007, p. 83). The powers of the Security Council and the right of each of the P-5 to use a veto meant that during the Cold War, the UN could only take action in any dispute if both the US and Soviet Union agreed to do so. The superpowers often negotiated outside the UN framework, or they used that framework for propaganda purposes. Unlike the EU, the UN's decision-making process was heavily skewed towards one institution – the Security Council. The end of the Cold War raised hopes that the UN would become more effective in dealing with conflict situations. As for the EU, the mushrooming of ethnic conflict and other security challenges altered the UN's agenda and increased its work burden significantly.

In fact, the end of the Cold War led to US dominance over the Security Council, tempered by Russian and Chinese opposition. Thus, the US was the driving force in intervening in Iraq in 1990, Somalia in 1992 and Haiti in 1994. It successfully spearheaded the argument that human rights and humanitarian disasters constituted separate threats to security (Resolution 803), thus enabling the doctrine of R2P. Under Resolution 1368, also spearheaded by the US, the right to act forcefully against terrorism provided de facto legitimization for intervention in Afghanistan (Mingst and Karns, 2007, p. 92). Similarly, Resolution 827 to establish the International Criminal Tribunal for Former Yugoslavia followed strong US lobbying and support.

However, the familiar narrative of Security Council dominance masks other aspects of the UN system. For example, in 1998, the International Criminal Court was established (ICC) to deal with systematic crimes against humanity, following many years of lobbying by a coalition of NGOs supported by the General Assembly (Mingst and Karns, 2007, p. 202). The ICC is a court of last resort and any individual, group of organization can bring cases before it. The US and China opposed its establishment on the basis that it infringed sovereignty and should be subject to Security Council oversight (Mingst and Karns, 2007, p. 202). However, despite this opposition, the ICC was established (Mingst and Karns, 2007, p. 202), implying that under certain conditions, consensus on the Security Council is not always necessary for institutional and political change.

Similarly, while the Assembly has been criticized for being a consultative talking-shop, a majority of states on the Assembly can block issues from the Security Council's agenda. For example, Indonesia blocked East Timor from the Security Council's agenda until 1999 and Sri Lanka also blocked its conflict with the Tamils from the Security Council's agenda. For this reason, six of the longest wars since 1946 have not been defined by Security Council as threats to peace. Another General Assembly tool is the 1950 'Uniting for Peace Resolution' enabled it to take responsibility where Security Council was unable to act (Malone, 2008, p. 118). Although the Resolution was actually proposed by the US to allow it to intervene in Korea, by-passing a Russian veto on the Security Council, it has become a potential resource for the Assembly and was used 'most famously' (Malone, 2008, p. 118) in 1956 to stop UK and French military action in Suez (see Chapter 3). Since 1956, the Uniting for Peace Resolution has been used for various measures including the condemnation of armed interventions in Afghanistan, the call for ceasefires in India and Pakistan and condemnation of some of Israel's policies on Gaza (Zaum, 2008, p. 163). The Assembly's Fifth Committee, with responsibility for financial and administrative affairs can also block UN administrative reform, by majority vote. The Security Council's relationship with the Assembly has been contentious and the Assembly has often addressed Middle Eastern issues when the Security Council has failed to do so (Zaum, 2008, p. 163). The Assembly also elects the Security Council's non-permanent members (Zaum, 2008, p. 163).

The third problem with solely focusing on the role of the Security Council is that the UN's increased work load since the early 1990s has caused it to burden-share its responsibilities. The complexity of the UN's agenda has also contributed to burden-sharing – peace-building often involves institutional and political state-building so the UN's tasks have become more complex. Like the EU's foreign policy agenda, the UN requires civilian and military expertise in devising and implementing policy (Malone, 2008, p. 122). Since the late 1990s, the UN has also increasingly used Special Envoys and Mediators in conflict cases. The need for expertise and information is exacerbated also by its increased engagement with actors in conflict zones (Hulton, 2004, p. 241).

Since 2000, the Security Council has conducted 13 missions in conflict zones so as to help them better understand conflict on the ground and also to enhance their effect on local actors (Hulton, 2004, p. 241). Each Mission is headed by the Special Representative of the Secretary-General (SRSG), following consultation with the Department of Political Affairs (DPA) in the UN and the Department of Peacekeeping Operations (DPKO) (Peck, 2004, p. 326). The SRSG's success depends on developing strong relationships with outside actors and with the UN's various institutions (Peck, 2004, p. 326). Thus, the Security Council has regular briefings from UN Secretariat officials, with emphasis on achieving more strategic and interactive policy process (Hulton, 2004, p. 247). In 1993, then under-secretary-general for DPKO, Kofi Annan, established the Policy Learning and Evaluation Unit in the DPKO, with a view to ensuring effective policy evaluation (Goulding, 2002).

The Security Council has also delegated increasingly to regional organizations and to NGOs to manage conflict (Newman, 2008) p. 183). In addition, informal groups of states have emerged as potentially influential lobbying actors in the UN system, outside the formal Security Council structures (Prantl, 2005). For example, there are

'Groups of Friends' – likeminded states who support UN offices and 'contact groups' – self-selected and ad hoc coalitions (Prantl, 2005). These groups help iron out unintended consequences and provide information to the Security Council (Prantl, 2005), but their predominance has led to complaints that they have 'usurped the role of the full Council' (Malone, 2008, p. 129) and that the secretary-general 'has been "unhelpfully constrained by them" at times' (Malone, 2008, p. 129).

The above trends have also had implications for the UN Secretariat and the UN committee system. Agenda-setting, information monopolies and expertise become increasingly important in a densely packed and challenging security policy environment. Under Kofi Annan, the Secretariat and the UN's administrative system generally became a specific focus of analysis in the light of the UN's challenges. In the next section, the Secretariat and the UN's committee system are examined so as to determine their role in UN policy to conflict zones.

Clearly, the Security Council is at the apex of the UN system, with various other consultative bodies, as well as the Secretariat. The Secretariat is headed by the secretary-general and under-secretary-generals. It is identified as a principal organ of the UN under Article 7 of the Charter (Newman, 2008, p. 176). Articles 7 and 97–101 sets out the secretary-general's powers and appointment procedure by the General Assembly with the instruction of the Security Council (Newman, 2008, p. 176). Under Article 98, the secretary-general must perform the functions entrusted to him/her by General Assembly, Security Council and other organs (Newman, 2008, p. 177). Over time, these functions have increased and the secretary-general has delegated authority over peacekeeping missions and security and human rights (Newman, 2008, p. 177).

The two departments with explicit responsibility for conflict and security are the DPA and the DPKO. The Office of Special Political Affairs (OSPA) was re-named the Department of Peacekeeping Operations in 1992 (Goulding, 2002, p. 31), under the new Secretary-General Boutros Boutros-Ghali. The DPA was also created by Boutros-Ghali with the aim of assuming 'responsibilities previously held by half a dozen different departments' (Goulding, 2002, p. 31). Under Perez de Cuellar, peace-making was moved to the secretary-general's office, but the creation of the DPA heralded its move to a separate department (Goulding, 2002, p. 31), although Boutros-Ghali also created the post of two under-secretary-generals to act as political advisers (Goulding, 2002, p. 31).

Originally the DPA was a conference service for members and for the Secretariat overall (Rubin and Jones, 2007, p. 404). However, increasingly it was called upon to engage with conflict prevention, mediation and resolution. It is perceived to be the focal point of prevention in the UN system, which will mobilize the resources of UN bureaucracies where necessary (Rubin and Jones, 2007, p. 406). It also has the power to convene meetings with delegates of key states, meet with them individually or organize informal meetings, or hold 'friends' groups' meetings. Two types of prevention have been identified by the UN: structural prevention to reduce risk through sound governance and institution-building and systematic prevention to address global risks of conflict that transcend particular states (Progress Report on the Prevention of Armed Conflict, 2006).

As Chapter 3 shows, in interstate wars, where the interests of the major UN powers are not involved, the DPA can play a significant role. For example, in the Israel–Lebanon war in 2000, the secretary-general and the DPA 'were able to mobilise the Security Council around a coherent strategy largely developed by the special coordinator of the Secretary-General' (Rubin and Jones, 2007, p. 395). However, its record in intra-state war is far weaker (Rubin and Jones, 2007, p. 395), as mediating 'treats both governments and opposition as parties to the conflict, rather than granting the government a monopoly of legitimate representation' (Rubin and Jones, 2007, p. 396). Therefore, the DPA rarely gets state consent to intervene (Rubin and Jones, 2007, p. 396). However, there have been some UN successes, as Chapter 3 shows.

The Secretariat is also empowered to conduct research into a given policy area, to brief the secretary-general and member states and also to engage in strategic planning. In practice:

> UN officials 'present ideas to tackle problems, debate them…, take initiatives, advocate for change, turn general decisions into specific programmes and implement them. They monitor progress and report to national officials'.
>
> (Weiss, 2010, p. 41)

Like the European Commission, the Secretariat has been heavily criticized for its alleged ineptitude and for lacking a strategic approach to conflict prevention. It also has faced allegations of cronyism and corruption. In the next section, a critique of the Secretariat and an overview of resultant reforms are provided.

Reforms of the Secretariat

Two themes have governed the Secretariat's history: 'a battle over its independent nature and an almost constant restructuring accompanied by calls for its reform' (Jonah, 2008, p. 160). The British civil service model of an independent civil service governed the foundation of the League of Nations' Secretariat (Jonah, 2008, p. 160). The UN Secretariat was also meant to be independent, 'a great experiment in international administration' (Jonah, 2008, p. 161), despite Soviet objections (Jonah, 2008, p. 161). In its early days, its independence was compromised by Secretary-General Trygve Lie succumbing to US pressure in the McCarthy era. However, Lie's successor Dag Hammarskjöld removed the Federal Bureau of Investigation from UN premises and reinvigorated Secretariat morale (Jonah, 2008, p. 162). However, there was a clear global North–South divide about the merits of an independent civil service: 'the South prefers a less independent civil service as it believes an independent civil service would reflect Northern bias' (Jonah, 2008, p. 165).

Another key divide, whether the majority of contracts in the Secretariat should be permanent or fixed, emerged. The Soviet Union favoured short-term contracts to allow nationals participate in the Secretariat on secondment and so as to enhance Soviet influence of the Secretariat (Jonah, 2008, pp. 163–64). Hammarskjöld agreed on 75 per cent permanent contracts and 25 per cent short-term contracts (Jonah, 2008, p. 164). Under Kofi Annan's reform proposals, a reversal of this was prescribed, but it was strongly resisted not only on careerist grounds but on the grounds that institutional memory and independence from political control would be jeopardized (Jonah, 2008, p. 164). However, under Kofi Annan also, the role of the DPKO was strengthened, and its recruitment autonomy and other powers were increased (Jonah, 2008, p. 165).

Apart from the above problems, there have been constant allegations of corruption made against the UN Secretariat, exemplified by the Oil for Food and sexual exploitation in the Congo. The

Independent Inquiry Committee into the Oil-for-Food Programme (IIC) revealed a 'culture of responsibility avoidance and resistance to accountability' in the Secretariat (IIC, 2005, p. 70) and called for its 'radical overhaul – its rules, structure, system and culture' (IIC, 2005, p. ii). It revealed corruption at managerial level, particularly with respect to procurement and also revealed a high level of cronyism in the Secretariat (Jonah, 2008, p. 270).

The IIC's damning report led to a series of reforms in the UN Secretariat, including the establishment of ethics, oversight and accountability offices (Frohlich, 2007, p. 154). The DPKO introduced a zero-tolerance policy for sexual exploitation and abuse (Frohlich, 2007, p. 153). The General Assembly adopted a draft resolution in 2006 to streamline the work of the Secretariat and the Fifth Committee, the Committee for Programme and Coordination (CPC) and the Advisory Committee on Administrative and Budgetary Questions (ACABQ). Again, it faced initial opposition from states in the South which claimed that by altering the work of these committees, their sources of influence over a Security Council–dominated system were further undermined (Frohlich, 2007, p. 156).

Another criticism of the Secretariat arises from the need to gain consent from governments for Secretariat intervention. This necessity implies that only when there is persistent violence does the UN intervene, creating the moral hazard whereby, that groups believe that violence 'is necessary to gain recognition' (Rubin and Jones, 2007, p. 400). Indeed, 'The Secretariat's lack of clear rules regarding how to treat the use of violence by non-state actors may actually induce violence' (Rubin and Jones, 2007, p. 400). Related to the problem of an absence of rules is the problem of overly rigid implementation of rules. The case of Rwanda mentioned in Chapter 1, highlighted how procedural rules impeded the DPA from helping to prevent genocide:

> Knowing when to ignore standard bureaucratic operating procedures and to make waves is an essential part of effective leadership that can break down the UN system's bureaucratic barriers.
>
> (Weiss, 2010, p. 46)

In addition, the DPA–UNDP relationship is fraught (Rubin and Jones, 2007, p. 402) and there is 'little evidence of actual implementation of...a coordinated approach' (Rubin and Jones, 2007, p. 402). Each unit in the UN has different, but overlapping purposes and budgetary systems impeding proper coordination (Rubin and Jones, 2007, p. 402). National interests impede cooperation, but so too do 'bureaucratic and funding problems' (Rubin and Jones, 2007, p. 402). One practitioner wrote that there were 'great variations from agency to agency' in the UN bureaucracy (Pitt, 1986, p. 27), 'In each, a distinct subculture tends to emerge, partly influenced by people...partly by the situation....There is a rapid turnover of staff' and great complexity. (Pitt, 1986, p. 27).

The complexity of the UN Secretariat and its resultant problems was highlighted by Marek Goulding, who as under-secretary-general for Political Affairs (1986–92) found:

> My task was made more difficult by the fact that I had no direct autonomy over two administrative divisions on whose performance the efficiency of the peacekeeping operations was critically dependent. The Office of Field Operational and External Support Activities (OFOESA) which later became the Field Operations Division (FOD) in the Department of Administration and Management was responsible for providing peacekeeping operations with personnel and logistical support of any kind. The Peacekeeping Financial Division in the Budget Office was responsible for all the financial issues. Both Divisions were under the responsibility of the Department of Administration and Management and would take no orders from the OSPA...the director of the FOD had also established a high degree of autonomy within his department. Bureaucratic and diplomatic skills were therefore needed to win the administrators' cooperation, especially when procedural corners had to be cut at the beginning of a new operation.
>
> (Goulding, 2002, p. 30)

The Boutros-Ghali reforms that created the DPKO and the DPA aimed to solve this problem, but the DPA comprised 'disparate elements' (Goulding, 2002, p. 30). The problem remained of 'where the boundary lay between the two new departments in the case of conflicts where a peacekeeping operation had been deployed, or was under discussion' (Goulding, 200, p. 31). For example in 1992, the under-secretary-general for peacekeeping was responsible for peace-making in 13 cases where peacekeeping operations had been deployed (Goulding, 200, p. 31), but the UN approach was that the DPKO was responsible for operational matters and the DPA was responsible for political matters (Goulding, 2002, p. 32). The DPKO drafted all reports on peacekeeping presented to the Security Council, but these reports were vetted by the DPA, causing 'understandable resentment in the DPKO' (Goulding, 2002, p. 334) and complaints from staff in both the DPKO and the DPA about 'alleged iniquities' (Goulding, 2002, p. 334).

Another criticism is that the DPA does not have the capacity to undertake its prevention and resolution tasks (Goulding, 2002, p. 334). In particular, unlike the UN High Commission for Refugees (UNHCR), it lacks a field presence (Weiss, 2010, p. 50). Therefore, it is not informed quickly enough about who makes decisions in a potential spoiler group, what degree of manoeuvre a decision-maker has in a group and to what extent the group is ideologically committed, or merely opportunistic (Rubin and Jones, 2007, p. 406).

Finally, the DPA's staff do not have research skills, but if it is to adopt a more strategic and approach to conflict prevention such skills are necessary (Rublin and Jones, 2007, p. 405):

> Its research capacity is limited; its knowledge about member states and their disputes is selective ... what we lacked was a systematic procedure for enlisting the help of governments, academics, journalists and NGOs in briefing Secretariat officials when a new crisis broke.
>
> (Goulding, 2002, p. 340)

One prescription is that, given the DPA's power to convene formal and informal meetings and given the increasing prevalence of informal 'groups of friends' in the UN system, to engage more deeply and enhance cooperation with key relevant states, for example ex-colonial powers in a given region, and/or with the EU as well as with funding agencies, such as the World Bank (Goulding, 2002, p. 340).

The above criticisms have not gone unnoticed by various UN secretary-generals and the P-5. For example, strategic planning was deepened in 1988, when then Secretary-General Perez de Cuellar established an Office for Research and Collection of Information

(ORCI), (Williams, 2010, p. 436). In 1997 Kofi Annan established the Strategic Planning Unit (SPU) in the Executive Office of the Secretary-General (Williams, 2010, p. 436) to provide 'best-available policy relevant information and research' and 'to enhance the quality, responsiveness and coherence of policy within the UN, including the Secretariat, programs and funds' (Williams, 2010, p. 436). The SPU had three staff, including an assistant secretary-general (Williams, 2010, p. 436). It drafted the secretary-general's annual priorities to ensure that they were supported by four other UN offices-the executive committees on Peace and Security, on Humanitarian Affairs, on Economic and Social Affairs and the UN Development Group (Williams, 2010, p. 437). The SPU also coordinated strategic reports from other units and liaised with national foreign offices and policy planning units, prepared planning papers for key policy issues and drafted the Secretary-General's Annual Report on the Working of the UN (Williams, 2010, p. 437).

A key success was the SPU's establishment of the Global Commission on International Migration (Williams, 2010, p. 439) and the identification of Kofi Annan's key priorities for his second term, through brainstorming meetings and liaison (Williams, 2010, p. 441). Overall, the SPU helped the secretary-general lobby, broker and implement deals (Williams, 2010, p. 444). It was given adequate independence to perform these tasks, but 'the tendency of various components of the system to promote their own agendas made it difficult to develop a coherent organization-wide approach to strategic planning' (Williams, 2010, p. 447).

Various other reforms have occurred with the aim of improving the UN's bureaucracy and its effectiveness in conflict prevention and resolution. For example, in 2000, the Brahimi Report strengthened the planning and management of peacekeeping, information gathering for conflict prevention and created strategic deployment stocks and troops to be ready for crises. In 1992, Secretary-General Boutros-Ghali proposed An Agenda for Peace which led to additional military staff (Mingst and Karns, 2007, p. 248) and recommended that the DPKO should increase its size and skill bases to manage civilian and humanitarian aspects, as well as military aspects of missions (UN, 1992). In 2004, reform of peacekeeping, peace-building and conflict prevention was presented in the High Level Panel on Threats Challenges and Change (HLP) (Rubin and Jones, 2007, p. 391). Recommendations were made to improve planning, information-gathering and analysis to prevent conflict and to increase the size and skill bases of the DPKO to manage civilian and humanitarian aspects, as well as military aspects of missions (UN, 1992). A Peace-Building Commission (PBC) was established comprising government representatives, and international financial institutions and supported by a new office in the Secretariat – the peace-building support office (Rubin and Jones, 2007, p. 392).

In 2006, Kofi Annan presented his reports *Investing in the United Nations* and *Comprehensive Review of Governance and Oversight* within the UN to the General Assembly. The first report aimed to improve accountability and efficiency, as well as to re-vamp human resource management to ensure that staff had adequate field skills for managing complex mandates, (UN, 2006, p. 1). It also delegated responsibility to the deputy secretary-general, rather than UN senior officials being 'directly answerable to the Secretary-General' (UN, 2006, p. 2). The *Comprehensive Review of Governance and Oversight* aimed to improve management and oversight of the UN and improve accountability. Similarly, in 2011, Secretary-General Ban Ki-moon reported that the UN Chief Executives Board for Coordination had been asked to collaborate on a system-wide reform effort and that senior UN managers had also been asked to provide ideas about how the UN system should change (UN, 2011, p. 16). Ban Ki-moon reported that engagement with civil society had increased including more than 6,000 NGOs and 650 universities (UN, 2011, p. 18). In addition, 'an advanced network of private sector experts' to help implement development and security globally, supporting the work of the Global Compact that was created in 2006 to develop corporate responsibility (UN, 2011, p. 19). Despite the above reforms and initiatives, the UN Secretariat's role, as well as that of the UN generally in conflict resolution and prevention continued to be heavily criticized (Rubin and Jones, 2007, p. 394).

Indeed, part of the UN's problem has been the vast number of reform efforts: 'By the sheer quantity of deliberations, debates, studies and resolutions devoted to it, reform has become one of the enduring pastimes and primary products of the UN system' (Luck, 2003). From 1995 to 97, the General Assembly had five working groups dealing with different aspects of reform (Luck, 2003), and in 1997, a volume of all reform measures since the UN's foundation amounted to 3,400 pages. Kofi Annan was criticized for launching his third major reform measure without implementing the two previous ones. For some critics, the key to meaningful reform is to tackle the question of 'who decides', rather than that of 'who implements?', the latter question being met with incremental refinements (Luck, 2003). The relatively fruitless reform efforts are fundamentally hampered by the absence of consensus and support among UN states generally and the P-5 specifically. In particular, 'the key to the success of the Secretariat is its leadership' (Jonah, 2008, p. 170), but that leadership is dominated by the Security Council (Jonah, 2008, p. 170).

Thus, the renewal of Ban Ki-moon's tenure as secretary-general for a second term in 2011 was criticized for occurring at a closed door meeting, where the P-5 could exercise a veto (Chowdury, 2011, p. 1). This decision-making rule implies that the 'very human temptation for a second term is so overwhelming ... that the secretary-general's main effort is wholly conditioned by the desire' and 'the wishes ... of the P5 get the priority attention' (Chowdury, 2011, p. 1). In turn, this situation encourages 'the possibility of a lacklustre leader to emerge' (Chowdury, 2011, p. 1). Similarly, one practitioner has noted that the Security Council has been loath to recommend a strong and independent secretary-general (Jonah, 2008, p. 170), but has expected that the secretary-general 'will perform miracles' (Jonah, 2008, p. 170). While at times the P-5 may inadvertently appoint a very proactive secretary-general, for example, Dag Hammarskjöld (Jonah, 2008, p. 171), such events are rare. Overall, as the next section shows, there are clear differences between the EU's institutional framework and that of the UN, but also some similarities.

Conclusion: Comparing the EU and UN's institutional framework

The obvious difference between the EU and UN's institutional framework is that the UN enshrines sovereignty and the P-5's veto, and the EU disperses power among various institutions, although intergovernmental politics is dominant. The second difference between the EU and UN is that the EU's policy processes are more flexible than those of the UN. The above overview of the evolution of EU foreign policy and the role of the Commission highlights how various crises in the 1990s precipitated changes in the role of committees and of the Commission. While the creation of the EEAS was provided for formally under the Lisbon Treaty, many of the changes that occurred in the EU's foreign policy-making process were informal and at times constituted unintended consequences, at least from the European Council's perspective. For example, Nugent has observed that the Commission has proved adept at maximizing opportunities to extend its influence in foreign policy, when other actors and institutions did not intend that the Commission's influence would increase (Nugent, 2001). EU treaties have provided for reform, but for reform of decision-making, designating that specific new policy sectors will be subject to the Community method, or curtailing Commission influence in certain sectors.

In contrast, the UN has been subject to many formal reforms of its administrative system, but very few reforms of its decision-making system. The UN Charter has been amended only three times since the UN's foundation (Luck, 2003, p. 3), so 'there has been no answer … to the core question of who decides over the past three decades' (Luck, 2003, p. 50). However, Luck observes that many changes to the UN's administrative system have occurred informally (Luck, 2003, p. 48) and that the system 'is highly adaptable to changing world conditions' (Luck, 2003, p. 48). Moreover, 'when reform fails to keep pace with changing needs, or conditions, entrepreneurial UN officials, Member states and civil society representatives are all adept at circumventing the rules and procedures to get things done' (Luck, 2003, p. 48), indicating a degree of flexibility. Also like the EU, 'the course of reform tends to be decidedly unpredictable. Rarely does a reform wave end up where its initiators expected' (Luck, 2003, p. 49). Again, just as the EU's administrative reforms have had unintended consequences, so too do unintended consequences occur in the UN's administrative system. UN and EU reform are also highly politicized, even when reform relates to apparently routine administrative issues (Luck, 2003, p. 5). Intra-institutional turf battles and competition for resources create heightened sensitivity among UN and EU bureaucrats and national affiliation of senior administrators raises national sensitivities – Catherine Ashton, for example, was criticized for appointing a large number of UK diplomats to the EEAS and not providing adequate representation to Germany. Another similarity between the EU and UN's systems is that both have been criticized for being highly compartmentalized, implying that multiple divisions may be dealing with the same functional area.

At the human resource level there are also differences and similarities. In particular, a key difference is that a higher proportion of UN administrative staff are on non-permanent contracts, whereas the EU's international bureaucracy has a higher proportion of permanent staff. Low morale constitutes a similarity between both systems at the human resource level and both bureaucracies are often targets of external criticism, if not scapegoats. Also, as the above sections showed, both the EU and the UN have been subject to reforms to consolidate functional administration and to achieve increased coordination, for example, the Lisbon Treaty, 2007 and Perez de Cuellar and Kofi Annan's reforms to the UN Secretariat in the 1990s and early twenty-first century.

While the above literature review highlights the existence of differences and similarities between the EU and UN's systems, there are not many in-depth empirical analyses of the EU's bureaucratic system and foreign policy and even fewer analyses of the UN's bureaucratic system (Luck, 2003). This chapter has shown that there are reasons to compare both bureaucracies and that the UN's bureaucracy, like the EU's has potential agenda-setting and lobbying powers. Questions remain about whether this potential is realized, if so, under what conditions and about the indicators identified in Chapter 1 – what are the formal and informal rules governing each unit for a given policy? There are gaps in the literature about relative flexibility and the conditions under which it occurs. For example, the UN's bureaucratic response to Rwanda was far from flexible, despite Luck's claims about entrepreneurial UN staff circumventing formal rules. In the next chapter, an overview of EU and UN involvement in conflict zones is provided, highlighting some general themes, before presenting the case study findings.

3
The EU, UN and Conflict Resolution: Overview

As Chapter 1 explained, while both the EU and UN were faced with the challenges of ethnic conflict after the Cold War, historically the UN was regarded as the main organization responsible for peace and security and the EU was more focused on building an economic union among its members. In this chapter, an overview of the EU and UN's involvement in conflict resolution and security issues is provided, highlighting the UN's history of intervention since the 1948 and the evolution of the EU's role since the 1990s.

The UN and conflict resolution

Chapter 2 detailed the various ways in which the Security Council can intervene in a conflict, under the UN Charter. The UN has three main methods in its efforts to resolve conflict: peaceful settlement, the deployment of UN peacekeeping missions and Security Council ratification of military intervention. Under Article 2 of the UN Charter, its key role is to settle conflicts peacefully (Mani, 2008, pp. 301–02). It aims to do so through various means, including negotiation, fact-finding and mediation, (Mani, 2008, pp. 304–07). In deploying these methods, particularly if the parties to a conflict do not want a settlement, the Security Council plays a crucial role, as Chapter 2 showed. Since the 1990s, as Chapters 1 and 2 also showed, the use of these methods has increased significantly.

There have been 53 UN missions since 1948 and 33 of these missions have occurred since 1989 (UN, 2013, http://www.un.org/en/peacekeeping/operations/current.shtml). Until the 1990s the UN's main role was its deployment of peacekeeping operations to conflict zones. The rationale behind peacekeeping forces was that they would keep both sides of a conflict separate to allow peaceful mediation to occur. The first peacekeeping operation was in 1948 to Israel and neighbouring states (the Suez Crisis). France, the UK and Israel attacked Soviet-backed Egypt, claiming a right to use force to keep the Suez Canal open (Weiss et al., 2007, p. 30). The Security Council failed to ratify UN intervention, as France and the UK vetoed it, but under the Uniting for Peace Resolution (see Chapter 2), the General Assembly authorized the UN to intervene (Weiss et al., 2007, p. 30). In 1956, the first UN Emergency Force (UNEF1) oversaw the disengagement of the peacekeeping forces and continued to act as a buffer between Israel and Egypt (Weiss et al., 2007, p. 30). The UN peacekeeping force was regarded as the main means of containing local conflict and it was prohibited from using force except in self-defence, although it also 'contributed to the freezing of the conflict' (Weiss et al., 2007, p. 28), as in Cyprus (Weiss et al., 2007, p. 28). In 1949, the UN's peacekeeping operation was deployed to India and Pakistan and in 1960 to the Congo and 1964 to Cyprus.

During the Cold War, peacekeeping was relatively successful, as most conflicts were inter-state, not intra-state and were easier to resolve (Doyle and Sambanis, 2008, p. 325). Often the peacekeeping operations monitored a truce, so as to allow the UN's Good Offices to mediate, or protected a buffer zone (Doyle and Sambanis, 2008, p. 325). In addition, the peacekeeping operation's presence aimed to facilitate economic and social cooperation, capacity building and institutional reform (Doyle and Sambanis, 2008, p. 327). Overall, 500,000 UN military, police and civilians served in peacekeeping operations during the Cold War and 700 were killed (Weiss et al., 2007, p. 33). From 1948 to 1978 there were 13 peacekeeping missions (Weiss et al., 2007, p. 39). When Ronald Reagan was elected US president in 1979, US–UN relations entered a sour and turbulent phase and US support for UN intervention waned (Weiss et al., 2007, p. 40). The end of the Cold War marked a re-birth of the UN's involvement. In the 1990s, the UN became increasingly involved in peace-building and mediation and the Good Offices of the Secretary-General became increasingly dominant. In the next section, a brief summary of UN intervention from 1950 to 1990 is provided, followed by an overview of UN mediation efforts since the 1990s.

The expansion of the UN's agenda after the Cold War led to the formulation of the Agenda for Peace under Secretary-General Boutros Boutros-Ghali, in 1992 (Doyle and Sambanis, 2008, p. 324). The Agenda for Peace ended the UN's traditional distinction between peacekeeping operations (first-generation operations) and mediation and encompassed 'a far more ambitious group of second generation operations that rely on the consent of the parties, but engaged in activities once thought to be only within the scope of domestic jurisdiction, such as elections monitoring' (Doyle and Sambanis, 2008, p. 325). It also provided for third generation operations, 'that operate with Chapter VII mandates and without a comprehensive agreement' (Doyle and Sambanis, 2008, p. 325) from the parties to a conflict.

Indeed, the UN's record after the Cold War was not entirely unsuccessful. Its role in Namibia, El Salvador, Mozambique, Nepal and Eastern Slavonia had positive effects (Doyle and Sambanis, 2008, p. 325). In Nepal, the DPA desk officer:

> Used second-track approaches and discreet contacts with political parties in parliament, civil society and the press to create a constituency for UN involvement. Based on this work, Under-Secretary-General Lakhdar Brahimi visited the kingdom and the UN also established a human rights mission.
>
> (Rubin and Jones, 2007, p. 396)

The existence of a strong civil society in Nepal contributed to the DPA's success in this case (Rubin and Jones, 2007, p. 396). However, the peace process itself resulted from domestic change, rather than UN mediation, the UN was a facilitator and monitor of the peace process (Rubin and Jones, 2007, p. 396). Indeed, in Nepal, the UN failed to win consent for the use of the Secretary-General's Good Offices, although the DPA was allowed to mediate. In contrast, in Niger, the UN 'applied some lessons from Nepal' in appreciating the degree of preparation needed and also in identifying more modest aims (Rubin and Jones, 2007, p. 397). In particular, the UN has been more successful in institution-building, as it does not require state consent. For example, in Niger, a joint programme was established between the DPA and the UNDP, the first of its kind and the UNDP administers a Bureau for Conflict Prevention and Recovery to strengthen capacity to prevent conflict in developing countries (Rubin and Jones, 2007, p. 397), by increasing local, regional and national capacities to prevent conflict (Rubin and Jones, 2007, p. 401).

Another UN success was El Salvador, where, 'the Council gave international endorsement to the UN-brokered negotiations between the government of El Salvador and an insurgent movement, the Farabundo Marti National Liberation Front (FMLN)' (Antonini, 2004, p. 423). This endorsement followed human rights abuses, political and economic deprivation and a resort to armed forces, during the 1980s. In August 1987, the 'Procedure for the Establishment of a Firm and Lasting Peace in Central America' was established under the president of Costa Rica, Oscar Arias (Antonini, 2004, p. 424). In response, the Security Council gave a mandate to the Secretary-General, Perez de Cuellar, to use his Good Offices to mediate a solution (Antonini, 2004, p. 424). However, the murder of six Jesuit priests and their housekeeper in 1987 by soldiers under military command increased pressure to resolve the conflict (Antonini, 2004, p. 425). In December 1991, agreement for a 'verifiable' ceasefire was reached with Marek Goulding (Antonini, 2004, p. 429). The peace accord was signed in January 1992 (Antonini, 2004, p. 430), followed by the UN's establishment of the UN Observer Mission in El Salvador, (ONUSAL) to oversee implementation of the accord (Antonini, 2004, p. 430). However, by October 1992, the deadline for full relinquishing of armed conflict had not been met. Goulding and Special Envoy, Alvaro de Soto actively mediated and in December 1992, the armed conflict had come to an end (Antonini, 2004, p. 432). Various obstacles occurred in subsequent years, but by 1995, when ONUSAL withdrew, many commitments had been kept and a smaller UN mission (MINUSAL) was established to monitor the implementation of remaining commitments (Antonini, 2004, p. 434).

The El Salvador case was regarded as a UN success and a 'pioneering experience' (Antonini, 2004, p. 435). It illustrated 'the independent nature of UN action when states give the world organization the room to maneuver' (Weiss et al., 2007, p. 54). The fact that the P-5 supported the process was a key factor in it success, but the mediation efforts of de Cuellar, Goulding, de Soto and their team were also praised (Weiss et al., 2007, p. 54), although very little specific analysis of that role has been provided. Similarly, the UN's role in Mozambique was praised.

The UN Operation in Mozambique, (ONUMOZ), launched under Resolution 797, was 'one of the most ambitious, multifaceted missions undertaken by the UN up to that time' (Ajello and Wittmann, 2004, p. 437). The UN did not play a role in the initial 1992 Rome agreement governing Mozambique, but it was crucial in providing technical and political help to advance the process (Ajello and Wittmann, 2004, p. 439). The UN established a Supervision and Monitoring Commission chaired by the Special Representative of the Secretary-General (SRSG). The commission was 'empowered to act on all matters related to implementation of the peace agreement' (Ajello and Wittmann, 2004, p. 439).

In the Mozambique case, the SRSG used all power available to him and was accused of exceeding his remit, but 'he interpreted his mandate broadly to ensure that ONUMOZ took the initiative early on' (Ajello and Wittmann, 2004, p. 439). His proactive approach ensured that the process was kept on track and delays were not used to derail it (Ajello and Wittmann, 2004, p. 439). Communication between the Special Representative and the Security Council was also praised (Ajello and Wittmann, 2004, p. 440). The SRSG also coordinated strategy with the diplomatic community in Mozambique, creating a united front to the Security Council (Ajello and Wittmann, 2004, p. 441). His intense communication and coordination efforts led to the Security Council speaking with one voice at crucial moments. In Mozambique, he ceased to be viewed as a remote irrelevant UN delegate, but as influential, representing the international community (Ajello and Whitmann, 2004, p. 442). Moreover 'with hard work from the UN Secretariat in New York, the final text of the Secretary-General's Report generally remained unchanged from the SRSG's draft and was always consistent with needs in the field' (Ajello and Whitman, 2004, p. 443).

This consistency was also assured by the SRSG briefing Security Council local ambassadors who were based in Maputo, the 'shadow Security Council' (Ajello and Whitman, 2004, p. 443). This briefing ensured support from the Security Council in New York (Ajello and Whitman, 2004, p. 443). Overall, the Mozambique case was an example of successful UN intervention, with no one state leading the mission although a concert of sympathetic states was involved (Ajello and Whitmann, 2004, p. 448). The key condition for UN success was the will of the parties to reach agreement. However, the end of the

Cold War also meant that the P-5 wanted to have a success story and were very supportive. The role of the SRSG was also praised, in his shrewd strategy and briefings of the Council and of internal actors (Ajello and Whitmann, 2004, p. 448).

However, in contrast to the El Salvador and Mozambique cases, the UN's role in Cambodia fell between success and failure – an example of the UN's limitations, but also possibilities (Berdal and Leifer, 2007, p. 64). Cambodia history was marred by rival claims over its legitimate government (Berdal and Lefier, 2007, p. 33). In Cambodia, the UN made feeble attempts during the Cold War to resolve the conflict between the Khmer regime and Vietnamese government (supported by Russia), whose military forces had invaded Cambodia. However, in 1985, under Mikhail Gorbachev, Russia began to disengage from Cambodia and other cases, allowing the UN to play a more effective role (Berdal and Leiffer, 2007, p. 38). In 1989, the Australian government 'began to explore ... a proposal by US Congressman Stehen Solarz for a direct UN role to overcome the impasse in power-sharing' (Berdal and Leiffer, 2007, p. 39) and in 1991, under the Paris Agreement, a diluted version of the plan was endorsed by the P-5 (Berdal and Leiffer, 2007, p. 39). Under the agreement, a UN transitional authority for Cambodia (UNTAC) was set up with all powers necessary to implement the power-sharing agreement (Berdal and Leiffer, 2007, p. 41). The UN was partially successful in that free and fair elections occurred in 1993 (Berdal and Lefier, 2007, p. 60). However, Cambodia, although it made considerable progress in the 1990s, compared to its violent past, continued to suffer from human rights violations (Berdal and Leifer, 2007, p. 64). Moreover, there were criticisms of the UN Secretariat's role. There was a 'paucity of staff' (Berdal and Leifer, 2007, p. 52) in the DPKO and weak strategic planning and military–civil cooperation within the UN (Berdal and Leifer, 2007, p. 52). There were also inadequate reporting channels and chains of command between the UN in New York and UNTAC (Berdal and Leifer, 2007, p. 57).

Thus for some observers, the UN's role in Cambodia was a UN success story (Doyle and Sambanis, 2008, p. 327), because eventually free and fair elections occurred and a power-sharing government was formed, but for others the UN was only partially successful (Berdal and Leifer, 2007, p. 64). In addition to criticisms of the UN's role in Cambodia, the UN was deeply criticized for its failure in Rwanda and Bosnia (see Chapter 2) and indeed, criticisms of the UN's role in

Cambodia pale in significance compared to criticisms of its role in these cases.

The UN has also enforced peace and peace enforcement was the justification used in the Gulf War in 1990, when under Chapter VII, the Security Council ratified military intervention, led by the US and UK (Doyle and Sambasis, 2008, p. 327). Enforcement is defined as 'operations that seek to impose the will of Security Council by direct military, or economic action' (Bellamy, 2005, p. 22). In the absence of consent from the conflicting groups, the UN 'must in effect conquer the warring factions' (Doyle and Sambanis, 2008, p. 332), In other cases, the UN has some support, but not from all sides and imposes distinct arrangements for one side, or more, for example humanitarian corridors of relief (Doyle and Sambanis, 2008, p. 332). In many cases, economic sanctions, or blockades are backed up by military force, or its threat, for example, in the Gulf War in 1990 and in the Balkans in the 1990s (Pugh, 2008, p. 372).

The mushrooming of ethnic conflict in the 1990s led to a shift in emphasis from traditional UN peacekeeping to calls for stronger peace enforcement. The key example of this change was the failure of UN–US intervention in Somalia from 1992 to 1995, UNOSOM11) (Pugh, 2008, p. 374). The original mandate was to provide security to allow humanitarian aid to reach Somalia (Pugh, 2008, p. 374). However, the US dominated the UN's military command and control structure and lobbied successfully to change the UN's rules of engagement (Pugh, 2008, p. 374).

Similarly in 1992, under Resolution 758, the UN Protection Force in the Balkans (UNPROFOR) was accorded 'Chapter VII enforcement powers' (Pugh, 2008, p. 374) to take control of Sarajevo airport. However, the UN lacked military effectiveness and NATO conducted airstrikes, unauthorized by the Security Council, in 1994 (Pugh, 2008, p. 375). In contrast, in Rwanda, as chapters 1 and 2 mentioned, UN intervention was blocked by France and the UK (Pugh, 2008, p. 375):

> The reluctance of Western political elites to provide political and material support for the UN Assistance Mission for Rwanda (UNA-MIR) meant that the UN Secretariat lacked the backing to undertake population protection and weapons raids. Members of the UN Secretariat adopted a defeatist approach....
>
> (Pugh, 2008, p. 375)

Thus, in many cases the UN used Chapter V11 to authorize enforcement, but in other cases enforcement was not used, for example, Rwanda and Darfur, highlighting the role of the P-5's interests in determining whether the UN intervenes (Pugh, 2008, p. 377).

Indeed, the problems faced in gaining P-5 support for UN proactivity in the post-Cold War system have been starkly highlighted by the UN's record in the Israel–Palestine conflict and also its response to the Arab Spring and its aftermath from 2011.As regards Israel and Palestine, 'the abundant literature . . . contains scant reference to the role of the UN' (Jones, 2004, p. 391), indicating that by the 1990s, despite relatively significant UN performance in earlier years, the UN appeared to be peripheral (Jones, 2004, p. 391). During the Cold War, a draft resolution to create a new UN force in Israel was blocked by the Soviet Union (Jones, 2004, p. 395). Arab lobbying blocked the deployment of UN forces in the Sinai in 1979 and Israeli forces blocked the movement of UNIFIL personnel in Lebanon in 1983, ushering in the period of UN marginalization (Jones, 2004, p. 395).

While the end of the Cold War appeared to open opportunities for peace in the Middle East, efforts were US-led, rather than UN-led. The UN and EU were given observer status, not participant status at the Madrid Peace Conference in 1992, under the leadership of George Bush. Following stagnation in the Madrid process (Muller, 2012, p. 41) an Israeli–Palestinian framework agreement was reached in 1993 and the Oslo Accords were signed in a ceremony hosted by President Clinton (Müller, 2012, p. 42) – the UN was not involved (Jones, 2004, p. 395).

However, the failure of the Oslo Accords, the assassination of Israel's Prime Minister Yitzhak Rabin, the election of the right-wing Benjamin Netanyahu and the resettlement of most of the West Bank (Müller, 2012, p. 43) contributed to increased UN activity. The then Secretary-General Boutros Boutros-Ghali appointed Terje Roed-Larsen as special coordinator for the occupied (Jones, 2004, p. 395). Kofi Annan's reign as secretary-general also saw a reinvigorated UN role, where he lobbied UN states to allow Israel become a member of its West European Group (Jones, 2004, p. 396) Kofi Annan also reappointed Roed-Larssen to the post of special coordinator (Jones, 2004, p. 396). For some observers, 'the combination of Annan's effort to restore relations with Israel and the reappointment of Roed-Larsen . . . rapidly created new political space for the (Security)

Council' (Jones, 2004, p. 396). Roed-Larsen persuaded Israeli Prime Minister Barak to work within UN Resolution 425 and Roed-Larsen and UNIFIL monitored the border to ensure full Israeli compliance (Jones, 2004, p. 397). This heightened UN role, with significant UN Secretariat involvement, was weakened after the 9/11 terrorist attacks (Jones, 2004, p. 397) and the US repeatedly used vetoes or their threat to prevent Security Council resolutions (Jones, 2004, p. 397). Similarly, the Security Council failed to reach agreement on recognizing Palestinian statehood in 2011 and US President Obama was criticized for his unsupportive speech to the General Assembly. However, the Assembly eventually voted in favour of granting observer status to Palestine.

In the attempt to circumvent Security Council dissent and the primacy of state sovereignty under international law, the concept of Responsibility to Protect (R2P) was outlined by the Canadian-sponsored International Commission in Intervention and State Sovereignty (ICISS), proposing that UN intervention should occur where the population of a region is at risk of a gross erosion of human rights, for example, genocide, or ethnic cleansing, regardless of whether the region is a sovereign state. R2P 'was one of the few substantive items to survive the negotiations at the 2005 World Summit' (Pugh, 2008, p. 398). There is a division of opinion as to whether R2P has been used effectively to date, or whether it is used as a justification for US, or P-5 state interest: 'Ill-considered rhetoric of pre-emptive strikes and Iraq as an example of "humanitarian intervention", risk draining support from R2P rather than adding to the legitimacy of such enterprises' (Thakur, 2006, p. 262).

Similarly, despite R2P, the UN's response to the Arab Spring was curtailed by dissent among the P-5 on the Security Council. In Libya in 2010, the UN was slow to respond to a humanitarian crisis. However, eventually the Security Council used R2P to justify intervention in Libya. Resolution 1970 had unanimous support for a substantial package of measures (arms embargo, asset freezes, travel bans and referral of the situation to the International Criminal Court) (Weiss, 2011). Moreover, 11 Council decisions have involved the R2P norm, and six of those took place in 2011 after Libya – for South Sudan, Yemen and Syria (Weiss, 2011).

The Syrian case also highlighted the UN's poor response, as a mounting humanitarian crisis developed in 2013 and the P-5 could not reach agreement on intervention, mainly hindered by a Russian veto. For Weiss, despite all that progress, the international actions (or inactions) aimed at protecting non combatants in Syria indicate that a robust R2P response certainly is not automatic. (Weiss, 2012)

While the previous sections have examined peacekeeping operations and military intervention, the UN has also been deeply involved in 'soft' intervention, either in conjunction with military intervention, or on its own. Thus, the UN has provided humanitarian aid to conflict zones and it has implemented sanctions against specific states.

Sanctions were first used against Rhodesia in 1966 and only used again in 1977 against South Africa, during the Cold War (Cortright, Lopez and Gerber-Stellingwerf, 2008, p. 349). From 1990 to date, sanctions were used more far frequently starting with Iraq in 1990 (Cortright et al., 2008, p. 349). While the rationale behind sanctions it to use non-military means under Charter VII to resolve a conflict, sanctions against Iraq highlighted the trade-off between that aim and minimizing distress to civilians (Cortright et al., 2008, p. 350). For some participants, sanctions against Iraq after it invaded Kuwait, were effective, as they forced the Iraqi regime to allow UN weapons inspection (Cortright et al., 2008, p. 351).

However, the oil for food scandal, describe in Chapter 2, undermined the credibility of sanctions and the US insistence that sanctions would continue as long as Saddam Hussein was in power, rather than being contingent on Iraqi cooperation with UN also weakened their legitimacy (Cortright et al., 2008, p. 351). The most devastating effect of sanctions against Iraq was their impact on innocent civilians. Thousands of preventable deaths among children occurred (Garfield, 1999).

From 1994 targeted sanctions were used (Cortright et al., 2008, p. 358). The UN published a list of targeted individuals who would face travel bans and a freezing of assets in various states, including, Liberia, Angola, Sierra Leone, Afghanistan (Cortright et al., 2008, p. 359). In Iraq, Libya and the ex-Yugoslavia, the UN froze governments' assets. The Yugoslav case was heralded as a particular success. A multinational monitoring regime was established by the Conference in Security and Cooperation in Europe (CSCE) and the EU to implement UN sanctions. The EU established the

Sanctions Assistance Missions Communication System in Brussels (SAMCOMM). SAMCOMM developed a computerized satellite system 'made available and funded by the US' (Cortright et al., 2008, p. 360). The EU–UN–US cooperative system 'established a substantial institutional capacity for monitoring and enforcing sanctions' (Cortright et al., 2008, p. 360) and constituted 'the first time that major regional organizations stepped in to assist the UN' (Cortright et al., 2008, pp. 360–61).

Indeed, according to the UN's official report on the sanctions regime 'this unique and unprecedented formula of coordinated inter-institutional cooperation at the regional level...was identified as the main reason for the effectiveness of sanctions in the case of the former Yugoslavia' (UN Security Council 1996, letter dated September 24, paras. 48 and 49).

While the above level of inter-organizational cooperation did not occur again, the UN did establish independent expert panels and monitoring mechanisms to improve the implementation of sanctions (Cortright et al., 2008, p. 361). The first panel was established to implement an arms embargo against Hutu rebels in Rwanda in 1995 (Cortright et al., 2008, p. 362). Subsequent panels were created for Sierra Leone, Afghanistan, Liberia, Somalia and the Democratic Republic of Congo (DRC). In Liberia, the panel recommended that sanctions be imposed on the Charles Taylor regime for its role in undermining sanctions in Sierra Leone and in supporting rebels there (Cortright et al., 2008, p. 362). These UN efforts were subsequently built upon by Swiss, German and Swedish governmental efforts, from 1998 to 2001, to improve sanctions regimes (Cortright et al., 2008, pp. 362–63).

However, despite improvements, differences between the P-5 have left important issues unresolved. In particular, in 2000, no agreement was reached on whether sanctions should be subject to a strict time limit, (the French preference) to avoid the outcome in Iraq when sanctions were implemented indefinitely, or whether no time limits should be added (the US and UK preference) (Cortright et al., 2008, p. 364). Similarly, the US and UK wanted to maintain the use of veto in with respect to sanctions, but France and Russia wanted to introduce majority rule (Cortright et al., 2008, p. 365). Thus, while changes have occurred, UN sanctions reform has been hindered by dissent on the P-5.

The above overview has highlighted the UN's multifaceted role in conflict resolution, indicated also by the quadrupling of Security Council resolutions between 1987 and 1994 and the tripling of its peacekeeping operations during this period (Doyle and Sambasis, 2008, p. 333). Its success has been patchy. Assessments of peacekeeping operations have found that by the mid-1990s, only 11 out of 39 operations were successful, and nearly half (19) were labelled as failures (Diehl, 2008, p. 126). However, Fortna (2004) in examining all cases of war from 1945 to 2004 found that peacekeeping operations can reduce the renewal of conflict by 30 to 95 per cent, controlling for the severity of the conflict. Other studies have found that peacekeeping operations reduce the likelihood of conflicting groups reaching a settlement, because they freeze the conflict and prevent a hurting stalemate from occurring (Greig and Diehl, 2005). Moreover, the UN's peace-building operations have been criticized for regarding elections and the trappings of Western democracy as the badge of success, when often domestic institutional capacity has hindered UN efforts, even if elections occur (Paris, 2004). More attention should be paid to capacity-building in these cases (Paris, 2004). The EU has also been criticized for its limitations in conflict resolution, as the next section shows.

The EU and conflict resolution

Since 2000, there have been 30 EU civilian and military missions across the world (European External Action Service, 2013, http://www.eeas.europa.eu/csdp/missions-and-operations/completed/index _en.htm). In this section, the evolution of EU foreign policy is examined from the 1950s onwards. The failure of the attempt to establish a common European army and foreign policy in 1953 contributed to the evolution of the EU's technocratic and economic focus. EU's first common policies were in trade and in agriculture (the Common Agricultural Policy, CAP). As Chapter 2 explained, the functional emphasis was necessitated by the need to maintain political support for the new institution by forging common policies on the basis of perceived common interests. As interdependence increased in the post-war years, the range of common interests also increased and the EU expanded both in membership and in its policy range. However, EU foreign policy was slow to develop until the 1990s and the EU 'developed throughout the Cold War first and foremost as an economic actor' (Marsh and Mackenstein, 2005, p. 51). In the next section, key events in the evolution of EU foreign policy are highlighted.

During the Cold War, dependence on NATO for military protection made the EU's attempts to develop a European foreign policy seem irrelevant (Keukeleire and McNaughton, 2008, p. 10) and led to emphasis on the EU as a 'civilian power' (Duchene, 1972) not a military power. Yet, member state preferences in the EU were divided between 'Atlanticists' who sought to develop cooperation with the US and act as the US' partner through NATO and 'Gaullists' who sought to develop the EU as an independent foreign policy actor, not influenced by the US. The outcome of these various preferences and the association of foreign policy as a key badge of sovereignty led to the evolution of an intergovernmental EU foreign policy in the 1970s and 1980s, not a supranational common policy (Keukeleire and McNaughton, 2008, p. 11).

The first initiative in foreign policy was the establishment of EPC in 1970–73. EPC was necessitated by the overlap between the EU's common economic policies in trade and agriculture and its external relations with non-EU states. As early as 1966, the European Commission represented the six EU states in the General Agreement on Tariffs and Trade (GATT) negotiations (Keukeleire and McNaughton, 2008, p. 43). Thus, the Luxembourg Report in 1970 emphasized 'the need to intensify political cooperation' (Keukeleire and McNaughton, 2008, p. 44). However, the Luxembourg Report and subsequent EPC were modest in content. They established a system of regular exchanges of information between states and aimed to coordinate EU members' views (Keukeleire and McNaughton, 2008, p. 44). While EPC was regarded as a vital stepping stone to later EU foreign policy initiatives (Smith, 2001, p. 86–88), its weakness was highlighted by the EU's response to the oil crisis in 1974. The nine EU states could not agree on a unified response and individual states acted independently of each other, with the Netherlands playing a lead role. Indeed partially in response to the EU's failure to respond effectively to the Oil Crisis, the intergovernmental European Council was established in 1974, spearheaded by Giscard D'Estaing, then president of France and Schmidt, then Chancellor of West Germany, who argued that the Europe's interests were not served by the Commission making 1000s of statements each month. By the 1980s, the EU had failed to respond effectively to 'the major crises at the time, such as the Middle East, Afghanistan and Poland' (Keukeleire and McNaughton, 2008, p. 49).

While EPC was weak and the European Council was an inter-governmental initiative, the Council, including its Presidency, the Commission and the EU's committee system all gradually became central to a deeper foreign policy from the 1990s, as Chapter 2 showed. The establishment of the CFSP under the Maastricht Treaty in 1992 'created major expectations (Keukeleire and McNaughton, 2008, p. 51), although it was a compromise between those who favoured deeper integration (France and Germany) and those who opposed it (the UK and Denmark)' (Keukeleire and McNaughton, 2008, p. 51). However, it was predominantly intergovernmental in substance and its weakness was exposed when Germany unilaterally recognized Croatia in 1993. The failure of the EU to respond ade-quately to the Balkans crisis also highlighted the superficial nature of the CFSP. However in 1994 to 1995, the Council Presidencies, 'with active support of the Commission…mapped out the major lines of policy towards most regions in the world' (Keukeleire and McNaughton, 2008, p. 52), but often the results of these policies were disappointing, as the next sections show.

For example as regards Israel, the EU 'historically upheld Israel's right to statehood' (Tocci, 2008, p. 100), but developed policy on Palestine also. In 1973, the EU affirmed 'the legitimate rights of Palestinians' (Tocci, 2008, p. 100) and in 1980, the EU Council's Venice Declaration backed Palestinian right to self-determination (Tocci, 2008, p. 101). However, it was met with anger from Israel and a cool response from both the Palestinian Liberation Organiza-tion (PLO) who argued that the statement did not go far enough and a cool response from the US (Muller, 2012, p. 35). In response, the EU 'withdrew from involvement in Middle East peacekeeping dur-ing most of the 1980s' (Müller, 2012, p. 35). Like the UN, the EU was a peripheral actor in both the Oslo Accords and the sets of peace negotiations. It was viewed as being involved in economic aspects of peace talks, as it had developed strong economic links with Israel, but the US was the lead political actor (Müller, 2012, p. 35). However, also like the UN, the EU responded proactively to the failure of the Oslo Accords. The Commission issued a report stating that the divi-sion of labour between the EU and the US had worked imperfectly and 'acknowledged the need for the EU to participate in all fora set up to assist bilateral negotiations between the parties' (Müller, 2012, p. 43). In 1996, the EU appointed a Special Envoy to the peace processes (Müller, 2012, p. 44) and in 1999, the EU's Berlin Declaration mentioned the EU's readiness to recognize a Palestinian state (Müller, 2012, p. 45).

Thus in 2001, the EU set out a two-state solution (Tocci, 2008, p. 101) and from 2002 to 2005 it 'vigorously pursued conditionality in the attempt to pursue Palestinian reform' (Tocci, 2008, p. 123). Yet the effect of economic policy was disappointing and the Commission was critical of the Palestinian Authority's slow reform process and its abuses of human rights and democracy (Müller, 2012, p. 49). However, for Tocci, from 2000 the EU's role was increasingly constrained, as Palestinian suicide attacks grew in frequency and the US was viewed as neglecting the crisis (Tocci, 2008, p. 112). Thus 'in the absence of a decisive US engagement in the Israeli–Palestinian arena, the EU proved unable to effectively put a halt to the destructive cycle of retaliation and counter-retaliation that unfolded between Israel and the Palestinians' (Müller, 2012, p. 52). These factors were exacerbated by the dominance of French, UK and German preferences in forging policy to Israel and Palestine (Müller, 2012, p. 3).

However, in contrast to negative appraisals of the EU's role in Israel–Palestine, Müller argues that although unsuccessful in resolving the conflict, the EU's policy to the Middle East became increasingly consistent and coherent from the mid-1990s, despite different preferences among its members and it increasingly played an active role in negotiations (Müller, 2012, pp. 67–68). In particular, the creation of the Middle East Quartet in 2002, comprising the UN, US, EU and Russia strengthened the EU's role (Müller, 2012, p. 6). It facilitated increased EU–US cooperation and the 2002 Roadmap Initiative incorporated EU ideas (Müller, 2012, p. 54).

Overall, the EU was criticized for ineffective responses to conflict and as Chapter 2 showed agreed various Treaty changes to deal with these criticisms. In particular in 1998, 'ESDP qualitatively changed the nature of the CFSP. It allowed the CFSP move from a declaratory foreign policy ... to a more action-oriented foreign policy focused on pro-active crisis management' (Keukeleire and McNaughton, 2008, p. 54). 'By the end of 2003, the EU had embarked on no fewer than four overseas missions, including two police missions and two military missions and in 2004 it launched its biggest ever mission, Operation EUFOR-Althea in Bosnia Herzegovina' (Howorth, 2007, pp. 207–08). Both the European Neighbourhood Policy (ENP) and the Lisbon Treaty sought to build upon these developments, as the next section shows.

In response to the 9/11 attacks, in 2003 the European Council adopted the 'European Security Strategy' presented by High Representative Javier Solana (Keukeleire and McNaughton, 2008, p. 59). It aimed to deal with the post-9/11 security threat and also to develop positive relations with neighbouring states – European Neighbourhood Policy (ENP) (Keukeleire and McNaughton, 2008, p. 59). However, in 2003, despite both the Amsterdam Treaty and Solana's strategy, EU responses to the Iraq War in 2003 were deeply divided, with the UK and Spain supporting the war and other states, led by France and Germany being deeply opposed.

The ENP was launched in 2004 to coincide with the 2004 enlargement process. Applicant states were not subject to the ENP (Whitman and Wolff, 2010, p. 6) and it 'was intended to strengthen existing regional and sub-regional cooperation' (Whitman and Wolff, 2010, p. 7). Its aims were to spread stability and security in the EU's neighbourhood, but although it offered financial assistance, its benefits were perceived to be too modest to bring about change in its neighbourhood (Whitman and Wolff, 2010, p. 13).

Moreover, in the midst of division and despite the failure to ratify the Constitutional Treaty in 2005, plans for EU foreign policy reform accelerated. Battle Groups to enable fast deployment in a crisis, comprising many representatives from EU member states forces (Howorth, 2007, p. 108). In 2008, the Lisbon Treaty provided for the new EEAS, headed by Catherine Ashton, as Chapter 2 outlined. The EEAS was faced with many immediate challenges, not least the humanitarian disaster in Haiti in 2009. Ashton was 'heavily and often unfairly criticized by many within the EU for her lack of action' (Allen and Smith, 2010, p. 210). However, in the first year she was faced with turf wars between the Commission and the Council, neither of which wanted to hand over powers to the EEAS (Allen and Smith, 2010, p. 210).

By 2012, these turf wars had not abated and the EEAS and its High Representative were 'condemned to a Janus-faced existence' (Hadfield and Fiott, 2013, p. 172). It was established to support both the Council and the Commission, but the Council retained decision-making powers and the Commission retained implementation and policy initiation powers as well as external representation in other domains (Blockmans, 2012, p. 7). Moreover, as the EEAS Executive Secretary, Pierre Vimont stated:

> The EEAS is not a fully-fledged institution . . . for the Commission, as such we do not have the legal status to deal with the different operational and financial resources that it manages.
>
> (House of Lords, 2013b, p. 12)

In addition, the creation of the EEAS coincided with the immense economic crisis in the EU leading it to observe its first year report that:

> The political and economic context for the launch of the EEAS has been particularly challenging. The global economic crisis and tensions within the Eurozone together with the Arab Spring have dominated the international agenda.
>
> (EEAS, 2011, p. 6)

Thus the EEAS and the EU overall were criticized in their responses to various crises. In Libya in 2011, when General Gaddafi took military action against Libyan citizens, France took the lead in pushing for international action against Gaddafi, but 'whilst the EU was prepared to make critical statements and provide humanitarian assistance, the member states were quite bitterly divided against the desirability of using military force' (Allen and Smith, 2012, p. 165). In 2012, clashes between rebel forces in Libya and the new National Transitional Council and the murder of US Ambassador Christopher Stevens and three other American citizens also met with a weak EU response (Hadfield and Fiott, 2013, p. 173). Ashton was also criticized 'for her tardiness in condemning' (Hadfield and Fiott, 2013, p. 173) newly elected Mohammed Morsi's weakening of democratic institutions in Egypt. As regards Syria, the EU did react quickly in removing the military option in response to friction over NATO's earlier intervention in Libya (Hadfield and Fiott, 2013, p. 173) and it imposed sanctions on Syria (Hadfield and Fiott, 2013, p. 173).

A core problem in the EU's response to Syria was that the ENP, the EU's usual policy tool in dealing with the Middle East, was not a policy for crisis – management (Whitman and Juncos, 2012, p. 151). Hoping to overcome this weakness, in 2011, Baroness Ashton and the Commissioner for Enlargement Štefan Füle presented 'A New Response to a Changing Neighbourhood' (European Commission, 2011a) to the EU's key institutions (Whitman and Juncos, 2012, p. 152). The review of the ENP led to the conclusion that a new approach was needed to build and consolidate healthy democracies and mentions the need for 'stronger political cooperation on…security and…conflict resolution matters' (European Commission, 2011a, pp. 1–3).

The EU's response to the UN General Assembly's agreement to give Palestine observer status in the UN also met with a divided response: Ashton expressed support for Palestine to become a full member of the UN, but in the UN, only 14 states in the EU voted in favour of Palestine (Hadfield and Fiott, 2013, pp. 173–74).

In contrast, Baroness Ashton was commended for her management of the Serbia–Kosovo relationship (see Chapter 6) and the enlargement process in the Balkans was heralded as a success. Indeed, as chapters 1 and 2 showed, enlargement policy has evolved as the cornerstone of EU foreign policy. In addition, while the EU's response to Arab Spring was criticized, as regards the CSDP, by 2013, the EU had deployed 16 missions.

Conclusion

Overall, the above overview of EU and UN involvement in conflict resolution since the 1950s highlights some general themes raised in the historical and institutional overview in Chapter 2. If assessing the EU and UN on the basis of their success in conflict zones, the record is quite negative. The UN, perhaps understandably given its longer history of involvement and its *raison d'etre* under the Charter, has had some successes, as noted above. The EU, as Chapter 6 shows has been praised for its strategy towards the Balkans from 2010. Yet overall there have been many failures and weaknesses. Clearly member state preferences in both the EU and the UN have undermined attempts to respond to crises quickly and effectively and clearly the US has been a lead actor in many cases, for example in the Middle East.

However, beneath a broad brush assessment of success and reasons for failure, other themes are highlighted by this chapter. The EU's increasing involvement in conflict zones and its evolution as a foreign policy actor is particularly stark. Its institutional evolution is also very obvious and the pace of EU institutional change surpasses that of the UN. However, both the EU and UN's histories provide examples of institutional entrepreneurship and leadership; for example, the role of the UN Secretariat in policy to the Middle East in the mid-1990s was striking, as was the Commission's role in the same period. Thus, while many EU and UN attempts to resolve conflict have failed, the above overview also highlights the actual and potential influence of international bureaucrats in conflict situations, under certain conditions. In the next chapter, the extent of EU and UN bureaucratic autonomy and influence is determined in the cases of Northern Ireland, Cyprus and Kosovo.

4
Northern Ireland

In 1998, Northern Ireland became the poster child for international intervention, when the Good Friday/Belfast Agreement (GFA) was signed, bringing the 30-year violent conflict to an end. While the UN was not involved in conflict resolution in Northern Ireland, the EU heralded the GFA as an example of the EU's ameliorating role. It was observed that 'without the embedding of both states in the wider system of European integration and without the models of politics offered by the EU, it is unlikely that both states and other political actors could have found the political capacity and the institutional models to craft the Good Friday Agreement' (Laffan, 2003, p. 14). Indeed, in 1998, Northern Ireland was the only example of a successful peace process within the EU, for which the EU took some credit.

In this chapter, the role of the EU is examined in Northern Ireland, so as to determine the impact of EU institutional processes in conflict resolution from 1988 to 1998. The assumption is that while there have been problems in implementing the GFA 'on the ground', and while there is still inter-communal division, the GFA did bring an end to 30 years of violent conflict in Northern Ireland, and thus Northern Ireland is a template of success within the EU. As it is the first example of a peace process within the EU, it is useful to examine the EU's role as a benchmark by which to compare its subsequent policy processes to conflict in the Cyprus and Kosovo cases. Specifically, two questions are addressed in this chapter: firstly, what were the EU's bureaucratic processes in the 1990s to Northern Ireland, and did these bureaucratic processes change in later conflict cases – the

Cyprus and Kosovo cases? Secondly, is there a difference between EU processes to conflict when the UN is not involved and policy processes when both the EU and UN are involved, as in the Cyprus and Kosovo cases?

In this chapter, it is argued that the EU's policy process to Northern Ireland was primarily intergovernmental and that the Commission played a relatively minor role in conflict resolution in Northern Ireland. In the first section of the chapter, a history of the conflict in Northern Ireland is provided. In the second section, an overview of EU policy to Northern Ireland from 1973 to 1998 is provided, and in the third section, the EU's policy process to Northern Ireland is examined. In conclusion, it is argued that state preferences were the sole factors in explaining EU policy outcomes to Northern Ireland.

The Northern Ireland conflict: Historical overview

The roots of the conflict in Northern Ireland lay in divisions between Irish nationalists, who wished to form of a united and independent Irish state with 32 counties, and British nationalists, that is, unionists, whose allegiance was to the UK. The Anglo-Irish Treaty in 1921 provided for partition of Ireland into Northern Ireland (six, but not all nine, counties of Ulster) and Ireland (26 counties) reflected an attempt to reconcile unionist and nationalist claims.

A unionist regime was built in isolation from Ireland (Tannam, 2013). Irish nationalists suffered extensive discrimination during regime consolidation: through gerrymandering and exclusion from fair participation in key institutions, the nationalists responded in various ways, including apathy and parliamentary abstention (Farrell, 1977). By the 1960s, however, Northern Ireland's nationalists had mobilized behind a campaign of civil disobedience, based on the tactics of the civil rights movement in the US. When this movement was met with extreme opposition from a majority of unionists, support for the use of violent means by the Provisional Irish Republican Army (IRA) increased.

Communication and cooperation between nationalist politicians in both parts of Ireland declined after partition (Tannam, 1999, pp. 43–49). There was bureaucratic resistance among the new Irish civil service and political leaders, where it was argued that cross-border cooperation was an implicit recognition of the border and also (as time passed) that Northern Ireland was a competitor for tourists and foreign investment (Tannam, 1999, pp. 43–9). The then Irish Prime Minister Sean Lemass and his Northern Irish counterpart, Terence O'Neill, attempted to develop cooperation, but their attempt failed under political pressure from unionists (Tannam, 1999, p. 61). The civil rights movement in Northern Ireland attempted to reform undemocratic aspects of the Northern Ireland regime, for example, allocation of local housing and an end of gerrymandering of votes. However, Northern Ireland had descended into violence by summer 1968 (Arthur and Jeffrey, 1996, p. 9), with growing violent opposition from unionists and increased nationalist support for the IRA's violent means. In October 1968, a peaceful civil rights march in Derry/Londonderry, led by John Hume, leader of the Social Democratic and Labour Party (SDLP) from 1972, was attacked by the police, backed by paramilitaries, when the marchers entered Protestant areas. Jack Lynch, the then Irish Taoiseach, called for UN intervention (Tannam, 1999, p. 63), but his request was vetoed by the British government on the grounds that UN intervention would erode British sovereignty. In 1972, Direct Rule from Westminster was imposed.

   Between 1969 and 1998, over 3,000 people were killed in Northern Ireland, with atrocities in England and Ireland also, for example the Birmingham bomb, 1974. British and Irish membership of the EU in 1973 led to claims that both the British–Irish relationship and the conflict in Northern Ireland would be fundamentally transformed in a new EU framework (Fitzgerald, 1968). Two key claims were made: the EU would alter the normative framework within which British–Irish and Northern Irish politics was conducted, making national identity less significant. In addition, the EU would increase cross-border cooperation between Northern Ireland and the Republic of Ireland, as it brought both parts together in an economic union and possibly in a federal union at a later date (Fitzgerald, 1968). Some of these EU-inspired ideas, for example, institutionalized cross-border cooperation, were present in the first British–Irish initiative to resolve the Northern Ireland conflict – the Sunningdale Agreement in 1973 which became central to John Hume's approach to conflict resolution.

   The Sunningdale Agreement provided for a two-tier Council of Ireland – a council of ministers with seven Irish and seven Northern Irish ministers with executive powers in designated areas.

Sunningdale was significant because in that the UK government recognized an Irish dimension to solving the conflict, for the first time (Keatinge, 1986). Ireland also recognized Northern Ireland's constitutional status in the UK. However, this recognition was not a commitment to provide for Irish constitutional recognition of Northern Ireland (O'Duffy, 2007, p. 100).

Unlike subsequent agreements, the Sunningdale Agreement was 'British-led' and was 'geared initially towards devolved power-sharing in Northern Ireland, followed by a belated side-payment to nationalists in the form of a Council of Ireland linking Northern Ireland and the Irish Republic' (O'Duffy, 2007, p. 98).The underlying assumption for British policy-makers was that the conflict in Northern Ireland was an internal one: the Irish government and the British–Irish relationship were not core components of conflict resolution. Security measures continued to be heavily stressed by the British government and commitment to end internment was overturned (O'Duffy, 2007, p. 102). Twin declarations were made by both governments about the status of Northern Ireland, but these were made separately by both governments. When the Sunningdale Agreement failed in the face of unionist opposition, divisions in British–Irish preferences and policies were revealed once more. The UK government continued to emphasize internal solutions to the conflict, such as increased security and emergency powers. Despite EU membership, British–Irish cooperation floundered until the 1980s.

The early 1980s were marked by clear divisions of opinion. Irish politicians were deeply concerned about the impact of hunger strikes by nationalists in Long Kesh prison in 1982 and the administration of justice in Northern Ireland. Despite joint initiatives, for example, the historic meeting between the Irish Prime Minister Charles Haughey and the British Prime Minister Margaret Thatcher in May 1980 and the establishment of an Anglo-Irish Intergovernmental Council in 1981, both governments used the media to publicize their differences of opinion. Megaphone diplomacy reached its loudest point in 1984, when Thatcher vociferously rejected proposals from the nationalist parties' New Ireland Forum Report (O'Leary and McGarry, 1993). However, in 1985 the Anglo-Irish Agreement (AIA) was signed and, as the next section shows, it signified a new departure in the British–Irish relationship and was partially influenced by EU approaches to shared policy-making.

The AIA provided for an Irish civil service secretariat in Belfast to provide a legally enshrined consultative role on specific cross-border issues and for an Anglo-Irish Intergovernmental Council (IGC) to meet regularly, comprising heads of government and relevant ministers, where appropriate. Thus, it reflected, albeit modestly, EU joint policy approaches. The Secretariat and the IGC were intended to reflect an 'Irish dimension' to resolving the conflict in Northern Ireland and reflected a compromise between Irish preferences for joint authority over Northern Ireland (again influenced by the EU's institutional framework) and British reluctance to cede sovereignty (O'Leary and McGarry, 1993, p. 239).

Unlike the Sunningdale Agreement, the AIA was ratified at the UN as an international treaty, implying that both states were bound to the terms of the Agreement unless both agreed to change it. The AIA also marked a key change in that British–Irish governments began to play a joint leadership role. In particular, while Irish governmental preferences continued to be influenced by the SDLP from 1985 both governments began to take the lead in constraining and/or creating extreme nationalist and unionist choices politically. A carrot-and-stick approach underpinned successive British–Irish initiatives from this time. If nationalists and unionists agreed to support British–Irish initiatives, they would be rewarded: they would gain power or some bargaining leverage. If they refused, they would be excluded – a policy of coercive consociationalism (O'Leary, 2004 p. 97.) Thus, rather than British–Irish preferences simply reflecting unionist/nationalist preferences, British–Irish governments began to adopt a strategic leadership role from 1985, attempting to shape nationalist and unionist behaviour. For many observers and participants in the relationship, membership of the EU contributed to the development of this joint relationship (Arthur, 2000). 'Moreover, increased efforts were made to receive EU money for cross-border projects' (Tannam, 1999, p. 81).

However, the AIA did not satisfy Irish governmental demands for a stronger Irish dimension, giving the Irish government only consultative power in designated areas. It also reflected differences between British and Irish governmental approaches to the conflict. The Irish government 'primarily sought to reform Northern Ireland by advancing minority interests and aspirations in the administration of justice', but the British government continued to emphasize security arrangements and minimizing loss of sovereignty (O'Leary and McGarry, 1993, p. 246).

The post-1985 period witnessed concerted British–Irish attempts to develop new institutional arrangements and build upon the provisions of the AIA. By 1993, it was evident that the Irish government was more willing to accept a referendum on constitutional change. Similarly, in the Downing Street Declaration, the British government stated that it had no selfish or strategic interest in Northern Ireland.

In 1995, the New Framework for Agreement, or Joint Framework Document (JFD), included a commitment to establish joint cross-border institutions possibly with executive powers over specific functional areas of activity. The issues of whether sovereignty would be eroded by the JFD and its cross-border provisions and whether Irish constitutional change would be provided for received particular attention. Immediately after the JFD, the British Prime Minister John Major emphasized that cross-border proposals did not imply joint sovereignty. Unlike previous negotiations, Irish constitutional amendment was obviously on the bargaining table in the 1990s and was referred to quite openly by Irish political leaders. The linkage of Articles 2 and 3 of the Irish Constitution to the establishment of cross-border institutions was implicitly accepted by Anglo-Irish policy-makers, as shown by the GFA in 1998.

Of all British–Irish initiatives, the GFA had most signs of EU influence. The GFA provided for a power-sharing executive proportional representation through the single transferable vote (PR-STV) Strand 2 of the GFA was of key relevance to cross-border cooperation. The North South Ministerial Council (NSMC) was established to develop 'consultation, co-operation and action within the island of Ireland – including through implementation on an all-island and cross-border basis – on matters of mutual interest within the competence of Administrations, North and South' (GFA, 1998).

The NSMC resembled the EU style of policy-making in some respects. The plenary meetings of the NSMC comprised the Irish prime minister, the Northern Irish first minister and deputy first minister. Like the EU, emphasis was on reaching decisions in designated areas by consensus (Coakley, 2002, p. 8). Sixty areas of cooperation were discussed in the negotiations which preceded the GFA, but only 12 areas were agreed upon (Coakley, 2002, pp. 8, 12). The designated areas of cooperation comprised areas where an economic need for cross-border cooperation was recognized – for example, trade – but where various objections existed to establishing implementation bodies. Some objections were driven by unionist alarm at a perceived large Irish dimension (Coakley, 2002, p. 8).

Moreover, the Special EU Programmes Body (SEUPB) replaced the administrative arrangements to implement and monitor EU cross-border programmes (Coakley, 2002, p. 15). The inclusion of the SEUPB implementation body implied reflected the overlaps between the British–Irish dimension of cross-border cooperation and the EU dimension.

A British–Irish Council was provided for, comprising representatives the British and Irish governments, devolved administrations/governments in Northern Ireland, Scotland and Wales and the Crown territories of the Channel Islands and Isle of Man and if established, elsewhere in the UK (GFA, 1998). There was also a new British–Irish Intergovernmental Conference which subsumed both the Anglo-Irish Intergovernmental Council and the Intergovernmental Conference established under the AIA (Good Friday Agreement, 1998). The following years were not without crises, including a rise in dissident republican violence, but bilateral cooperation typified responses to these crises.

Several aspects of the GFA overlapped with EU policy domains. Cross-border economic cooperation within the EU was a component of Strand 2 of the agreement, which dealt with relations between Northern Ireland and the Republic of Ireland. Cross-border institutions with executive power were established over six designated areas of policy, the SEUPB was set up to manage all aspects of EU funding packages, trade and business development (InterTrade Ireland), food safety, language and Irish lighthouses. Like the European Council, the NSMC gave ministers 'considerable discretion to reach decisions' but they remain 'ultimately accountable to their respective legislatures' (O'Leary, 1993, p. 162). Under Strand 1 of the agreement, which dealt with Northern Ireland's internal institutions, the d'Hondt electoral system used for the allocation of portfolios to assembly members was adapted in part from the European Parliament's (EP's) system of allocating political offices according to shares of seats (O'Leary, 2003, p. 292). The similarities between aspects of the EU and the content of the GFA, contributed to observation that the EU had influenced the formulation of the GFA and the peace process I Northern Ireland. In the next section an overview of EU policy to Northern Ireland is provided, before assessing the role of the Commission in policy to Northern Ireland.

The EU and Northern Ireland

In 1973, when Ireland and the UK joined the EU, political parties in Northern Ireland were divided about the EU's potential role in Northern Ireland (Hainsworth, 1979, p. 470). However, by the late 1980s, various EU institutions, most notably the EP had become more vocal in their approach to Northern Ireland. For example, in 1982, the EP condemned the use of plastic bullets in 1982 (O'Leary and McGarry, 1993, p. 214). In 1983, the EP's Political Affairs Committee commissioned a report chaired by the Dutch Member of the European Parliament (MEP) Nils Haagerup on resolving the conflict in Northern Ireland (Haagerup, 1984).

The Haagerup Report sought to address 'one of the gravest political and social problems existing in the Community' (Haagerup, cited in Hayward, 2006, p. 267) and aimed to 'explain the situation of conflict in Northern Ireland to non-British and non-Irish MEPs and also 'to show how the EU could be of assistance in addition to its economic support' (Haagerup, 1984, p. 5). The report defined the conflict as being one of 'conflicting national identities' (Haagerup, 1984, p. 7) not a religious conflict between the two communities in Northern Ireland and recognized 'the legitimate Irish interest in the achievement of lasting peace and stability in Northern Ireland' (Haagerup, 1984, p. 6). It also expressed awareness that improvement required close British–Irish cooperation (Haagerup, 1984, p. 6) and reiterated the 1981 resolution that the EU had 'no competence to make proposals for changes in the Constitution of Northern Ireland' (Haagerup, 1984, p. 5B). British and Irish governments should 'use their influence with the two communities in Northern Ireland to bring about a political system with an equitable sharing of government responsibilities, which would accommodate the identities of the two traditions, so upholding the ideals and the concept of tolerance vis-à-vis minorities' (Haagerup, 1984). Haagerup emphasized the role of the IGC, established in 1981 to achieve this cooperation (Hayward, 2006, p. 270).

The Haagerup Report also emphasized the desirability of the EU's limited role in resolving conflict in Northern Ireland, prioritizing British–Irish cooperation as the preferred method of conflict resolution (Hayward, 2006, p. 271). It prescribed new arrangements in Northern Ireland and stated that these arrangements should 'facilitate further cooperation between the European Commission and the relevant authorities and elected representatives in Northern Ireland 'in matters related to the economic development' (Hayward, 2006, p. 271). The Commission and the Council of Ministers were asked to 'undertake a major review of all its current and planned projects in Northern Ireland and in the Border areas of the Republic, to present an integrated plan for a major contribution to the development of Northern Ireland, in conformity with the overall objectives of the European Community' (Haagerup, 1984, p. 7).

The Haagerup Report, although 'cautious' (Guelke, 1988, p. 160) and 'studiously moderate' (Guelke, 1988, p. 160), signalled the first time an EU institution made a comprehensive statement on Northern Ireland. As the next section shows, Haagerup's main recommendations became the cornerstone of the Commission's and the EU's approach to the conflict in Northern Ireland: that the EU's role was an economic one, relying on the Commission and Council of Ministers to fund economic projects in Northern Ireland and the border counties and that British–Irish cooperation was central to conflict resolution. However, in 1988, EU reform led many commentators to believe that the Commission's economic role would become more significant in resolving conflict and that the Commission would have a deeper political role, as the next section shows.

The European Commission and Northern Ireland: Policy content

Two main factors potentially altered the Commission's policy approach to Northern Ireland. Firstly, under the Single European Act (SEA) (1986), the EU aimed to achieve a single European market (SEM) by 1993, removing all barriers to trade (Single European Act, 1986). The SEM was argued to provide opportunities to businesses in Northern Ireland and the Republic to cooperate so as to stem threats from larger economies in Europe and to maximize the benefits of the SEM (Tannam, 1999, p. 100). Secondly, the SEA laid the basis for EU regional policy reform that also provided potential incentives for cross-border cooperation (Tannam, 1999, p. 102). EU aid was to be concentrated on the new Objective One regions in the EU. The Republic of Ireland as a whole was identified as an objective one region, as was Northern Ireland. In order to receive maximum funding from the EU, administrative arrangements to ensure partnership and subsidiarity were demanded. Specifically, cross-border cooperation was a condition to receive aid, providing an incentive for cross-border cooperation between Northern Ireland and the Republic of Ireland and for intercommunity cooperation in Northern Ireland.

Thus, special cross-border programmes were introduced which would not simply be back-to-back projects, but had to be formulated jointly by two state authorities. These programmes had to be overseen by a monitoring committee, which represented sub-national, central and Commission representatives. In 1990, the Commission introduced the Interreg programme:

> to assist both internal and external border areas of the Community in overcoming the special development problems arising from their relative isolation within national economies and from the Community as a whole.
>
> (European Commission, 1990)

Applications for Interreg aid were open to all EU member states, including the Republic of Ireland and the UK. An Interreg programme was agreed on the Irish–Northern Irish border regions, which included all of Northern Ireland (apart from Belfast) and the Irish counties which adjoin Northern Ireland. Thus, Northern Irish and Irish policy-makers were given the incentive to cooperate with each other if they were to receive EU aid. Such money clearly upgraded common interests between Northern Ireland and the Republic of Ireland. If these regions did not cooperate with each other, they would both lose EU money. Thus, the SEA was a catalyst for a deeper economic role in Northern Ireland, as prescribed by Haagerup. Moreover, the peace process and the GFA itself deepened the Commission's role further, as the next shows.

The Peace Package

In 1994, in response to the burgeoning peace process in Northern Ireland, the EU agreed to create funding to underpin the fragile ceasefires. The Commission established a task force to undertake a 'Special Support Programme for Peace and Reconciliation for Northern

Ireland and the border counties of Ireland' (European Commission, 1995) the 'Peace Package', so as to assist practically, the Irish border counties and Northern Ireland (SEUPB, 2003, p. 98). In July 1995, the European Commission approved the allocation of 350 one million pounds (sterling) for expenditure on cross-community and cross-border cooperation in Northern Ireland and in the Irish border counties. The aim of the initiative was

> [t]o reinforce progress towards a peaceful and stable society and to promote reconciliation by increasing economic development and employment, promoting urban and rural regeneration, developing cross-border co-operation and extending social inclusion.
>
> (Eurolink Supplement No. 9, 1995, p. i)

The programme was innovative in many ways. It represented EU commitment to helping alleviate ethnic conflict in two of its member states. A clear priority was that measures to alleviate social exclusion would be prioritized. A strong emphasis was placed on 'getting the money on the streets' of deprived Northern Irish areas, partly because it was argued that economic deprivation contributed to paramilitary violence in Northern Ireland. It was also hoped that the possibility of gaining financial benefits for maintaining peace would provide an incentive for paramilitary leaders and their supporters to maintain the cease-fires.

Thus, social inclusion measures to alleviate poverty among the poorest communities constituted the major share of the peace programme – 30 per cent (Eurolink Supplement, 1995, No. 9). Moreover, the role of the Commission in initiating and supporting the above policies appeared to imply that it played a relatively autonomous role in the conflict in Northern Ireland.

The Commission dimension was further strengthened financially when it was agreed that Peace 1 would be continued for until 2004 and then extended to 2006 (known as PEACE 2), providing 500 million euro to the border regions (400 million to Northern Ireland and one million to the six Irish border counties) (SEUPB, 2003, p. 124). In addition, Interreg, LEADER and other Community initiatives provided funding to Northern Ireland and the Republic of Ireland. Northern Ireland was allocated 890 million euro under EU initiatives, some of which were specifically for cross-border cooperation (SEUPB, 2003, p. 125). Thus, the 1990s saw a continuation and a strengthening of the Commission's role in Northern Ireland through conditionality. However, clearly as in the Haagerup report, the Commission's emphasis was technocratic and economic, not political. Despite this qualification, for some observers the case of Commission's role in Northern Ireland provided evidence that the Commission was becoming a more autonomous actor with respect to EU policy to Northern Ireland and also that it was increasingly aware of its potential to ameliorate conflict through conditionality.

The Commission's policy process to Northern Ireland

Between 1990 and 1995, as this section shows, a change occurred in the Commission's approach to Northern Ireland. However, as this section also shows, British–Irish strategy and John Hume's influence underlie apparent Commission influence. Overall the Commission's input was minimal, and the package was in many ways an intergovernmental initiative funded by the EU.

In the early 1990s, the Commission's approach to Northern Ireland was mainly economic, as the previous section showed. There were some examples of the Commission appearing to flex its muscle, but these were rare and not very significant. On the one hand, from the late 1980s, the Commission was aware of using its economic cross-border programmes to advance reconciliation and to help alleviate suffering in Northern Ireland. Interreg was central to Commission officials' rhetoric when asked about the Irish–Northern Irish cross-border relationship, and the negotiations that preceded the first Interreg programme were cited as evidence of the Commission's effect on the Irish–Northern Irish cross-border relationship. The Commission drafted its proposals for the Interreg initiative in February 1989. Irish and Northern Irish civil servants, excluding members of the Northern Ireland Office and the Anglo-Irish Division, were invited to meet with the Commission in that same year. Both sets of civil servants engaged in a process of horse-trading under the watchful supervision of the Commission (Tannam, 2006).

However, despite this apparent influence and interest, in interviews conducted by this author in the early 1990s, the Commission consistently emphasized that Northern Ireland was a British–Irish problem. The then president of the Commission, Jacques Delors, when asked about the EU's management of the crisis in the former Yugoslavia, replied: 'We don't even understand Northern Ireland, never mind Yugoslavia' (Delors, cited in Tannam, 1997, p. 20). Moreover, some practitioners observed that in general the Commission was afraid of getting involved in the conflict. Therefore, the Commission was cautious and any initiatives reflected British, Irish and Northern Irish lobbying.

In particular, both the Haagerup Report and the Commission's approach to Northern Ireland were deeply influenced by John Hume. The SDLP's first policy document on Northern Ireland, *Towards a New Ireland* (Murray, 1998, p. 209) proposed a federal framework that later was linked to support for a European federal framework and a Europe of the Regions. Hume's argument was that 'Irish unity can be engineered in the context of a European nation-state' (Murray, 1998, p. 214) and that the nation-state is 'no longer a sufficient political entity to allow people to have adequate control over the... forces that affect people's opportunities and circumstances' (Murray, 1998, p. 214). The adoption of the Haagerup Report by a majority of the EP was 'widely interpreted... as a triumph for John Hume's lobbying of European opinion' (Guelke, 1988, p. 160) and 'the significant political result of the debate was to put added pressure on the Government to reach agreement with Republic of Ireland through the Anglo-Irish process' (Guelke, 1988, p. 160). Indeed, the strong presence of Hume's stamp on the report led many unionists to argue that the Haagerup Report was a partisan document (Fitzgerald, 2004, cited in Hayward, 2006, p. 268). Not surprisingly, the decision to establish the Haagerup committee was encouraged by the Irish government (Fitzgerald, cited in Hayward, 2006, p. 268) and the Report was greeted favourably by the Irish government whose policy approach echoed Hume's. However, it is noteworthy that for the Irish government, the British–Irish relationship took precedence over EU involvement in Northern Ireland, and the then Irish government did not want to be seen 'as pushing' the Haagerup Report (Fitzgerald, 2004, cited in Hayward, 2006, p. 268). The Commission also adopted a cautious approach to Northern Ireland and one that was determined by intergovernmental rather than supranational factors.

Overall, the Commission's approach until the mid-1990s was technocratic and functional, providing further evidence of the EU as an institution with 'shallow political roots' (Laffan, Smith and O'Donnell, 1999). In contrast, in 1995, in formulating the Peace Package, the Commission appeared to enjoy considerable autonomy and appeared to behave as a policy entrepreneur (Laffan and Payne, 2001).

The announcement of the Peace Package in 1995 to underpin the paramilitary ceasefires appeared to highlight increased proactivity in the Commission's approach to Northern Ireland, by highlighting the Commission's commitment and ability to alleviate the conflict in Northern Ireland. Jacques Delors approached Hume to ask if the Commission could help support the peace process (SDLP official, interview with the author, May 2, 2013). Hume suggested the idea of the Peace Package and also met with the other (unionist) Northern Irish MEPs, who met with Delors formally to agree on the programme (SDLP official, interview with the author, May 2, 2013).The Commission then met with British and Irish government representatives to agree the programme and work on the final package (SDLP official, interview with the author, May 2, 2013).

The Commission appeared to be deeply involved in the negotiations that preceded the announcement of the Peace Package (Laffan and Payne, 2001). An intensive six-week period of negotiations preceded the announcement of the package. These negotiations were conducted between the Commission, Northern Irish civil service departments, political leaders, Irish civil service departments and government leaders. John Hume, the leader of the SDLP, played a particularly active role in the negotiations, as well as a key group of Commission officials. The Commission was particularly concerned that the Peace Package had a clear purpose and did contribute to advancing reconciliation (SDLP official, interview with the author, May 2, 2013). Thus, it insisted that clear and extensive targets be included in the package (SDLP official, interview with the author, May 2, 2013). Its rationale was not only to achieve reconciliation but also to be able to 'sell' the Peace Package to EU member states. Similarly, in 2001, when Peace 11 was being negotiated, the Commission prioritized that its economic purpose be identified more fully and that partnership elements be included in the programme between unions, rural actors and sectoral representatives (SDLP official, interview with the author, May 2, 2013). For the Commission, partnership and definite economic targets would help gain support from EU member states again, particularly from Germany (SDLP official, interview with the author, May 2, 2013).

Thus, the Peace Package contained many innovative elements that appeared to be derived from Commission influence (Laffan and Payne, 2001). For example, it made partnership schemes between local councils in Northern Ireland a condition of receiving aid. It set up cross-border Commission offices to provide information on aid, and it devolved responsibility for the administration of the aid to intermediary agencies rather than to civil service departments, thereby emphasizing grass-roots involvement and inclusion of local communities. There were clear examples of the Commission using its financial influence to increase cross-border cooperation. For example, the Commission played a major role in influencing networks and the final Interreg submission in 2001 (Laffan and Payne, 2001, p. 98). The Commission demanded genuine partnership and cross-border cooperation. It initially rejected the first Interreg submission partly on the basis that there was insufficient attention paid to indicators of its impact and also because it lacked concrete examples of cross-border cooperation (Laffan and Payne, 2001, p. 116).

Unlike the administration of general EU regional programmes, the administration of the Peace 11 necessitated a full-time desk officer to engage with the formulation of the programme and to oversee implementation. In addition, four to five Commission officials were involved at various times in administering the programme (Tannam, 2006). Unlike the early Interreg brief, their task was directly related to a conflict situation and the task of resolving it; hence, a purely technocratic approach was not adopted, and in interviews, the Commission officials exhibited a deep knowledge of Northern Irish politics and society. They observed and analysed Irish and British bureaucratic obstacles to maximizing the potential of the Commission's influence and limits to the extent to which an EU strategy to Northern Ireland could be developed (Tannam, 2006). These limits were caused by intergovernmental constraints and tensions within Northern Irish politics. The ability to analyse these obstacles and to discuss them in a wide-ranging manner was interpreted as an advance in Commission officials' understanding of the complexity of conflict resolution in Northern Ireland, compared to its perception of Northern Ireland in 1992.

Commission officials involved in the Peace Programme were in contact with officials involved in the European Commission's the then new Conflict Prevention Unit. While the Conflict Prevention Unit had a smaller budget than Peace 11 (Tannam, 2006), the Peace Programme was seen as a template for Commission's work in other conflict areas, including Palestine and Cyprus, and hence there was communication between both sections, although the contacts were at an early stage.

Thus, a change occurred in the Commission's approach to Northern Ireland between 1988 and 1995. The Peace Packages signified a deeper understanding and involvement of the Commission in Northern Ireland. For some observers, the Commission was more autonomous and behaved as a supranational entrepreneur with respect to Northern Ireland. However, as the next section shows, the Peace Packages represented a political decision influenced by Irish and British governments and Northern Irish parties, particularly John Hume (Tannam, 2006). This decision was a high-level political one, involving EU member state agreement. Thus, while the Commission's understanding of and involvement in conflict resolution in Northern Ireland appeared to increase from 1995, the dominant role of British and Irish governments was stressed by officials in explaining the Commission's approach, and the political intergovernmental nature of the Peace Programme was emphasized.

British–Irish influence on the Commission's policy approach

The predominant role of intergovernmental preferences was highlighted when the apparently autonomous role of the Commission changed after the GFA. In particular, the SEUPB was accountable to the new Northern Irish devolved government, and the Irish government played the primary role. Executive control of the GFA was strong and while Commission officials had voting power over the EU monitoring committees under Peace I (1994–1999), they merely became advisers with no voting power for Peace 11 (Tannam, 2006). Thus, whereas in Peace I the Commission emphasized partnership and communication between itself and local communities in policy formation, the more centralized Peace II provided fewer avenues for local communities to influence policy-making in alliance with the Commission.

Under the GFA, the implementation bodies had core responsibility to implement programmes and, indeed, for some Irish and Northern Irish observers, the role of local partnerships lessened and that of central administration increased. Accountability conditions were served by giving a central role to the Department of Finance in the Republic of Ireland and the Department of Finance and Personnel in Northern Ireland (Tannam, 2006). The Commission's role was less central. As the next section shows, the strong influence of SDLP, British and Irish governments over the Commission's approach to Northern Ireland reflected the evolution of a very intense and dominant British–Irish relationship that underpinned the peace process itself. Therefore, although the Commission did become more involved in Northern Ireland from the mid-1990s and although it did show a greater interest in the political aspects of conflict, its influence was always dependent on British–Irish policy to Northern Ireland.

British–Irish preferences and conflict resolution in Northern Ireland

British cooperation increased significantly from the mid-1980s, and by the 1990s British–Irish governmental cooperation often occurred informally and more frequently, indicating a significant level of cooperation. This cooperation formed the basis of the peace process and was crucial in explaining the Commission's approach to Northern Ireland.

Civil servants' accounts of the British–Irish policy-making process highlighted its increased informality and continuity since the AIA (Tannam, 2011). One official observed that the biggest change in the conduct of British–Irish relations was their informality (Tannam, 2011). For example, in the 1990s, the Irish Taoiseach met with his British counterpart at short notice and with very little preparation, compared to prime ministerial interaction in the 1980s (Tannam, 2011).

Similarly, another official observed that by the 1990s the bargaining process was very much an intellectual exercise, whereby officials on both sides met to resolve a current issue and to approach the problem with a common view in an effort to conceptualize jointly the core of the problem (Tannam, 2001). Policies were more likely to emerge jointly from British–Irish discussions.

The predominant role of the British–Irish relationship influenced all aspects of EU, including US policy to Northern Ireland. As regards US influence on the peace process, the US 'operated for the most part in tandem with the wishes of British and Irish governments' (Guelke, 2012, p. 426) Indeed prior to the 1990s, with 'modestly important exceptions' (US Presidents Jimmy Carter and Ronald Reagan; Senators Edward Kennedy and Daniel Moynihan; and Speaker 'Tip' O'Neill), 'interest in the American connection to the conflict in Northern Ireland concentrated on fund-raising and support for the republican cause' (Murray, 1998, p. 357). As in the EU, John Hume developed close contacts with key US politicians, most notably Edward Kennedy (Murray, 1998, p. 228), and along with Irish diplomatic support, gradually influenced US opinion towards constitutional nationalist means and to support Irish governmental policy to Northern Ireland. Bill Clinton's election as president in 1992 heralded a more proactive and very visible US interest in Northern Ireland, but even the role of Senator George Mitchell was strongly determined by UK and Irish preferences (Guelke, 2012, p. 425). For example, the Mitchell Draft was presented by Mitchell 'as his work', but in fact, 'the two governments had drafted Section 2 and he was told not to alter it' (O'Kane, 2007, pp. 152–53). The British–Irish relationship and its policies dominated external/international actors' role in Northern Ireland.

Thus, the Commission's view of how to deal with Northern Ireland was based on its consultations with British and Irish governments and with John Hume. The policy agenda was also tightly controlled by officials in the Anglo-Irish Division of the Department of Foreign Affairs in Dublin and by officials in the Northern Ireland Office in Belfast and officials in Westminster. All EU policy issues from Irish civil departments, of relevance to conflict resolution in Northern Ireland, went through the Irish Anglo-Irish Division for approval (Tannam, 2006).There was evidence of strong Irish influence over British–Irish bargaining outcomes and over Commission's policy through consensual means (Tannam, 2001, p. 509). O'Leary, in his capacity as former adviser to the former Northern Ireland Secretary Mo Mowlam, observed that from 1989 to 1998 many policy ideas setting the British–Irish bargaining agenda emanated from the Anglo-Irish Division (Tannam, 2011). Again, many of these ideas – sharing sovereignty, joint authority, recognition of multiple identities – can be traced to John Hume's approach from the early 1980s.

British governments began to accept the concepts of joint sovereignty and a strong Irish dimension to British policy-making for Northern Ireland, reflecting fundamental changes in British approaches to the state and to role of government (Bogdanor, 1999). These changes also reflected SDLP and Irish governmental preferences from the mid to late 1980s. Therefore, while the normative influence of the EU and the post-war model of conflict resolution is credited with influencing Hume's approach to Northern Ireland (Murray, 1998), Commission entrepreneurship and autonomy were not evident in the peace process in Northern Ireland, although the Commission's understanding of ethnic conflict grew from the mid-1990s.

Overall, the Commission's role in EU policy to Northern Ireland and the role of EU policy itself followed the lead of British and Irish governments. The EU's role did alter from 1988 to 1995: From 1995, the Commission viewed the case of Northern Ireland and other cases of ethnic divide as being not simply 'member state' issues, but perceived conflict zones to be of relevance to the European 'project' and as issues to which the Commission should pay attention. However, emphasis on the need for prior intergovernmental agreement before the Commission could carve a proactive role implied that the Commission's new approach in the 1990s was facilitated if not caused by EU member state commitment to the peace process in Northern Ireland. The underlying role of British and Irish governments implies that the Commission's role was not autonomous. However, it is noteworthy that the Commission's increased engagement with conflict in Northern Ireland preceded an era of deeper EU involvement in conflict zones generally. In the conclusion to this chapter, the implications of the Northern Ireland case are summarized, before examining specifically the EU's policy approach to Cyprus and the role of the Commission.

Conclusion: The EU and Northern Ireland – Implications for other conflict cases

There are various finding from the above analysis. Northern Ireland was the first case of EU involvement in conflict resolution. It differs from the other cases in this book in many ways, as subsequent chapters show. The UN Security Council was not involved in Northern Ireland, and UN involvement was minimal overall, although it was relevant to implementing human rights and international law in Northern Ireland. US involvement was often high profile in the 1990s, but policy of Northern Ireland was determined by British and Irish governmental preferences. The peace process was predominantly an intergovernmental process led by the kinship states – British and Irish governments. EU involvement was determined primarily by those governments and also very notably by John Hume. It is also noteworthy that the EU's policy process to Northern Ireland was not formulated on any of the formal EU committees, highlighted in Chapter 2. The EU policy process was governed mainly by meetings between Hume, British and Irish representatives and EU officials, outside the formal committee system. Only the more technical financial aspects of the Peace Packages were decided upon at formal committee level.

The Commission's autonomy and influence in the formulation process were not large. However, there was some evidence of an increase in the Commission's influence and understanding of the conflict in the mid to late 1990s. This change coincided with the creation of a separate desk office to deal with the Peace Package, and it also preceded the creation of conflict resolution unit in the Commission, reflecting the increased significance and incidence of importance of ethnic conflict from the 1990s. In this way, Northern Ireland forms a benchmark in the evolution of EU approaches to conflict, and it also sheds light on a successful conflict resolution process in the absence of UN involvement. In the next chapter, the case of Cyprus is examined, and the EU's increased role, as well as the predominance of the UN's, in conflict resolution is highlighted.

5
Cyprus

On April 22, 2004, 78 per cent of Greek Cypriots voted against the UN's federal plan for Cyprus, and on May 1, 2004, the EU granted membership to a divided Cyprus – in practice, to Greek Cyprus. Unlike the Northern Ireland case, Cyprus represents a case where the EU and UN's roles became uniquely intertwined in 2004 and where despite such interlinkage, as well as pressure from the US, the UK, Germany and Russia, resolution of the underlying conflict did not occur. In the aftermath of the referendum, both the EU and the UN were blamed: the EU for not making Cyprus' membership of the EU conditional on acceptance of the federal plan and the UN for including elements in the plan that were never going to be accepted by Greek Cypriots and for not engaging adequately with public opinion. However, while many accounts describe EU and UN policy in 2004 and criticize it, few accounts analyse the decision-making processes that led to those policies.

In this chapter, the EU and UN's policy processes are dissected, highlighting the role of the UN's Special Envoy and the Secretariat and the role of the Commission. In the first section, an overview of UN involvement in Cyprus is provided from 1964; in the second section, an analysis of the UN's decision-making processes in the 2004 Cypriot negotiations is provided; in the third section, an analysis of the EU's policy-making process to Cyprus is provided; and in conclusion, the EU and UN's processes are compared.

The UN and Cyprus

As this section shows, the UN's involvement in Cyprus did not begin until 1964, but since that date, the UN was the main international actor in mediating efforts. Cyprus was ceded to Britain by Turkey in 1878 (Richmond, 1998, p. 68), and until the late 1950s, the UN's involvement in Cyprus was opposed by Britain and the US. Greek Cypriot leaders brought the issue of *Enosis* (unity with Greece) to the UN in 1949 (Richmond, 1998, p. 68) and lobbied UN General Assembly members in 1952 and 1953 (Richmond, 1998, p. 68), but attempts to foster UN support failed and in 1950, the newly appointed Archbishop Makarios began to lobby Greece for support of *Enosis* (Faustman, 2001, p. 5). In 1951, the Greek prime minister declared Greece's support for *Enosis* (Faustman, 2001, p. 5). The Greek Cypriot nationalist EOKA (*Ethniki Organosis Kyprion Agoniston* – National Organization of Cypriot Fighters) increasingly used violent tactics to achieve its aims (Faustman, 2001, p. 5), targeting British military and civilians in Cyprus (Richmond, 1998, p. 72), and along with US support for *Enosis*, contributed to the British decision to withdraw from Cyprus in 1958, culminating in the Treaty of Guarantee in 1959 and the facilitation of a UN role.

However, to Greek Cypriots' and Greek disappointment, the UN refused to side with their cause (Faustman, 2001, p. 40), and the 1959 Treaty of Guarantee strengthened the Turkish Cypriot position by providing for a power-sharing government whereby the Turkish vice-president and the Greek Cypriot president would have a mutual veto over aspects of legislation (Ker-Lindsay, 2005, pp. 9–10). It also gave Greece, Turkey and Britain a 'constitutional responsibility to guarantee the national territory, sovereignty and independence of the republic' (Ker-Lindsay, 2005, p. 10). Cyprus became independent on August 15, 1960 (Ker-Lindsay, 2005, p. 10). The constitution was argued to favour Turkish Cypriots so as to safeguard their security as a minority and it prohibited *Enosis* (Ker-Lindsay, 2005, p. 10). Constitutional reform proposals were put forward by the Greek Cypriot vice-president in 1963 but were strongly opposed by Turkish Cypriots led by Rauf Dentkash, who perceived the reform to be a declaration of war against Turkish Cypriots (Richmond, 1998, p. 78). Violence spread rapidly leading the British government, under the Treaty of Guarantee, to establish and patrol a Green Line to prevent civil war.

Greek Cypriots argued that the Green Line constituted partition (Richmond, 1998, p. 78). Turkish Cypriots, who had already withdrawn to enclaves, did so permanently after the creation of the Green

Line (Richmond, 1998, p. 79). The Treaty of Guarantee was effectively dead and serious fighting ensued between the newly formed Turkish Cypriot National Guard, supported by the Turkish Air Force and Greek Cypriots, culminating with UN intervention (the United Nations Peacekeeping Force in Cyprus, UNFICYP) in 1964 under Security Council Resolution 186 (Richmond, 1998, p. 94). The de facto partition of Cyprus following the 1974 Turkish invasion of Greek Cyprus is at the centre of competing ideological demands. For Turkish Cypriots, comprising one-third of the Cypriot population, the border is perceived as a protection of identity, but for Greek Cypriots it is seen as a means of Turkish oppression and curtailment of Greek identity (Richmond, 1998, p. 218). As the next section shows, the UN attempted to steer a neutral line in the conflict, but despite its sensitivity, various mediation efforts failed.

The UN and Cyprus: 1964–97

From 1964 onwards, the UN played a high-profile role in Cyprus. A UN mediator, Diego Cordovez, was also appointed under Resolution 186 and the resolution became the lynchpin of UN involvement in Cyprus, envisaging that peacekeeping would provide the stability to allow successful UN mediation (Richmond, 1998, p. 102). However, the UNFICYP became 'merely a mechanism for a consolidation of the status quo' – a de facto partition (Richmond, 1998, p. 103). Until the appointment of Diego Cordovez, the UN's view was that its Good Offices were to help develop ideas but were not about mediation, 'let alone arbitration' (Senior retired UN Secretariat official, interview with the author, July 3, 2013). Moreover, Greek and Turkish Cypriots did not accept that there was a 'hurting stalemate' or ripeness in their conflict that required UN mediation, although they consented to UN intervention (Richmond, 2001, p. 105).

Problems were compounded by the fact that Greek Cypriots felt vindicated when the UN intervened and saw the UN as their means to achieve international recognition of their sovereignty, but Turkish Cypriots felt undermined by the UN:

> In this manner, the UN peace making and peace keeping operations became drawn into the substantive issues of the dispute at an early stage.
>
> (Richmond, 1998, p. 97)

As the next section shows, by 1997, the concept of the UN's offices as a mediator had gained currency, and successive rounds of UN mediation efforts occurred (Ker-Lindsay, 2005, pp. 12–13), as well as numerous UN Security Council resolutions (Richmond, 1998, p. 116). However, they failed to deliver agreement, largely because each agreement was used as a political football by each side and point-scoring dominated negotiations. Following the failed series of UN-mediated talks between 1967 and 1974 and the foundation of the EOKA-B in 1972, a militant organization aiming for *Enosis*, the Greek Cypriot leader Makarios wrote to the military dictatorship in Greece, asking them to remove all officials from Cyprus. The Athens-based leader of the EOKA-B demanded the overthrow of Makarios, and in response, Turkish troops invaded Cyprus in July 1974 (Richmond, 1998, p. 116). From 1975 onwards, the effects of 1974 violence and the failure of mediation talks contributed to the UN supporting a federal solution to the Cypriot problem (Richmond, 1998, p. 133) as well as resulting in Turkish Cypriot's support for the UN's mediation role.

A landmark date occurred in February 1977 when Makarios and Dentkash signed an agreement 'confirming that a future Cyprus settlement would be based on a federation made up of two states (bi-zonal) and two communities (bi-communal), marking a monumental change for the Greek Cypriot government away from *Enosis* as a core aim' (Ker-Lindsay, 2005, p. 15). However, the agreement was rejected by Greek Cypriots on the basis that it did not enshrine 'the three freedoms': freedom of movement, freedom of settlement and the right to own property (Ker-Lindsay, 2005, p. 16), all core issues for Greek Cypriots, as they had fled their land in Northern Turkey after 1974.

In 1983, Dentkash's declaration of the creation of an independent non-aligned Turkish Republic of Northern Cyprus (TRNC) (Richmond, 1998, p. 165) increased tensions in Cyprus. Only Turkey recognized the new state, and Security Council Resolution 541 condemned the declaration. Mediation efforts in 1984, 1986 and 1989 all ended in failure (Richmond, 1998, p. 165).

However, despite the failure of talks, there were hopes by the 1990s, that because of the carrot of EU enlargement, the UN, including its Secretariat staff could play a far more active and autonomous role, especially given the end of the Cold War (Newman, 2001, p. 140). In addition, Security Council members began to express annoyance at the cost of peacekeeping and impatience about the lack of progress in Cyprus (Newman, 2001, p. 141). Related to the post-Cold War, EU enlargement added to the list of incentives to resolve the Cypriot conflict once and for all. However, as the next paragraph shows, UN efforts on the 1990s also ended in failure.

In 1992, the new Secretary-General Boutros-Ghali presented the Security Council with a draft plan comprising a bi-zonal, bi-communal federal settlement (Ker-Lindsay, 2005, p. 19) based on de Cuellar's 1989 'Set of Ideas', but this effort also failed (Ker-Lindsay, 2005, p. 20). Further efforts by Boutros-Ghali failed again in 1994 (Ker-Lindsay, 2005, p. 20). However, from 1997 to 2004, efforts continued, as undaunted, the new Secretary-General Kofi Annan reinvigorated UN mediation when he took office in 1997, heralding a new era of UN initiatives – the Annan Plans. Unfortunately, as the next section shows, these hopes were short-lived.

1997–2006: The Annan Plans

From 1997 to 2004, there were various attempts to resolve the Cypriot conflict, and all of these attempts were scuppered by Greek, or Turkish Cypriots, or by both sets of actors. However, despite this failure, the role of a small team from the UN Secretariat in the mediation efforts is noteworthy, particularly in the 2004 Plan.

1997–2001 Negotiations

Following Kofi Annan's appointment as secretary-general, the first meeting in three years between Greek and Turkish Cypriots occurred in upstate New York in January 1997. After the meeting, Annan offered a list of suggestions for future efforts under UN mediating auspices (Newman, 2001, p. 144), but the Commission's announcement that full membership negotiations would begin with Cyprus, but not with Turkey increased tensions. Dentkash announced in 1997 that he would no longer support a federal solution, but only a confederal one (Ker-Lindsay, 2005, p. 22). However, in 1999 a new *rapprochement* process between Greece and Turkey led to Greece lifting its veto over Turkish EU membership. Greek Cypriot–Turkish Cypriot proximity talks began at the behest of the UN in June 1999 (Ker-Lindsay, 2005, p. 23). Dentkash refused to meet for a sixth round of talks in 2001, criticizing the EU's role and later the UN's role (Ker-Lindsay, 2005, p. 23). Turkey also became increasingly tough in its stance about Cypriot EU membership, stating that if Cyprus joined the EU, it would annex Northern Cyprus (Ker-Lindsay, 2005, p. 23).

2002 Negotiations and Annan 1

As the next sections show, UN mediation efforts failed again in 2002 and led to a change in the UN's approach thereafter. To the surprise of observers, Dentkash asked Clerides to meet in November 2001 (Ker-Lindsay, 2005, p. 24). Formal talks began in January 2002 (Ker-Lindsay, 2005, p. 25), headed by UN envoy Alvaro de Soto, despite earlier objections from Dentkash, who perceived de Soto to be pro-Greek Cypriot. The leaders agreed to ten rounds of talks (Ker-Lindsay, 2005, p. 26). The first talks dealt with security, but the security issue ultimately stalled any further talks and the negotiations ended in failure (Ker-Lindsay, 2005, p. 26). In particular, the Greek Cypriots' confidence-building measure (CBM) of destroying an arms stockpile and de-mining parts of the buffer zone (Ker-Lindsay, 2005, p. 27) was not reciprocated. Indeed, the number of Turkish airspace violations grew and no reduction in troops numbers occurred (Ker-Lindsay, 2005, p. 27). Further talks about property were even more contentious and talks began to flounder (Ker-Lindsay, 2005, p. 27). Similar problems continued throughout all the rounds of talks, leading de Soto to state in April 2002 that June need not be the cut-off point for negotiations (Ker-Lindsay, 2005, p. 29).

The failure of the 2002 talks led to the UN unequivocally blaming Turkish Cypriots for the failure to reach agreement, revoking the UN's previous stance of maintaining neutrality in the negotiations (Ker-Lindsay, 2005, p. 32). This emphasis on Turkish Cyprus as the main obstacle to resolving the Cypriot conflict and on the need to lobby Turkey to influence Turkish Cyprus continued until the end of the Annan negotiations in 2004 and influenced both UN and EU bargaining strategies. It also conjoined the EU and UN in their strategies. The strategy adopted was to persuade Turkish Cyprus that if it rejected a UN agreement, Greek Cyprus would join the EU anyway and race ahead of Turkish Cyprus and Turkey. The underlying assumption by EU and UN officials, based on the negotiations, was that Greek Cyprus and Greece would not block an agreement. This perception was created and shaped by the actors closest to the Cypriot negotiators – de Soto and his team and thus in explaining the UN and EU's strategy, their role was crucial.

Consequently, in October 2002, the Commission stated in its accession progress report that Cyprus met all economic and political criteria to be a candidate for EU membership (Ker-Lindsay, 2005, p. 34). The election by substantial majority of more moderate Recep Tayyip Erdogan in Turkey in November 2002 and his statement that he would push for EU membership and *rapprochement* with Greece raised optimism about the Cypriot negotiations (Ker-Lindsay, 2005, p. 36), again under the assumption that Turkey and Turkish Cyprus were key to reaching an agreement.

Erdogan's election and the EU's enlargement strategy fuelled optimism about UN negotiations. For de Soto, meeting Erdogan after the Turkish election was 'like the clouds parting' (Senior retired UN Secretariat official, interview with the author, June 20, 2012), and following the Turkish election, Kofi Annan unveiled the Annan Plan 1, drafted by de Soto (Ker-Lindsay, 2005, p. 39). The Plan dealt with security and international relations, the territorial structure of the state and the constitutional and political system, and it provided for a referendum in both areas of Cyprus to be held on March 30 (Ker-Lindsay, 2005, p. 39). While not without their criticisms, both Greek and Turkish Cypriots were relatively positive about the Plan (Ker-Lindsay, 2005, p. 10) and the European Council decided in December that Cyprus would be admitted to the EU on May 1, regardless of whether the Plan was approved (Ker-Lindsay, 2005, p. 44). Moreover, while Turkey lobbied for its accession to start in 2003, the European Council decided that it would consider Turkish membership in December 2004, again placing more pressure on Turkey and Turkish Cyprus than on Greek Cyprus (Ker-Lindsay, 2005, p. 45). Thus, the EU and UN approach polarized elite behaviour in Cyprus. De Soto invited both sides to meet with the Guarantor powers, but the meeting failed to deliver an agreement (Ker-Lindsay, 2005, p. 45). Clerides received a hero's welcome in Greek Cyprus:

> [T]he terms of the accession agreement were such that even without settlement the EU would have deemed the whole of the island to have joined-even if the *acquis communautaire* would be suspended over Northern Cyprus.... In other words Cyprus would join the Union united in theory...and Turkey would be deemed to be in occupation.
>
> (Ker-Lindsay, 2005, p. 46)

As the next paragraphs show, criticism of Dentkash led to renewed negotiations and strengthened the EU and UN's perception that Turkish Cyprus was the main obstacle to reaching a UN-mediated settlement. In response, Dentkash agreed to meet again to formulate another agreement – the 2004 Annan Plan.

However, Dentkash merely repeated his previous demands (Ker-Lindsay, 2005, p. 49). International pressure mounted for an agreement, and de Soto flew to New York to meet Annan, Prendergast, Sir David Hannay, British envoy to Cyprus and the US State Department coordinator, Thomas Weston (Ker-Lindsay, 2005, p. 50):

> In every capital mammoth efforts were being made by the EU, UN, US and Britain to bring all sides into line in the hope that a deal could be reached.
>
> (Ker-Lindsay, 2005, p. 52)

The Head of the European Commission Romano Prodi also threw his weight behind international efforts to reach agreement and stated that whether or not an agreement was reached Cyprus would be join the EU on May 1, 2004 (Ker-Lindsay, 2005, p. 55). Greek and Turkish governments stated their commitment to reach a deal (Ker-Lindsay, 2005, p. 53), but Dentkash made it clear that a deal was still not in sight (Ker-Lindsay, 2005, p. 53).

Meanwhile, in the Greek Cypriot election, the former EOKA member Papodopoulos gained 51.5 per cent of the vote, although it was agreed that Clerides would continue to represent Greek Cyprus at the talks (Ker-Lindsay, 2005, p. 52). In February, Kofi Annan visited Cyprus for the second time in 2004 to start joint meetings with both sides (Ker-Lindsay, 2005, p. 52) and held separate meetings with Dentkash and Papodopoulos (Ker-Lindsay, 2005, p. 54). No agreement was reached and further meetings were scheduled for March (Ker-Lindsay, 2005, p. 54). Given the tight time frame, de Soto was doubtful that a comprehensive agreement would be reached in March (Ker-Lindsay, 2005, p. 55). Despite intensive and long meetings throughout February and March, de Soto emerged on March 9, to state that the talks had collapsed (Ker-Lindsay, 2005, p. 56). While Papodopoulos had agreed to put the Plan to referendum, Dentkash had refused and called for an entirely new set of talks (Ker-Lindsay, 2005, p. 56). Again, Dentkash's behaviour fuelled the EU and UN's belief that Turkish Cyprus was the obstacle to resolving the Cyprus conflict.

In an attempt to limit damage caused by Papodopoulos negotiating position, the Green Line was opened and Greek Cypriots were allowed stay up to three days in hotels in Northern Cyprus (Ker-Lindsay, 2005, pp. 60–63). Further measures were introduced by both Greek and Turkish Cypriot governments, including measures to promote freedom of movement, access to medical care and protection of cultural heritage (Ker-Lindsay, 2005, p. 63). However, Dentkash remained opposed to re-opening UN-sponsored talks (Ker-Lindsay, 2004, p. 66). The EU provided a €12 million package for Northern Cyprus to help support a breakthrough (Ker-Lindsay, 2005, p. 66), but in an apparently negative vein, de Soto was posted to Western Sahara indicating a diminishing of UN efforts in Cyprus (Ker-Lindsay, 2005, p. 69). As the next section shows, this negativity was short-lived, as the US and Turkish pressure led to a resumption of talks in February 2004. As the next section also shows, the UN, specifically de Soto and his team, was centre stage in these negotiations, but the EU supported UN efforts and later became more central when the talks failed.

2004 Negotiations

In January 2004, following US Erdogan told Dentkash that Turkey would no longer allow Dentkash to block a settlement (Agence France-Presse, 2004a). As a result, on January 13 Dentkash stated that the UN plan was still on the table (*Independent*, 2004a). Erdogan requested that Kofi Annan re-start negotiations (Agence France-Presse, 2004b) and if an agreement was not reached that Annan would 'fill in the blanks' (Agence France-Presse, 2004b). Turkey also requested that de Soto would not be the envoy, but Annan refused to drop de Soto from the negotiations.

Despite these problems, Annan invited Dentkash and Clerides to New York for a meeting (*Defense and Foreign Affairs Daily*, 2004). Both Greek and Turkish Cypriots resented the demand that they give a 'prior commitment to hold a referendum on a compromise text over the heads of the negotiators' (Agence France-Presse, 2004c). One Turkish Cypriot paper reputedly commented that 'Annan spells out everything in minute detail. All that's left are the signatures' (Agence France-Presse, 2004c). The first set of talks ended in stalemate in February 2004 with both sides opposing the UN's right to 'fill in the blanks' (*Irish Times*, 2004a). In turn, the UN blamed both sides: 'they clearly showed that they wanted to do away with the Annan Plan' (Ker-Lindsay, 2005, p. 85), and the first set of talks lasted only 30 minutes (*Channel NewsAsia*, 2004). However, the crisis was averted when Erdogan rang Dentkash to persuade him to attend the negotiations (BBC Summary of World Broadcasts, 2004a).

Therefore, on February 13, 'in a major breakthrough' (*Associated Press Worldstream*, 2004a), both sides agreed to resume full negotiations (Associated Press Worldstream, 2004a) and to hold referenda simultaneously before May 1, 2004 (Federal News Service, 2004). Annan presented a 'take-it-or-leave-it' timetable document' (Federal News Service, 2004) to which all agreed. De Soto was to continue as Envoy (Federal News Service, 2004), despite Greek Turkish opposition. The EU offered to accommodate any settlement reached, and the Commission offered technical assistance (Federal News Service, 2004). The Commission's DG Enlargement Head, Gunter Verheugen, arrived in Cyprus on the eve of the resumption of talks (Ker-Lindsay, 2005, p. 87). De Soto also visited Brussels frequently in this period (Agence France-Presse, 2004d) and commented in Brussels that there was no 'Plan B' if the UN deal was rejected in referendum (XINHUA General News Service, 2004a).

In effect, Turkey and Annan and de Soto believed that a political agreement had already been reached (Ker-Lindsay, 2005, p. 86). Similarly, US State Department envoy, Thomas Weston stated, 'It is almost certain now that there will be a settlement on the island on Cyprus' (*The Australian*, 2004). However, following separate talks with Dentkash and Clerides on March 1, Australian Special Envoy for Cyprus, Jim Short, commented that 'nothing has been achieved' (Associated Press Worldstream, 2004b) and that time was running out (Associated Press Worldstream, 2004b).

By early March, the then Under-Secretary-General Sir Kieran Prendergast had arrived in Cyprus to aid stalling negotiations (Associated Press Worldstream, 2004c). Weston, striking a more negative tone than in February, warned that a 'no' vote would be 'a heavy burden to bear' and was criticized by both leaders for using threats and meddling (Agence France-Presse, 2004e). It emerged that Papadopoulos had reservations about Dentkash's demands to enhance bi-zonality and sovereignty of the two areas (Ker-Lindsay, 2004, p. 89). Dentkash also opposed any UN control of 10 per cent of Northern Cyprus that would be given to Greek Cypriots under the Annan Plan (Agence France-Presse, 2004e). Dentkash then submitted a nine-page letter demanding that Cyprus re-apply for EU membership (Agence France-Presse, 2004e). The Commission 'quickly confirmed that there was no need for a new application' (Ker-Lindsay, 2005, p. 90).

Point-scoring continued among the two leaders from then on, despite de Soto's positive statements (Ker-Lindsay, 2005, p. 90) and despite the UN's announcement that a referendum would be held on April 20, later changed to April 21, 2004 (Ker-Lindsay, 2005, p. 92). Failure to progress led de Soto to announce that proximity talks would replace face-to-face between the two leaders (Agence France-Presse, 2004f). De Soto also stressed that he did not think the UN 'could consider the possibility of extending the negotiations' (Agence France-Presse, 2004g). Annan stated that it was likely that he and his team would be finalizing the agreement, as it seemed unlikely that Greek and Cypriot leaders would do so themselves (EUObserver.com, 2004). De Soto also added a few days later that Greek and Turkish involvement in the talks would occur, if both sides could not reach agreement by March 22 (Associated Press Worldstream, 2004e). If there was still no agreement after a week, then the UN would finalize the agreement (Agence France-Presse, 2004e). Clearly, in the first two months of 2004, the UN was highly and intensively active in Cyprus, attempting to troubleshoot the many impediments raised by Greek and Turkish Cypriots. This involvement was heightened from March to April, 2004, culminating in the Annan Plan and referendum.

Final stage of 2004 negotiations

The final stage of the Annan Plan negotiations began on March 15, when de Soto asked the two sides to prioritize their demands. On March 16, he asked the leaders to separate out easy issues from 'difficult': issues (Ker-Lindsay, 2005, p. 93) from a list of divisive issues identified by the UN. A brief halt to meetings was called to let the leaders examine the list and to allow de Soto consult with Sir Kieran Prendergast who has just arrived in Cyprus (Ker-Lindsay, 2005, p. 93) to assess the situation on behalf of Kofi Annan.

However, 'by this point attitudes were hardening on both sides' (Ker-Lindsay, 2005, p. 94) and 'Ankara considered as insufficient the new document presented by... Alvaro de Soto' (BBC Summary of World Broadcasts, 2004b). Turkish Cypriots and Turkey were concerned that the EU had reneged on its agreement to accept derogations from the EU's *acquis* over Northern Cyprus (BBC Summary of World Broadcasts, 2004b) and that the Commission refused to renegotiate Cypriot accession (BBC Summary of World Broadcasts, 2004b). They were also concerned that their wish for a reduction in the number of Greek Cypriots who would be allowed to return to the North had not been included in de Soto's document and that more specific references to the different ethnic communities were needed (Agence France-Presse, 2004g). The Greek Cypriot media also 'launched a tirade against de Soto' (Agence France-Presse, 2004g) claiming that his paper addressed core issues that should have been outside the talks (Agence France-Presse, 2004g). In the midst of less than satisfactory outcomes, 'four-way' talks were announced to begin in Switzerland between Greek Cypriot, Turkish Cypriot, Greek and Turkish leaders and the second round of talks began in late March in Switzerland (Ker-Lindsay, 2005, p. 95).

Problems multiplied, as Greek Cypriots perceived the UN to be pandering to Turkish Cypriot demands (Ker-Lindsay, 2005, p. 96) and felt that the UN was pressurizing Papadoupolos to sign the UN plan (Ker-Lindsay, 2005, p. 96). When the latter left the talks to attend a meeting in Brussels, the UN submitted a document to sign to the remaining Greek Cypriot negotiations in his absence, which incensed Greek Cypriots (Ker-Lindsay, 2005, p. 96). Despite the hours of negotiations put in by de Soto and his team, substantive and tactical problems continued to dog the talks. The bargaining agenda was further complicated by the EU dimension, as the next section shows.

While the UN was at the coalface of negotiations, the European Commission also found itself in stormy waters. EU law and the substance of UN negotiations became very intertwined from 2004. Under the *acquis*, all Cypriots would have freedom of movement and therefore could go to Turkish Cyprus. Turkish Cyprus feared that their majority in a bi-zonal federation would be swamped by wealthier and numerically stronger Greek Cypriots and therefore requested that the *acquis* be suspended permanently. It could not allow a derogation of the *acquis* over Northern Turkey on legal grounds and also because Greece and Greek Cypriots said they would not support an agreement if this derogation occurred (Ker-Lindsay, 2005, p. 97). The EU arrived at a compromise that there would be an adaptation act to be put in place that would create indefinite transition periods, so that Northern Cyprus would not be automatically covered by EU law over Greek Cyprus. While an advance, for Turkey this compromise was not satisfactory. Greek Cypriots also continued to oppose direct talks, but de Soto stated that an agreement 'was still possible' (*Associated Press Worldstream*, 2004e) bemoaned the absence of 'give-and-take' among the Greek and Turkish Cypriot leaders (Agence France-Presse, 2004i). Despite all these complexities and difficulties, the May 1 EU enlargement deadline, particularly emphasized by the UK (Senior retired UN Secretariat official, interview with the author, July 3, 2013) spurred on the UN negotiators. Thus, on March 29, the fourth Annan Plan was unveiled by de Soto (Ker-Lindsay, 2005, p. 98), who described it a 'win-win' proposal (*Associated Press Worldstream*, 2004e). However, as the next paragraphs show, despite efforts to 'sell' the Plan to Greek and Turkish Cypriots, it was rejected by Greek Cypriots on April 1.

The Annan Plan and Referendum

In unveiling the Plan, de Soto explained that it had been drawn up by the UN on the basis of a synthesis of all negotiations that had occurred (*Associated Press Worldstream*, 2004e). Turkish Cypriots were more favourably disposed to the Plan, although they had criticisms. However, Greek Cypriots responded by stating that the Plan favoured Turkish Cypriots (Ker-Lindsay, 2005, p. 99), because it announced further cuts to the number of Greek Cypriots who could return to Northern Cyprus and there was a possibility of permanent Turkish military presence on the island (*Associated Press Worldstream*, 2004g). They argued that de Soto 'had just gone ahead and filled in the blanks' (Ker-Lindsay, 2005, p. 99).

Even moderate Greek Cypriots increasingly opposed the Plan (Ker-Lindsay, 2005, p. 99). Greek Cypriots fears were exacerbated by newspaper reports that 'Turkey claims victory in Cyprus Negotiations' (Agence France-Presse, 2004j) and that 75 per cent of Turkish Cypriots' demands had been met by the fourth Annan Plan (*Irish Times*, 2004b). On March 30, the two sides gave their official responses to Annan and de Soto met with the Greek Foreign Minister (*Irish Times*, 2004b). Annan and his team refined the plan and met with Verheugen (*Irish Times*, 2004b) who had provided an official Commission response to the plan. Prodi announced formally that no permanent derogations would be provided, but instead that there would be transition periods (Ker-Lindsay, 2005, p. 101). Despite the Commission's qualification, Turkey supported the Plan (Ker-Lindsay, 2005, p. 101). The Greek response was more muted (Ker-Lindsay, 2005, p. 102), but its Foreign Minister, Petros Molyviatis, warned of repercussions if Greek and Turkish Cypriots rejected the Plan stating that 'there will be no new initiative for a long time' (Agence France-Presse, 2004k).

De Soto briefed the Security Council on April 2 and stressed that the plan was based on Greek and Turkish Cypriot preferences and that the UN only added items where no agreement was reached (Agence France-Presse, 2004k). The Council did not endorse the plan and stated that the outcome would have to be decided by the Greek and Turkish Cypriots (Agence France-Presse, 2004k). On April 7, Papadopoulos rejected the Plan (Ker-Lindsay, 2005, p. 104), in a 'blistering attack' stated that there were no guarantees that Turkey would abide by the Plan and advising Greek Cypriots to vote 'No' (Ker-Lindsay, 2005, p. 104). Internationally, many felt that Papadopoulos had deliberately misled the UN and EU (Ker-Lindsay, 2005, p. 105). Divisions in Papadopoulos' AKEL (Progressive Party of Working People) party emerged and it finally opposed the Plan (Ker-Lindsay, 2005, p. 105).

However, Britain and the US attempted to secure support for the Plan. In an attempt to assure Turkish Cypriots that the Plan would be fully implemented, if agreed at referendum, Britain and the US co-sponsored a Security Council resolution to create a new UN peacekeeping mission that would monitor implementation of the Plan and to impose an arms embargo on the island so that it would be fully demilitarized (XINHUA General News Service, 2004b). However, Russia, backed by China, vetoed the Resolution, although Annan and de Soto strongly supported it as necessary (Agence France-Presse, 2004l). Russia 'which has strong ties with the Greek Cypriot South where many Russian companies are registered' (Agence France-Presse, 2004l) and exported arms to Greek Cyprus, stated that passing the resolution would have represented a UN attempt to influence the vote (Agence France-Presse, 2004l).

It was felt that Papadopoulos had deliberately prevented the resolution by lobbying Russia, so as to prevent the yes campaign from winning the election (Ker-Lindsay, 2005, p. 109). The referendum result was announced on April 24, 64.9 per cent of Turkish Cypriots endorsed the Plan, but 75.8 per cent of Greek Cypriots opposed it. The 20-strong team of negotiators led by de Soto 'packed their bags' the next day, feeling 'despondent and exhausted' (*Daily Telegraph*, 2004), and on May 1, Cyprus was granted membership of the EU. The UN's mediation efforts had failed as before, but perhaps in more disappointing fashion given the optimism generated by the EU's enlargement process. Clearly, the UN negotiations were closely connected to the EU's enlargement strategy to Cyprus and its approach to the Cypriot conflict. In the next section, the EU's policy to Cyprus is examined before comparing EU and UN decision-making processes.

EU and Cyprus

Unlike the UN, the EU did not play a role in conflict resolution efforts in Cyprus before the 1990s. During the Cold War Cyprus was non-aligned and its efforts not to antagonize Russia prohibited EU membership (Karatas, 2011, p. 17). Indeed, 'EU member states did not want to get involved in the Cyprus conflict at all' (Karatas., 2011, p. 24) for fear of igniting latent tensions in Mediterranean region. The UK's membership of the EU in 1973 precipitated an association agreement between Cyprus and the EU, providing for a Customs Union (Karatas, 2011, p. 24). The EU 'briefly attempted to play a crisis – management role during the summer of 1974' (Verney, 2009, p. 126), but its fledgling entry into foreign policy under the new EPC framework was weak and its neutrality in the conflict was compromised by Greece's application for EU membership in 1975 (Verney, 2009, p. 126) and by the UK's membership from 1973 (Karatas, 2011, p. 25). The events of 1974 also delayed the implementation of the Customs Union agreement until 1987 (Karatas, 2011, p. 25). In general, until the end of the Cold War, the EU operated as 'a supportive by-stander to the UN negotiations' (Verney, 2009, p. 128) and its rhetoric, 'reflecting that of the broader international community' (Verney, 2009, p. 127), condemned the creation of the TRNC. Cyprus ranked 'quite low' (Verney, 2009, p. 128) on the EU's policy agenda.

However, the end of the Cold War precipitated increased EU involvement in Cyprus, as it did in other conflict zones (Ker-Lindsay et al., 2011, p. 19). From the 1990s, the EU's approach to Cyprus was two-pronged. It focussed on improving the Greek–Turkish relationship and ensuring that democracy and human rights were protected in Turkey (Tannam, 2012) and also it directly focussed on Cyprus by providing incentives for Cypriot conflict resolution. Turkey applied for EU membership in 1987 (Ker-Lindsay et al., 2011, p. 20) and in 1990, Cyprus applied for EU membership (Ker-Lindsay et al., 2011, p. 17). The motivation was primarily political, as Greek Cypriots urged by Greece 'perceived the application as a way to bring new impetus to the deadlock' (Ker-Lindsay et al., 2011, p. 19) after '26 years of fruitless UN negotiations' (Ker-Lindsay et al., 2011, p. 19). For Greek Cypriots, the EU would also provide security against any possible Turkish military action (Ker-Lindsay et al., 2011, p. 20). Turkish Cypriots, backed by Turkey strongly opposed the application, arguing that the Greek Cypriot application 'violates the international and constitutional ban on *Enosis*' (Karatas, 2011, p. 23) and that fully implementing the EU's *acquis* contravened international law (Karatas, 2011, p. 23). For Turkey, if Greek Cyprus joined the EU, there were potentially two vetoes against Turkish EU membership (Karatas, 2011, p. 24).

In line with its previous approach to Cyprus and to other conflicts' the Commission's action was 'to avoid deeper involvement' – 'calculated inaction' (Karatas, 2011, p. 24). The Commission did not give its *avis* on Cyprus' 1990 application until 1993 (Karatas, 2011, p. 24). In the *avis*, conditionality formed a major part of Commission's policy:

> The Commission feels that...as soon as the prospect of settlement is surer, the EU is ready to start the process with Cyprus that should eventually lead to its accession ... The situation should be reassessed in view of positions adopted by each party in the (UN-led) talks and that the question of Cyprus' accession to the Community should be reconsidered in January 2005.
>
> (European Commission, 1993)

The Commission's approach, while hesitant reflected the view that:

> The accession period for all EU states is the crucial one for the Commission to exert its influence, whereby the threat of not being a member is a crucial incentive for domestic change.
>
> (Demetriou, 2004, p. 4)

Turkish membership was also made conditional on resolution of the Cyprus issue:

> Cyprus' integration with the Community implies a peaceful, balanced and lasting settlement of the Cyprus question... and that as soon as the prospect of a settlement is surer, the Community is ready to start the process.
>
> (Schimmelfennig, 2006, p. 202)

However, the 1997 Luxembourg European Council summit antagonized Turkey when it authorized accession negotiations to begin with ten countries, including Cyprus, but excluding Turkey (Evrivades, 2003, p. 249). The Council conclusion was that the 'political and economic conditions allowing accession negotiations to begin' were not satisfied (Luxembourg Presidency, 1997, Conclusions, p. 5). The Council also stated that:

> Strengthening Turkey's links with European Union also depends on that country's... establishment of satisfactory relations between Greece and Turkey; settlement of legal disputes, support for negotiations under the aegis of the UN on a political settlement in Cyprus....
>
> (Luxembourg Presidency Conclusions, 1997, p. 6)

This decision was reversed in 1999 in Helsinki, when Turkey was granted formal candidacy, but no formal date for the start of negotiations was given (Evrivades, 2003, p. 249). It was hoped that the EU's provision of economic incentives would precipitate increased Greek Cypriot–Turkish Cypriot cooperation, as well as Greek–Turkish cooperation (Schimmelfenig, 2006, p. 202). To bolster economic incentives, various aid packages were provided by the EU for Greek Cyprus, Turkish Cyprus and for Turkey, on condition that a solution to the Cypriot conflict was reached. However, in 1999, the carrot-and-stick approach altered with the decision that resolving the Cyprus conflict should be separated from Cypriot and Turkish accession negotiations and in 2003, the Commission's *avis* formally supported Cyprus' membership of the EU in 2004 (*Official Journal of the European Union*, 2003).

Overall from 1999, the thrust of EU policy including that of the Commission was to provide economic carrots to both parts of

Cyprus and Turkey, but to assume that Greek Cyprus would sup-port the Annan Plan, so most pressure should be exerted on Turkish Cyprus and Turkey, using enlargement as the tool. In turn, follow-ing the Greek Cypriot rejection of the Plan, EU efforts sought to reverse their previous assumptions and reward Turkish Cyprus for their support of the Plan and to minimize the economic impact of a divided Cyprus entering the EU. For example, on April 29, 2004, it approved an aid package of 259 million euro for Northern Cyprus (Associated Press Worldstream, 2004i). The EU quickly eased trade restrictions on Northern Cyprus (Associated Press Worldstream, 2004i) 'after thirty years of economic isolation' (*Independent*, 2004b). The European Commission also announced its plans to set up a mission in Northern Cyprus (Agence France-Presse, 2004m). At the same time, the EU's activity in 2004 was not merely technocratic and functional.

For example, the EU was unanimous and forthright in its con-demnation of Greek Cyprus' vote. EU High Representative for For-eign Affairs, Javier Solana praised the 'courageous' Turkish Cypriots (Agence France-Presse, 2004n) and Verheugen said that he felt 'cheated' by Papadopoulos (BBC Summary of World Broadcasts, 2004c) and that it was 'nothing short of tragic that (reunification) has now failed because of the Greeks' (Associated Press Worldstream, 2004i). Moreover, at various times in the UN talks, the EU played a key role. For example, the mediation efforts of the Danish Pres-idency and particularly the then Danish Foreign minister, Joschike Fischer (*European Voice*, 2002a) were commended for averting a cri-sis. Fischer placated Turkish demands for a definite start date to its accession negotiations by inserting the words 'without delay' into the text, stating that accession talks would begin (*European Voice*, 2002a). While Turkey lobbied for a definite date, the Commission urged the Council not to set a date, as it would be blamed by Turkey if its progress report did not recommend membership when that date was reached (*European Voice*, 2002a). Austria, Sweden, the Netherlands and Luxembourg were also opposed to a definite date being stated, on the basis of their concerns about Turkish human rights, so Danish diplomatic intervention was a successful compromise and regarded as a significant success, as 'consensus within the Union on the desirabil-ity of a new member state, particularly an important, yet problematic applicant such as Turkey, does not emerge overnight' (*European Voice*, 2002b).

European Commission involvement in Cyprus gradually became intense, with frequent high-level meetings between de Soto and the Commission, as well as EU member state representatives. Prodi himself visited Cyprus to make a final push for the Annan Plan and Verheugen made frequent pleas for support for the Annan Plan, asking Cyprus not to throw away 'remarkable progress' and called on politicians to persuade the population to support the Annan Plan (Agence France-Presse, 2004o). Vergheugen also participated in the last stages of UN negotiations in Buergenstock (Cyprus News Agency, 2004) The overlaps between the EU accession talks and the UN negotiations were put into relief when the Council decided against offering a permanent derogation from freedom of movement (*European Voice*, 2002a) and Prodi reiterated that no permanent legal exemptions on freedom of movement could be granted (Associated Press Worldstream, 2004j). The Copenhagen Council stated that 'in the absence of a settlement, the application of the *acquis* to the northern part of the island shall be suspended, until the Council decides unanimously otherwise on the basis of a proposal by the Commission' (European Council, Presidency, 2002, p. 3). Thus, EU and UN policy to were interlinked.

Similarly, in the run up to the referendum, Solana said that relations with Cyprus would change if Greek Cyprus voted 'no' and that Turkish Cyprus would not left out in the cold (*Associated Press Worldstream*, 2004k). In the next section, the EU's policy process from 1999 to 2004 is analysed, with a view to determining the Commission's autonomy.

UN and EU policy processes, 2002–04

EU and UN strategy towards Cyprus overlapped from 2002 and 2004 and as the above section showed, senior Commission and Secretariat officials were in close contact with each other. It is striking that UN Secretariat staff, namely de Soto and his small team enjoyed considerably more autonomy and influence than Commission staff. In the next section, the role of the UN Secretariat is examined before examining the EU's policy process to Cyprus.

Even before the Annan Plan negotiations, many UN secretary-generals and Secretariat envoys were proactive in Cyprus. While the outcomes of UN mediation were unsuccessful, various secretary-generals showed the potential to maximize their autonomy from Security Council constraints. For example, Waldheim stated that Britain, France and the US 'had no intention of seriously seeking to halt the Turkish offensive and that UNFICYP's mandate was not enough for the developing situation' (Newman, 2001, p. 134), but that he took it upon himself 'to extend the very narrow mandate of UNFICYP – to act as buffer between the Greek and Turkish Cypriot communities – in order to mitigate as far as possible the hardships of conflict it was unable to prevent' (Waldheim, 1985, p. 85).

Similarly while ultimately unsuccessful, the proximity talks to achieve a federal bi-zonal bi-communal Cyprus, were 'handled well' (Newman, 2001, p. 138) by Secretary-General Perez de Cuellar in 1984, involving 'creative mediation' (Newman, 2001, p. 138). De Cuellar also played a role in arranging first face-to-face meeting between Greek and Turkish Cypriot leaders in six years, in 1984, although interference by Athens seems to have led conflicting expectations of the meeting (Newman, 2001, p. 139).

The above sections show that from 2002 to 2004, the UN's role in Cyprus was particularly intensive. It is noteworthy from the above overview that de Soto and his small team had significant discretion in devising bargaining tactics, setting the agenda of negotiations and also setting the rules of the 'game'. Indeed, the UN's attempts in 2002–2004 to reach a settlement in Cyprus were beyond mere mediation, whereby it would simply provide ideas and solutions in an open-ended framework. Instead, the UN's approach shifted from its traditional mediation role to one of arbitration (Ker-Lindsay, 2009, p. 161). There was a clearly defined timetable and the parties 'mandated the UN to decide the final terms of the Plan' (Ker-Lindsay, 2009, p. 161). While the Annan Plan was based on decades of negotiations, the parties did hand over 'an unparalleled degree of power and authority to the UN over the peace-making process' (Ker-Lindsay, 2009, p. 161). According to some observers, Security Council resolution 939 placed the secretary-general in a 'pivotal position in peace-making efforts' (Newman, 2001, p. 148), and its potential was realized in the Cyprus case, under Kofi Annan. The office had 'room for manoeuvre in the development of ideas for negotiation, coordinating CBMs, facilitating cooperation between the parties on missing persons and in making public statements' (Newman, 2001, p. 148).

The discretionary power left to de Soto and his team in 2001–04 was a function of various factors: the end of the Cold War allowed Boutros-Boutros- Ghali to abolish the Office of Special Political Affairs as it had inherited Cold War traditions of secrecy and tight control over staff (Senior retired UN Secretariat official, interview with the author, June 20, 2012). The impact of de Cuellar's strategy in dealing with the Security Council and in conflict resolution continued after his tenure (Senior retired UN Secretariat official, interview with the author, June 20, 2012). As Chapter 3 showed, de Cuellar was able to take strong (if not always successful) initiatives in Namibia, Cambodia and El Salvador and to negotiate the withdrawal of Soviet troops from Afghanistan (Senior retired UN Secretariat official, interview with the author, June 20, 2012). All these initiatives were handled by senior Secretariat staff (envoys) and small secretariat teams who reported directly to de Cuellar (Senior retired UN Secretariat official, interview with the author, June 20, 2012). De Soto himself learnt from his successful experience under de Cuellar in El Salvador (see Chapter 3).

According to UN Secretariat interviewees personality factors were also deemed to be important. De Cuellar was a UN bureaucrat whose skills were particularly evident in 'behind-the scenes' negotiations. He was skilled in providing enough information to the Security Council, so that they did not feel distrustful, but not so much that they might undermine his mediation efforts (Senior retired UN Secretariat official, interview with the author, June 20, 2012). He also allowed significant autonomy for his senior staff (Senior retired UN Secretariat official, interview with the author, June 20, 2012). The De Cuellar's reign as Secretary -General, before the creation of the DPA, led to' considerable flexibility and an absence of excessive bureaucratization (Senior retired UN Secretariat official, interview with the author, June 20, 2012). However, while the creation of the DPA may have increase bureaucratization and lessened flexibility (Senior retired UN Secretariat official, interview with the author, June 20, 2012), some of the hallmarks of de Cuellar's tenure continued and are evident in the Cypriot negotiations: providing information frequently to the Security Council, but not excessively, as an information overload would create insecurity among members and adopting an informal flexible consultation and policy-making approach.

The circumstances that facilitated a proactive Secretariat role in the above cases also influenced conditions in Cyprus. In 2003 and 2004, two reports, the first mainly written by Robert Dann, a Secretariat official in de Soto's office and the second by Sir Kieran Prendergast, then Head of the DPA. These reports described how Turkey and Cyprus' EU membership bids, Greek–Turkish *rapprochement* and a lessening of military control of Turkish government opened the door to settling the Cyprus problem (Senior retired UN Secretariat official, interview with the author, June 20, 2012). Of these conditions, EU membership was the biggest catalyst for the resumption of UN negotiations (Senior retired UN Secretariat official, interview with the author, June 20, 2012). The reports paved the way for the 2004 negotiations.

The actual negotiations, as Ker-Lindsay observed (see above) highlighted the Secretariat's role, specifically that of the Special Envoy. For example, de Soto argued that the Cypriot negotiations were best conducted by side-stepping the issue of whether resolving the conflict meant bringing two parts of Cyprus back together (the Greek Cypriot perception), or whether it would implied creating a new confederal state (the Turkish view). For de Soto, it was best to exclude this issue from negotiations (Senior retired UN Secretariat official, interview with the author, July 2, 2013).

Similarly, the ultimatum that if the two sides could not reach agreement, Annan would 'fill in the blanks' and the two sides must agree in advance to hold referenda was made by de Soto (Senior retired UN Secretariat official, interview with the author, June 20, 2012). In making these decisions, de Soto worked closely with a small team of senior officials – again Sir Kieran Prendergast, Robert Dann and also with senior EU officials, in particular Verheugen (Senior retired UN Secretariat official, interview with the author, June 20, 2012). De Soto also met with the P-5 Ambassadors and briefed them in New York regularly, and consequently 'most of whom were happy' to let him lead (Senior retired UN Secretariat official, interview with the author, June 20, 2012). His team sent a reporting cable every day to the Security Council, in line with de Cuellar's practice of reassuring the Security Council. De Soto also met regularly with Sir Kieran Prendergast and four, or five DPA staff, nominated by Prendergast (Senior retired UN Secretariat official, interview with the author, June 20, 2012) and also with the Head of the DPKO, 'more as a courtesy', as the DPKO's role was more minimal (Senior retired UN Secretariat official, interview with the author, June 20, 2012). The process was mainly informal and flexible, under de Soto's and Annan's leadership (Senior retired UN Secretariat official, interview with the author, June 20, 2012). The Annan Plan itself and all its drafts, as well as reports to the Security Council were all written by de Soto, in consultation with other Secretariat senior officials, particularly Kieran Prendergast.

The process was also tightly controlled, as de Soto made it clear that the negotiations were delicate (Senior retired UN Secretariat official, interview with the author, June 20, 2012). For example, if an EU official was visiting Cyprus, the EU had to contact de Soto's team first and be briefed on what to say (Senior retired UN Secretariat official, interview with the author, June 20, 2012). De Soto and his team's view was that they were grateful for EU help, but would not take instructions from the EU, or from the UK (Senior retired UN Secretariat official, interview with the author, July 3, 2013).

However, the UK and the US were key actors also and their role was vital in securing Denktash's decision to come to New York for opening talks in February 2004. The US supported Turkish membership of the EU and pressurized Turkey to influence Denktash (Senior retired UN Secretariat official, interview with the author, June 20, 2012) and the UK (Senior retired UN Secretariat official, interview with the author, June 20, 2012). De Soto had an open door policy to key national leaders (Senior retired UN Secretariat official, interview with the author, June 20, 2012), if they had concerns, or queries. In the actual proximity talks, the UN team issued 'talking points' to explain the overall plan (Senior retired UN Secretariat official, interview with the author, June 20, 2012). Where there were differences, de Soto spoke to each leader individually after the talking points (Senior retired UN Secretariat official, interview with the author, June 20, 2012).

The tightly controlled process also implied that in terms of the civil society/elite-driven cleavage, the process was clearly top-down. The tight framework and strictly controlled procedures were elite driven and negotiations comprised primarily Greek Cypriot and Turkish Cypriot prime ministers. Moreover, to maintain impartiality, the UN had to be careful not to appear to lobby for support of the referendum (Senior retired UN Secretariat official, interview with the author,

June 20, 2012). Therefore, it was decided not to engage with local actors and non-governmental organizations.

Specific decisions during the course of the negotiations, such as the opening of the Green Line also had strong UN involvement. The UN provided the framework for opening the Green Line. As a perceived success, the decision had many fathers (Senior retired UN Secretariat official, interview with the author, June 20, 2012). For example, Denktash's support can be explained by his attempt to keep his community on board following leaks that he had compromise excessively in the UN negotiations. However, the UN ensured that the opening satisfied basic requirements of both communities and that also respected the EU's *acquis* (Senior retired UN Secretariat official, interview with the author, June 20, 2012).

Thus, flexibility, working in a small team and informality were hallmarks of the Cypriot negotiations and these hallmarks empowered the UN Secretariat significantly, particularly the envoy. However, while EU membership, the US, the UK and France facilitated these conditions, as well as the tactics of de Soto, learnt from de Cuellar, the culmination of the talks also highlighted the constraints caused by the Security Council and key EU states, particularly the UK.

Russia clearly tolerated de Soto and his teams' autonomy, as all Security Council members wished for a solution in Cyprus and lessening the cost of UN peacekeeping on Cyprus had become a post-Cold War priority. In other words, de Soto and his team had a mandate from the Security Council. However, for de Soto, Russian support for a UN resolution would have turned the AKEL in favour of the Plan and Greek Cypriots would have followed suit. The Russian veto, following Papadopoulos' visit to Russia, prevented this outcome.

Thus, the Cyprus case highlights the relative autonomy enjoyed by UN Secretariat senior staff, but also the constraints under which they operated. In addition, for some senior Secretariat officials, the negotiations would have had more success if they had been open ended, without the May 1 deadline posed by EU enlargement (Senior retired UN Secretariat official, interview with the author, July 3, 2013). In many ways, circumstances were conducive for a settlement – both the Turkish and Greek governments were more amenable to a settlement and Greek–Turkish cooperation had increased (Senior retired UN Secretariat official, interview with the author, July 3, 2013). The carrot of enlargement was potentially influential (Senior retired

UN Secretariat official, interview with the author, July 3, 2013). However, not enough time was allowed to allow these changes filter through to the Cypriot conflict resolution process because the EU and particularly the UK was insistent on a fixed deadline for the talks (Senior retired UN Secretariat official, interview with the author, July 3, 2013). For some participants also the Annan Plan was too complex and was not understood by Greek Cypriots (Senior retired UN Secretariat official, interview with the author, July 3, 2013). The Plan resembled a Rubik's cube, where finding a solution that 'fit' was extremely difficult (Senior retired UN Secretariat official, interview with the author, July 3, 2013). When agreement was reached in one issue, it impeded an earlier agreement on another issue. Solving the puzzle necessitated far more time. The decision to reverse conditionality, but also to grant aid to Turkish Cyprus also meant that Greek and Turkish Cypriot leaders had very little incentive to cooperate (Senior retired UN Secretariat official, interview with the author, July 3, 2013). Therefore, for some participants, while the Security Council, Russia's veto proved problematic, the EU's approach to Cyprus, particularly the May 1 deadline was equally problematic. In the next section, the EU's policy process is examined.

EU policy process and Cyprus

The EU policy process from 1997 to 2004 was tightly controlled by member states and the PSC's role was less dominant, particularly in 2004, than that of COREPER 11 (Interview, Irish Department of Foreign Affairs, Dublin, June 25, 2013). In addition, under the Irish Presidency, a special working group dedicated to managing Cypriot membership on May 1, and the Annan Plan negotiations were established. This was a small group chaired by a senior Irish diplomat. The Commission's role in this group was relatively minor. National preferences held sway, particularly those of Greece, but also the British government's preference for a fixed May 1 deadline. Although the working group travelled to Switzerland for the final stages of the Annan negotiations, it was not included deeply in the negotiations and the UN team kept tight control over the process. Given the potential synergies between EU enlargement strategy and the Annan Plan, EU–UN cooperation was relatively minimal.

The reasons for the paucity of EU–UN cooperation, not only in the Cypriot but also in the Kosovo–Serbia case, as the next chapter shows, are argued to be partially a function of US influence in the UN, whereby US administrations tend to be wary of any apparent excessive sharing of foreign policy information. The weakness of cooperation is also a result of different approaches to conflict resolution, particularly 'on the ground'. Specifically, the EU's approach tended to be more pragmatic and functional, with a view to putting basic building blocks in place first (European Commission/EEAS official, interview with the author, July 19, 2013), such as economic infrastructure, whereas the UN tended to create a check list of ambitious democratic aims (Interview with UN Secretariat official, June 20, 2012). The UN's aims for many EU officials were not realisable unless economic factors were addressed first and indeed the democratic indicators used may not even exist fully in well-developed democracies (European Commission/EEAS official, interview with the author, July 19, 2013).

The dominance of Greek preferences in the EU with respect to Cyprus added to weaknesses in the policy process to Cyprus in 2004. On one level, the EU's policy reversals with respect to Cyprus from 1997 to 2004 rested on a Commission and Council assumption that if the Cyprus issue continued to be a part of accession negotiations, Turkish membership in particular would not be agreed. Turkish–Greek cooperation was assumed to be vital to resolving the Cypriot issue and more generally Turkish 'Europeanization' and Turkish democratization could be solidified by joining the EU. However, intergovernmental factors underlay the Commission's approach.

Greek lobbying of EU member states and the Commission has been argued to be vital to the EU's policy to Cyprus (Ker-Lindsay et al., 2011, p. 27). There were various strands to Greece's approach to the Cyprus issue in the EU. Firstly, shifts in the Greek–Turkish relationship led to Greece dropping Cypriot resolution as a condition for Cypriot and Turkish EU membership. Greek–Turkish animosity until the 1990s led to Greece opposing Turkey's bid to become an EU member until 1999. In 1995, following the 1994 Greek veto of Turkish membership of the EU's Customs Union, Turkey declared a *casus belli* against Greece because of its possible extension of territorial waters. In 1996, a cargo boat accident triggered a conflict about the status of the Imia inlet in the Aegean Sea culminating in the arrival of Greek and Turkish troops to the region and bringing Greece and Turkey 'to a near-war situation' Again, in 1997, Greece and Turkey threatened war over Cypriot purchase of missiles. These crises in the Greek–Turkish relationship in the 1990s affected Greek policy to Turkish and Cypriot membership at both the Luxembourg 1997 summit and the Helsinki 1999 summit and determined the Council's conclusions at these summits (Rumelili, 2004). Specifically the condition stipulated at the Luxembourg Council that Turkey should resolve the Cypriot conflict (see above) was clearly related to the tensions between Greece and Turkey at that time.

However, despite these slumps, Greek–Turkish *rapprochement* developed gradually. For example, when both states were faced with the devastating consequences of earthquakes in 1999, both governments at the UN co-sponsored a joint UN resolution to establish a Joint Standby Disaster Response Unit (Rumelili, 2007, p. 12). Thus, Greece supported the Helsinki Council's decision in 1999 to grant Turkey candidate status (Karatas, 2011, p. 34). A key incentive for Greek cooperation was a fear of growing a Turkish–Israeli military cooperation (Stivachtis, 2002, p. 37). Also, the EU had helped 'in containing excessive nationalistic elements in Greek foreign policy' (Karatas, 2000, p. 207). In addition, there was a perception among Turkish elites that cooperation would 'reap mutual benefits' to Greece and Turkey (Rumelili, 2007, p. 21). Thus, a reason for the EU weakening conditionality with respect to Cyprus conflict resolution was Greek–Turkish *rapprochement* – Turkish membership of the EU would be jeopardized if it was contingent on resolving the Cypriot conflict and therefore Greece supported Turkish membership. Greek policy reversals led to EU policy reversals on the Cyprus issue.

The second reason for Greek policy and its influence on the EU was that Greece, supported by the EU, believed that Turkish Cypriots were the main obstacles to conflict resolution. Therefore, the assumption was Greek Cypriots needed less convincing, but that the carrot of EU membership would have a catalytic effect on Turkish Cypriots to induce them to cooperate in UN negotiations (Ker-Lindsay et al., 2011, p. 34).

The perception that Turkish Cypriots were the main obstacle to agreement was strengthened by the greater intransigence of Turkish

Cyprus under Denktash, in the early stages of the Annan negotiations. The EU's perception was that Greek Cypriots were the victims
of irrational and dogmatic Turkish Cypriot behaviour. Dentkash's
intransigence added weight to this perception. Thus, Greece had
moral superiority with respect to the Cyprus issue and this moral
weight strengthened its bargaining power. However, this moral power
waned when Greek Cypriots rejected the Annan Plan, despite the
media prediction that Turkish Cyprus would not be offered a Customs Union with the EU because Greece would wield its veto (*Daily
Telegraph*, 2004), EU adherence to Greek preferences weakened after
the referendum and Greece could not block the customs union, or
block the EU's decision to open a mission in Turkish Cyprus.

In addition, it was hoped that the prospect of Greek Cyprus entering the EU as 'Cyprus', in the absence of Turkey and Turkish Cypriots
would entice Turkey to pressurize Turkish Cyprus to compromise.
In Turkish Cyprus, an increasing proportion of the population supported EU membership, and therefore 'based on a functional logic,
the EU hoped that as soon as the Turkish Cypriots perceived the
advantages of the EU accession more clearly, they would automatically join the accession track' (Karatas, 2011, p. 34). Similarly, Turkey
would 'soften its tone over the Cyprus issue' (Karatas, 2011, p. 34)
so as to join the EU. Thus EU conditionality was aimed more at the
Turkish Cypriots to induce them to cooperate in UN negotiations
(Ker-Lindsay et al., 2011, p. 34).

Fundamentally, Greek preferences held sway about relaxing
conditionality for Cyprus, because it used the EU's intergovernmental
structures to influence outcomes (Karatas, 2011, p. 28), particularly
by threatening to use a veto in final enlargement decisions. Thus, at
the Corfu European Council meeting in June 2004, Greece threatened to use its veto against the forthcoming EFTA enlargement
(Austria, Finland and Sweden) unless the EU allowed Cyprus to join
in 2004:

> Not only will there be not be any further enlargement if proce-
> dures for Cyprus' accession do not commence and are concluded,
> but it might also be difficult for other Community developments
> to proceed.
>
> (Greek Foreign Minister Pangalos, quoted by
> Athens News Agency, June 4, 2004)

The centrality of COREPER 11 and the creation of an ad hoc 2004 Council working group to deal with Cypriot enlargement and the Annan Plan negotiations highlight the intergovernmental nature of the EU' s policy process to Cyprus during this period, as opposed to comitology. Thus Greek influence was more easily facilitated by the process.

The ability of Greece to influence the EU so strongly also rested on tacit support from some other EU states. While the US strongly lobbied for Turkish membership of the EU and from 1995 linked Cypriot resolution to advancing Turkish EU membership, many EU states, including France and Germany, had 'doubts about Turkey's place in Europe' (Barkey, 2003, p. 239). The effect of this ambivalence was demonstrated in the Copenhagen Council conclusions (see above). Thus, Greek influence should be seen in the context of an absence of EU consensus on Turkish membership. Similarly, Sir David Hannay, former British Ambassador and UK Envoy to Cyprus, has observed that Cyprus has been a pawn in other states strategic games for decades (Hannay, 2006, p. 2).

Overall, in the Cypriot case, the Commission clearly lacked autonomy. Its *avis* altered significantly between 1993 and 1999 and its condition that the Cypriot conflict be resolved before entry was relaxed. These changes have been argued to result from Greek lobbying. Similarly, with respect to Turkish membership of the EU:

> The concerns raised by the Commission in its 2003 regular report on Turkey's progress towards accession, pertaining to international law issues, echo the Greek position which leads us to the conclusion that there is substantial input from one conflict party in this case.
>
> (Pace, 2005, p. 16)

Thus, in the Cypriot case intergovernmental politics constrained the Commission's autonomy and Greek lobbying, particularly its veto over future enlargements curtailed the Commission's role. Given these constraints, the Commission's approach was to provide economic and functional aid and to support the UN negotiations, but also to insist on a fixed deadline for de Soto's negotiations (Pace, 2005, p. 16). It must be noted, however, that the increasing support of Turkey and Turkish Cyprus for the Annan Plan seemed to indicate that EU policy and the Commission's approach were paying off (Karatas, 2011). Until the last weeks of the negotiations, very few officials expected Greek Cyprus to reject the Plan. In other words, ceding to Greek preferences reflected a strong perception that Turkish Cypriots and Denktash were the main obstacle to resolving the Cypriot conflict and that Greek Cyprus would vote 'yes' to the Annan Plan. The above analysis of the UN and EU's policy processes towards Cyprus provide various insights into the role of the Commission and of the UN Secretariat, as the final section of this chapter shows.

Conclusion

One of the main differences between the role of the UN Secretariat and the European Commission in the policy process to Cyprus was that senior officials in the Secretariat had far more autonomy than their Commission counterparts. Once the Security Council began to prioritize Cyprus in the 1990s, the Secretariat was empowered to find a solution. The Commission was far more constrained by intergovernmental politics, particularly by Greece. The Commission's ability to implement a strategic policy was constrained, and therefore conditionality rules were relaxed and the deadline of May 1 for Cyprus' entry could not be extended.

A second difference between the UN Secretariat and the Commission in Cyprus is that Secretariat was more flexible and informal. There were very few committee meetings and although de Soto and Annan reported formally to the Security Council, most communication was informal. The Commission and EU too operated informally generally, but the EU's governance structure provided for a greater number of committee and Council meetings. While Chapter 1 highlighted evidence that the committee system could empower the Commission, given the Commission's experience in the enlargement policy area, it is clear that in the case of Cyprus, the committee system acted as a check on Commission autonomy and facilitated Greek influence. For example, key decisions were often made on COREPER 11, not the PSC and they often followed Greek preferences, with support from other states.

However, a common factor in both EU and UN policy processes is the role of misperception. The policy priorities of the

Commission and UN Secretariat were not markedly different during the Annan Plan negotiations. Specifically, the belief that Turkish Cyprus would be the main obstacle to ratifying the Annan Plan dominated perceptions in the EU and the UN. Overall, as the above overview of the UN policy process showed, UN Secretariat staff took the lead in the negotiations and fed information to both the EU and to the Security Council. Thus their perceptions were highly significant. While Greek preferences explain the EU decision to make Cypriot EU membership unconditional on a settlement, the emphasis on enticing Turkish Cyprus to cooperate rested on an assumption that Greek Cyprus would support the Annan Plan. As Secretariat officials were so closely in touch with both Greek and Turkish officials, it is likely that the EU's perception of Greek Cypriots' preferences at the very least was not undermined by the UN team and at most was encouraged by them. Indeed, de Soto was very surprised when Papadopoulos rejected the Annan Plan publicly, as he argued that he had had no indication of opposition from him in private meetings. There was deep puzzlement as to the causes of the verbal public rejection and he surmised that pressure may have been brought to bear on Papadopoulos at a lengthy AKEL meeting (Senior retired UN Secretariat official, interview with the author, June 19, 2012).

Thus, in explaining the EU's policy to Cyprus not only Greek lobbying but also the role of perception, was crucial. Perception and misperception also explain the UN Secretariat's approach to the negotiations and as de Soto and his team had considerable autonomy, it was crucial in explaining the final policy outcome. Senior UN Secretariat staff as key negotiators had a monopoly of information about Greek Cypriot and Turkish Cypriot preferences, and therefore, UN officials' information framed the EU's approach.

Clearly also, the elite-driven policy process can explain misperception – civil society was not largely engaged. For the UN Secretariat, the weakness of engagement with local grass-roots actors was driven at least partially by the aim of not appearing to be partisan. Hence the argument that the UN principle of neutrality determines, if not constrains policy processes (see Chapter 1) was evident also in the Cypriot case.

UN staff were not to blame if misperception occurred. It appears that Commission had no evidence to contradict the UN's view. Moreover, it is striking in the above overview of the UN's negotiations that different national envoys had different assessments of progress; for example, the US envoy Weston and the Australian envoy presented very different assessments of the negotiations within two days of each other. Similarly, various envoys altered their assessments relatively frequently during short time periods. For both senior international Secretariat staff and national diplomats, there were clearly information gaps about Greek Cyprus's preferences, and neither Greek influence in the EU nor Russian preferences on the Security Council solely explain the outcomes of the Annan negotiations.

Overall, perhaps counter-intuitively in the light of the UN's image, Cyprus was a case where the UN Secretariat enjoyed relative autonomy and the Commission was more constrained by national preferences. The Security Council's consensus in favour of finding a solution under UN auspices and in favour of giving Kofi Annan and his staff a proactive role was an initial condition for the Secretariat's autonomy. However, the examination of UN Secretariat senior officials' role in Cyprus has highlighted other factors that gave considerable discretion to his team, particularly flexibility and informality. In contrast, an absence of consensus in the EU, particularly Greece's intense preferences with respect to Turkish membership and to Cyprus limited the Commission's autonomy. If the Commission had a monopoly of information and expertise, it did not seem to use it to assert its influence and COREPER 11 and an ad hoc Council working group comprised the key institutions in the EU's policy process. Moreover, the Commission's field knowledge was not as great as the UN Secretariat's knowledge, despite the Secretariat's elite-driven approach in the Annan negotiations. In the next chapter, the EU and UN's policy process to Kosovo and to Serbia is examined to determine the Commission and UN Secretariat's role.

6
Kosovo and Serbia

As previous chapters mentioned, the Balkans case severely dented the EU and UN's reputations, following genocide and ethnic cleansing on a scale not seen since the Second World War. While the 1999 NATO airstrike officially ended the conflict and the Dayton Accord was signed to indicate a peaceful resolution of the conflict, Kosovo and its relationship with Serbia were left over as unresolved issues and one that became increasingly unstable. Like Cyprus, both the EU and the UN became embroiled, albeit reluctantly in attempting to stabilize and democratize Kosovo. Kosovo's Unilateral Declaration of Independence (UDI) in 2008 was met with an incoherent and divided international response, whereby various EU and UN states refused to recognize Kosovo's independence, despite the 2010 International Court of Justice's (ICJ) verdict that the UDI was not in breach of international law.

In this chapter, it is argued that, as in the case of Cyprus, the EU and UN's policy processes to Kosovo and to Serbia have been markedly different. However, as opposed to the Cypriot case, the EU's process has increasingly shown flexibility and innovation that allowed it to agree on key initiatives, despite the failure of its members to agree to recognize Kosovo as a sovereign state. Indeed, it seems that the EU's policy-makers had learnt from the Cypriot experience. In contrast, the UN's policy process suffered from severe impediments. While, like Cyprus, the absence of consensus on the Security Council was a key constraint, the Kosovo case not only shows how bureaucratic factors impeded the UN's approach, but also shows that the Kosovo case also highlights the relative autonomy of the UN secretary-general, of UN envoys and teams in a conflict case.

The background to the case of Kosovo and Serbia is presented in the first section, before setting out the EU's and UN's policy responses. In the third section, the EU and UN's policy processes are examined. The key focus is on the period 2006–11, and various policy decisions are examined within this time frame: the UN's policy to Serbia and Kosovo from 1998 to 2006; the UN's role under the Ahtisaari process in 2007; the EU's resumption of Stability Association Agreement (SAA) negotiations in 2006; its agreement to deploy an EU mission to Kosovo, EULEX (European Union Rule of Law Mission in Kosovo), in 2008; and its response to the ICJ's 2010 judgement that Kosovo's UDI was not illegal.

Kosovo and Serbia: Background to conflict

The core divide in Kosovo is between Kosovo's Albanian community, mainly Muslim, comprising a majority of the Kosovo population and the Serb minority that are concentrated in North of Kosovo and comprise the minority within Kosovo. For Serbs, Kosovo is perceived to be part of Serbia, so the Albanian community comprises a minority within the Serb state. Under President Tito, the 1974 Yugoslav constitution provided a large measure of autonomy to Kosovo, giving it the same prerogatives as the six other republics in Yugoslavia (Bosnia, Herzegovina, Croatia, Macedonia, Montenegro and Serbia), except the right to secede (Phillips, 2012, p. 7). Thus, Kosovo had the right of veto at the federal level. Serbia strongly opposed Kosovo's status and when Tito died, Yugoslavia became a loose coalition of competing parties (Phillips, 2012, p. 7). The collapse of Communism saw the rise of Slobodan Milošević, who prioritized Serbian nationalism, especially towards Kosovo as a key electoral platform in Serbia (Phillips, 2012, p. 8). Constitutional amendments were made to repeal Kosovo's autonomy (Phillips, 2012, p. 9). In 1989, Milošević stated that armed battle could not be ruled out (Phillips, 2012, p. 11), and martial law was imposed on Kosovo (Phillips, 2012, p. 13). An Albanian Kosovoar grass-roots movement, the Democratic League of Kosovo (LDK) led by intellectuals, notably Ibrahim Rugova, formed a protest movement (Phillips, 2012, p. 13). In 1990, they declared Kosovo's independence and a new constitution (Phillips, 2012, p. 14). Serbia declared a new constitution affirming Kosovo as an inalienable part of Serbia (Phillips,

2012, p. 14) and Milošević deployed 80,000 troops and police across Pristina (Phillips, 2012, p. 16).

The early 1990s saw the proclamation of independence by a number of Yugoslav republics and the ensuing violence in Croatia (for example, the shelling of Dubrovnik) and genocide in Bosnia met with international neglect of Kosovo (Phillips, 2012, pp. 23–24). The Arbitration Commission of the Conference on Yugoslavia (the Badinter Commission) was set up at Germany's urging, under Robert Badinter, the president of France's Constitutional Council (Phillips, 2012, p. 23). The Badinter Commission recommended independence for Slovenia and Macedonia, but not Kosovo as it was not a republic (Phillips, 2012, p. 24).

The UN's initial response to the Balkans was that it was 'a European problem' (de Cuellar, quoted in Traube, 2007, p. 42). However, in Bosnia, Serb forces sought to consolidate control of Serb-dominated regions and a policy of ethnic cleansing began (Traube, 2007, p. 42). By 1992, tens of thousands of Bosnians and Croatians had been killed and hundreds of thousands had been driven from their homes (Phillips, 2012, p. 25). Barbaric atrocities shocked the world and the UN High Commissioner for Refugees passed a resolution condemning events in Bosnia (Phillips, 2012, p. 25) and appointed a Special Rapporteur to investigate. In 1992, the Security Council agreed to deploy UN military observers in Croatia in 1992 (Phillips, 2012, p. 25), and in June 1992 the mission was expanded and became known as UNPROFOR (Phillips, 2012, p. 25).

In August 1992, world leaders met in London to discuss the emergency in Bosnia and Herzegovina (Phillips, 2012, p. 27). A plan was proposed to sanction Serbia and provide emergency relief via humanitarian corridors to displaced people. The US would lead an effort to organize robust deterrence in the UNSC and the EU would be responsible for aid (Phillips, 2012, p. 27). The final deal, supported by Bosnia and Serbia, established no-fly zones, called for the decommissioning of heavy weapons around Sarajevo and tightening of sanctions against Serbia and called for the creation of a war crimes tribunal (Phillips, 2012, p. 27). Following strong Serbian objections to being identified as the aggressor, Serbia was identified as the aggressor in a verbal statement, but not in the actual plan (Phillips, 2012, p. 27).

The US supported the Carrington Plan, envisaging a loose association of former republics, agreed by consensus of all the former republics of Yugoslavia, with autonomy in each republic (Phillips, 2012, p. 28). However, the Carrington Plan did not afford sufficient protection to non-Serb minorities and was doomed to failure (Phillips, 2012, p. 27). The LDK, supported by human rights organizations, increased its lobbying of US officials and in 1992, a steering group on Balkan issues, later called the 'Contact Group' comprising the P-5 and Belgium, a non-permanent Security Council member, was established. Given Russia's objections to any territory seceding unilaterally, the quint was created, comprising the Contact Group members, minus Russia. However, it too failed to agree. Richard Holbrooke, then US Assistant Secretary for European Affairs, believed that Serbia would continue to act with impunity unless there was a credible threat of military intervention and lobbied for support for NATO airstrikes in the face of the passive international response (Phillips, 2012, p. 60). NATO's Operation Deliberate Force helped Bosnia gain territory in September and October, 1995, and the Dayton Talks began in November 1995 (Phillips, 2012, p. 60).

The Dayton Talks comprised the leaders of the ex-Yugoslavia, US Secretary of State Warren Christopher, Serbian President Slobodan Milošević, Croatian President Franjo Tuđman, Bosnian President Alija Izetbegović (Phillips, 2012, p. 60) and various European senior officials. The UN was not officially represented as Holbrooke advised Albright that 'the UN's involvement in the talks would further complicate them' (Holbrooke, 1999, p. 202), so Albright 'held the UN at bay' (Holbrooke, 1999, p. 202). The German representative, Wolfgang Ischinger, recollected that his 'instructions from the German foreign minister, Klaus Kinkel, were to include Kosovo in the Dayton Accords' (Perritt, 2009, p. 33), but it was 'impossible to implement' (Perritt, 2009, p. 33). Various US officials favoured making concessions to Serbia conditional on Serbia reforming its policy to Kosovo (Congressman Engel, cited in Phillips, 2012, p. 63). However, the Dayton Accord resolved the crises in Bosnia and Croatia, but left Kosovo out of the negotiations. The moderate LDK was greatly compromised by the Accord's results (Phillips, 2012, p. 63). Non-violent resistance was increasingly criticized by Kosovo's Albanians (Phillips, 2012, p. 67), and the Kosovo Liberation Army (KLA) announced its campaign of guerrilla warfare (Phillips, 2012, p. 68).

The US response was a twin strategy of stabilizing Kosovo and persuading 'the EU to think strategically about Serbia' (Phillips, 2012,

p. 75), so that Serbia could be persuaded of the benefits of EU membership, if it engaged in rapprochement with Kosovo (Phillips, 2012, p. 75).

As regards Serbia, the Clinton administration's approach was to transform it into an economically and democratically viable state to lead to *rapprochement* with Kosovo (Phillips, 2012, p. 75). The task seemed less daunting when opinion polls showed that Milošević's popularity was slipping in 1998 (Phillips, 2012, p. 76). However, in spring 1998, Milošević launched a brutal attack on Kosovo (Phillips, 2012, p. 89). The US reaction was to adopt more robust policy to Serbia (Phillips, 2012, p. 90). In March 1998, Rugova wrote to Madeline Albright, Secretary of State to say that he was willing to start negotiations with Milošević, with Holbrooke as mediator (Phillips, 2012, p. 91) and Milošević, under the threat of more biting sanctions, agreed to meet Rugova in May 1998. Violence continued, with Serbian forces targeting Albanian villages and the KLA counterattacking (Phillips, 2012, p. 92). In September 1998, Tony Blair, then UK prime minister addressed the UN General Assembly and warned about an impending humanitarian disaster in Kosovo, due to violence, weather and Serbian harassment of relief efforts (Blair, 1998). UNSC resolution 1199 was sponsored by the UK two days later demanding a ceasefire (Phillips, 2012, p. 92) and threatening a NATO airstrike. In response, Milošević agreed to a ceasefire (Phillips, 2012, p. 92).

In addition, UNSC Resolution 1203 established the Kosovo Verification Mission (KVM) to allow 2000 unarmed inspectors, under the auspices of the Organisation for Security Cooperation in Europe (OSCE), to monitor the ceasefire (Phillips, 2012, p. 95). According to the then US Special Representative for the implementation of the KVM, Pardew, the KVM was 'ad-hocery from start to finish' (Pardew, cited in Phillips, 2012, p. 96), as they were unarmed and verified only that Kosovo was a very dangerous place (Phillips, 2012, p. 96).

In January 1999, in response to the murder of six Serbian teenagers, Serbian forces massacred 45 Kosovo Albanians in Račak, a small village in central Kosovo (Phillips, 2012, pp. 98–99). The Racak massacre laid the ground for NATO's airstrike in 1999 and the Rambouillet Agreement (Phillips, 2012, pp. 100–01). The failure of the Dayton Accord to deliver peace and the deteriorating security situation led to the Rambouillet negotiations (January 1999 to March 1999)

(Chandler, 2000, p. 204). Thus in January 1999, Albright and the Russian Foreign Minister Igor Ivanov issued a joint statement to express US and Russian indignation at the massacre in Racak (Phillips, 2012, p. 101) and the then Head of NATO, Javier Solana stated that 'NATO stands ready to act' (Phillips, 2012, p. 101).

In March 1999, under the Rambouillet Agreement, the UN High Representative was to be the de facto ruler of the province with the power to remove elected representatives, curtail institutions and close down media organizations with no right of appeal (Chandler, 2000, p. 204). There was also to be NATO presence. The Kosovo delegation was deeply divided between the more moderate LDK and the KLA (Phillips, 2012, p. 103) and Thaci 'never even read the [Rambouillet] agreement' (Surroi, cited in Phillips, 2012, p. 104). Milošević too had no intention of negotiating and Russia also did not participate. When final diplomatic efforts failed in March 1999, Solana ordered NATO forces to commence airstrikes against targets in Kosovo and Serbia (Phillips, 2012, p. 107) and NATO intervened on March 23, 1999.

For many Albanian Kosovans, the airstrike constituted international recognition of the right to Kosovo's independence (Shala, 2000, p. 187). However, in fact, the dominant international view, epitomized by Albright, was to support autonomy for Kosovo, but not complete independence: 'We want Serbia out of Kosovo, not Kosovo out of Serbia' (Albright, quoted in Ker-Lindsay, 2009, p. 145). The NATO airstrike itself and the humanitarian crisis that ensued led the leaders of the G8 to draw up a seven point plan in 1999. The Plan still favoured autonomy, not independence and under Security Council Resolution 1244, provided for the establishment of the United Nations Mission in Kosovo (UNMIK) to administer Kosovo and to oversee the development of democratic self-governing institutions, so as to pave the way for a final settlement (Resolution 1244, S/RES/1244, 1999).

Given Russian objections to a proposed airstrike, the airstrike was not ratified by the UNSC, under a new resolution, but it was argued by the US and UK that UNSC Resolution provided for it. Milošević capitulated on June 9, 1999 and UNSC Resolution 1244 ended the war officially and provided for UNMIK as the executive, judicial and legislative authority for Kosovo (Phillips, 2012, p. 106). The ensuing years saw the increasingly discredited reign of UNMIK, the

UN-mediated Ahtisaari Plan in 2007 and, in 2008, the establishment of the EU's EULEX. In the next section, an overview of UN and EU policy to and involvement in Kosovo is provided, before examining EU and UN policy processes.

The UN's policy to Kosovo

UNMIK sought to 'establish a secure environment in which refugees and displaced persons can return in safety, the international civil service can operate, a transitional administration can be established, and humanitarian aid can be delivered' (UN Security Council Resolution 1244, 1999). Annex 1 provided for 'an interim political framework agreement for substantial self-government for Kosovo' (UN Security Council Resolution 1244, 1999). The resolution also called for the demilitarization of the KLA (Phillips, 2012, p. 115) and the return of an agreed number of Serbian and Yugoslav police to Kosovo (Phillips, 2012, p. 115). In addition, under Chapter VII of the UN Charter, 50,000 peacekeeping troops were deployed to Kosovo (KFOR) (Phillips, 2012, p. 117). These troops reported directly to NATO, constituting a separate military presence (Phillips, 2012, p. 117), but it coordinated its work with UNMIK (Phillips, 2012, p. 117).

Following his deployment to East Timor, the first SRSG, Sergio de Mello was replaced quickly by Bernard Kouchner (Phillips, 2012, p. 120). Under Kouchner, UNMIK's first 100 days were relatively productive. The KLA was transformed into un-armed KLC (Perritt, 2009, p. 54). The KLC was not allowed to participate in politics and the aim was that it would also comprise Serbs (Phillips, 2012, p. 121). However, UNMIK itself was 'an unwieldy amalgamation of international organizations . . . a joint venture between international organizations with complementary expertise' (Phillips, 2012, p. 120). Pillar 1 was the international civil administration, Pillar 11 was led by the UNHCR to deal with humanitarian issues (Phillips, 2012, p. 120), Pillar 111 focused on institution-building and was led by the OSCE and Pillar 1V was led by the EU and was responsible for reconstruction (Perritt, 2009, p. 54).

In 2001 Michael Steiner replaced Kouchner as SRSG (Phillips, 2012, p. 138) and 'instituted a policy of benchmarking, through which indicators (of democracy) were to be developed in eight areas of governance' (Knoll, 2005, p. 639). These standards included the functioning of democratic institutions, enshrining the rule of law, protecting the rights of minorities and developing dialogue with Serbia. In 2001, the new Constitutional Framework to establish Provisional Institutions of Self-Government in Kosovo (PISGs) did not cede control over areas that might erode Serbia's sovereign rights (UNSC, Regulation no. 2000/9). Steiner reported to the UN secretary-general in 2002 that his top priority was to transfer responsibilities from UNMIK to the PISGs (Phillips, 2012, p. 139). UNMIK's new constitutional framework 'envisioned a power-sharing arrangement with an elected assembly appointing a president and constituting a government headed by a prime minister. Twenty seats in 120-member assembly were reserved for minorities' (Perritt, 2010, p. 69). UNMIK had the right to veto PISG decisions and to nullify legislation passed in the new Assembly (Perritt, 2010, p. 70). The aim was to encourage Kosovo's parties to join in a grand coalition, so as to undercut KLA domination of the political sphere (Perritt, 2010, p. 70).

The rationale proposed by Steiner was that Kosovo could only become a fair and just society if democratic preconditions were met and that these democratic standards mirrored those set by the EU (Knoll, 2005, pp. 639–40). As regards status, the policy stated that status would be decided at a later date, on condition that democratic standards were met – a standards before status policy. For Rugova, the PSIG's 'were denied the competencies and budget' to achieve standards themselves (Knoll, 2005, pp. 639–40). In fact, 'most legislative and executive authority continued to be exercised by UNMIK' (Perritt, 2010, p. 70).

In addition, the attempt to dismantle parallel structures in Northern Kosovo, led to growing unrest in Kosovo. An announcement was made in 2003 that the Contact Group would review progress in achieving international standards, so that the process of determining Kosovo's final status could begin (Ker-Lindsay, 2009, p. 149). Despite this announcement, Kosovans, who already found that Steiner 'ignored government ministers and assembly members' (Perritt, 2010, p. 71), were deeply angered (Phillips, 2012, p. 139) and in 2004, violence swept Kosovo, killing 19 people and injuring a 1,000 people (Ker-Lindsay, 2009, p. 20).

The impact of the riots was 'enormous' (Ker-Lindsay, 2009, p. 20): 'the realisation that the international community was unable to stop the fighting transformed the whole debate over status' (Ker-Lindsay,

2009, p. 21). Resentment grew between UNMIK and KFOR (Ker-Lindsay, 2009, p. 21), with UNMIK making allegations that KFOR was ignoring the violence (Ker-Lindsay, 2009, p. 21). Although by 2003 there was 'substantial development of local political institutions' (Perritt, 2010, p. 70), there was also 'growing frustration within the PISG and Kosovar Albanian citizenry over the slow pace' (Perritt, 2010, p. 71) of devolution of power from UNMIK to local institutions. For Perritt, this delay was not only because of opposition to devolution from some national government, but also because of opposition from UN bureaucrats, 'especially UN lawyers' (Perritt, 2009, p. 71). The Contact Group intervened, governed by a perception that Steiner was allowing UNMIK to drift and Soren Jessen-Petersen was appointed SRSG in June 2004 (Phillips, 2102, p. 147).

By 2005, the US and all EU states, apart from Cyprus, Slovakia, Spain, Greece and Slovenia supported Kosovo's bid for independence from Serbia, despite initial reluctance to do so. Jessen-Petersen accepted the post on condition that he had 'a mandate to put status talks on the agenda' (Jessen-Petersen, cited in Phillips, 2012, p. 147). He felt that 'Mitrovica made it very clear that we had to move at an accelerated pace' (Jessen-Petersen, cited in Phillips, 2012, p. 147) and that he 'needed to tell Kosovans that status talks would get going' (Jessen-Petersen, cited in Phillips, 2012, p. 147). Jessen-Petersen developed a strategy to improve UNMIK's performance, to increase cooperation between all actors in the international community and to improve Kosovo's leaders' performance, so that Kosovo's Serbs would have an incentive to participate in PISGs (Jessen-Petersen, cited in Phillips, 2012, p. 147).

Emphasis on status continued when the Contact Group met in 2005 to assess Kosovo's progress towards independence. The Group recommended that Kofi Annan appoint an independent expert, not connected to UNMIK, to assess Kosovo's progress (Phillips, 2012, p. 157) and Kai Eide was appointed in June 2005 (UN Press Release, S/A, 927, June 6, 2005, 'Secretary-General Appoints Kai Eide as his Special Envoy to Undertake Comprehensive of Kosovo'). Eide was criticized for his 'reluctance to speak to UNMIK staff' apart from Jessen-Petersen (Phillips, 2012, p. 158) and also for ignoring civil society (Phillips, 2012, p. 158).

Eide's report concluded in October 2005, that progress was 'uneven' (Ker-Lindsay, 2009, p. 23). There were significant achievements in institution-building and the development of public services in health and education, but there were serious problems in the justice system, the rule of law and progress towards reconciliation (Ker-Lindsay, 2009, p. 23). Eide's optimism was met with scepticism from some observers who claimed that 'the centre of gravity of his report was critical of progress in Kosovo and that his conclusion was coerced by the United States' (Interview with European diplomat, cited in Perritt, 2009, p. 89). However, the Contact Group agreed on core principles to guide the status process and Martti Ahtisaari was appointed to replace Eide in 2005 (Phillips, 2012, p. 158).

From the start of the Ahtisaari negotiations, it was assumed that independence for Kosovo was the only solution (Phillips, 2012, p. 159):

> Members of the Contact Group, including Russia, were informed by Ahtisaari that the ultimate outcome would be a plan for Kosovo's independence. The challenge was brokering a mutually acceptable settlement between Serbia and Kosovo that would uphold the interests of Kosovo Serbs and allow their functional ties to Belgrade.
>
> (Phillips, 2012, p. 161)

Frank Wisner, the then-retired US diplomat, was appointed as Ahtisaari's assistant on the mediating team (Phillips, 2012, p. 161). Convincing the Contact group of the merits of an independence plan for Kosovo, backed by the US, was not easy, in the aftermath of the Iraq War (Phillips, 2012, p. 161): 'Germany was very careful...because of its coalition government...France was historically pro-Serb...but it changed course' (Ahtisaari, cited in Phillips, 2012, p. 161). China viewed Kosovo as a European problem (Wisner, cited in Phillips, 2012, p. 161). According to Wisner, Russia did not indicate that it would oppose independence, if properly negotiated (Phillips, 2012, p. 161). Indeed, 'Contact Group members' were hopeful that in 2006 a plan for Kosovo could be crafted in the West and sold to Russia with persuasive diplomacy (Perritt, 2009, p. 126). Ahtisaari set up the UN Special Envoys Office for Kosovo (UNSOEK) with a small team of advisers.

UNSOEK's first key task was to build Kosovo's diplomatic and negotiating capacity. While Serbia's diplomats were well trained, Kosovo's had little experience (Phillips, 2012, p. 165). Its members were deeply divided and according to Ahtisaari, although they all agreed on the aim of independence (Ahtisaari, cited in Phillips, 2012, p. 166).

Serbia's team was also divided between the more moderate Tadic, the then president and the 'virulent nationalist' (Phillips, 2012, p. 167), Vojislav Kostunica, the then prime minister. Kosovo Serbs were also represented, but they were instructed by Belgrade, so did not play an independent role (Phillips, 2012, p. 167). With no agreement reached in July, working groups met in September to discuss centralization and minority rights (Phillips, 2012, p. 167). However, UNOSEK's mediation efforts failed to deliver agreement (Phillips, 2012, p. 167). The Contact Group met at the UN General Assembly on September 20th (Phillips, 2012, p. 167). Ahtisaari, to help Tadic increase his support base, agreed to delay presenting his plan for Kosovo until after Serbia's parliamentary election on January 21, 2007 (Phillips, 2012, p. 168). With increasing fears from UN administrators that any delays in bringing a plan before the Security Council would provoke violence (European Voice, 2007a), the Ahtisaari Plan was unveiled in March 2007 (*European Voice*, 2007a).

The Plan provided for Kosovo's independence after a transition period under international supervision (UNSC, 2007). The EU's European Rule of Law Mission (EULEX) would take over this supervisory role, as well as a new International Civilian Representative and KFOR would continue to be responsible for security (Kosovo's independence after a transition period under international supervision) (UNSC, 2007). Kosovo could apply for membership of international organizations immediately (UNSC, 2007). Minorities would be promoted by law and devolution to local authorities would further protect Serbs located in the North (UNSC, 2007).

Reactions from Kosovo's leaders were negative, as there was strong opposition to devolving power to local government and concern about the 'number and boundaries of Serbian municipalities' (Phillips, 2012, p. 168). Serbia strongly opposed independence and Ahtisaari concluded that 'there was no will from the parties to move away from their previously stated positions…no amount of additional negotiation will change that' (Ahtisaari, cited in Perritt, 2009, p. 169). Therefore, after nearly a year of exhaustive negotiations, Ahtisaari formally submitted his 'Comprehensive Plan and Recommendations' to the UNSC on April 3, 2007 (Phillips, 2012,

p. 168), calling for the above provision, as well as the dissolution of UNMIK within 120 days and the replacement of Resolution 1244 with a new UNSC Resolution (Phillips, 2012, p. 169). Just before the Plan was formally announced, following Ahtisaari's outline of the plan in February, even moderate Serbian nationalists were outraged (*European Voice*, 2007b). Tadic reiterated that Serbia would never accept Kosovo's independence and that other countries also would have problems, hinting at Russia (*European Voice*, 2007c). All UNSC members, apart from Russia and China endorsed the Ahtisaari Plan (Phillips, 2012, p. 169). Russia opposed any new UNSC Resolution that undermined 'Serbia's state sovereignty' (Phillips, 2012, p. 169). Germany's Chancellor Merkel and Solana discussed the need for further negotiations if Russia would not agree to the Plan (Phillips, 2012, p. 169), but Ahtisaari argued that 'you don't have paradise with a peace agreement' (Ahtisaari, quoted in Phillips, 2012, p. 169) and that the process had been to facilitate dialogue: 'it was inevitable that they would not agree' (Ahtisaari, quoted in Phillips, 2012, p. 169). Kosovo's Albanians were disappointed (Ahtisaari, quoted in Phillips, 2012, p. 169) and increasingly called for a unilateral declaration of independence, irrespective of whether Serbia, or Russia, agreed.

In response to the failure to reach agreement (Phillips, 2012, p. 173), the then French President Nicholas Sarkozy called for a new round of negotiations to last 120 days, and the US agreed, but with the caveat that if no agreement was reached Kosovo could declare independence (Phillips, 2012, p. 173). The fifth draft of a UN resolution was viewed as a way of overcoming Russian and Serbian objections, by removing any reference to 'supervised independence', despite the Ahtisaari Plan's recommendations (*European Voice*, 2007d). However, Russia rejected all draft resolutions and by July 2007, 'it was clear that the process of realising Kosovo's independence would have to happen without the approval of the United Nations' (Phillips, 2012, p. 176), Ahtisaari's deputy, Albert Rohan stating that 'nobody can prevent Kosovo's independence' (*Associated Press Worldstream*, 2007a).

It was agreed, that with the endorsement of UN Secretary-General Ban Ki-moon, a troika made up of the United States, the European Union and Russia, would lead future talks (*Associated Press Worldstream*, 2007a). There was a dominant belief that moving negotiations from the Security Council to an informal group poten-tially brought better conditions for an agreement between the three (US, EU, Russia) (*European Voice*, 2007e).

However, the troika was divided, not just between Russia and the US, but between EU members also (*European Voice*, 2007e). Russia wanted the deadline for UNMIK's dissolution and for Belgrade–Pristina negotiations to be indefinite, but the US, Germany, the UK, France and Italy's preference for a fixed deadline dominated: 'there will be no delays after December 10. It should be possible to find a negotiated settlement, but if it is not possible, then December 10 is the decisive date' (Volker Stanzel, quoted in Deutsche Presse-Agentur, 2007). By November 2007, no agreement was envisaged between Kosovo and Serbia on the Ahtisaari Plan (Agence France-Presse, 2007), despite the December deadline and despite the absence of any men-tion of Kosovo's status on the Troika's 14 point negotiating document (XINHUA General News Service, 2007).

Thus, the troika, despite Russian objections, submitted its final report on December 10, 2007, supporting Kosovo's independence (Phillips, 2012, p. 179), but confirming a deadlock in Serbia and Kosovo negotiations (Associated Press Worldstream, 2007b). Russia urged the Security Council to support further talks, but met with opposition from the US and from many EU states, particularly the UK (Associated Press Worldstream, 2007c). The impasse led Ban Ki Moon to warn of the dangers of violence, if the status issue was not resolved (Associated Press Worldstream, 2007d). Moreover, the commitment to the December deadline, was argued to increase chances that Kosovo would make a UDI, if agreement was not reached (*European Voice*, 2007f) and indeed on February 17, 2008, following the failure to reach agreement in December, Kosovo declared its independence (Phillips, 2012, p. 182).

While the majority of EU states recognized Kosovo's independence, only a minority of UN states did so. In Serbia and in Serb enclaves in Kosovo, 'despair and disbelief' (Phillips, 2012, p. 183) were felt deeply and the UDI was denounced by both Tadic and Kostunica (Phillips, 2012, p. 183). At Russia's behest, a UNSC open meeting was called on February 18 (XINHUA General News Service, 2008a). Russia's then Foreign Ministry spokesman, Mikhail Kamynin argued that any debate on Kosovo on the Security Council 'should have a restraining influence on those forces that have been pushing Pristina towards independence' (RIA Novosti, 2008a). In the Security Council's debate on Kosovo's UDI, the Russian Ambassador stated that the UDI was a 'blatant breach of the norms and principles of international law' (XINHUA General News Service, 2008b).

The then US Secretary of State, Condoleezza Rice stated that Kosovo's UDI was not a precedent for other cases, as it was a unique case by virtue of the long duration of UNMIK's administration, the break-up of the Yugoslav state and ethnic cleansing against Kosovo Albanians (Rice, 2008). In the continued attempt to overcome Russian and Serbia objections, Ban Ki-moon stated that his intention was to 'reconfigure the structure and profile of the international civil presence to one that... enables the European Union to assume an operational role in Kosovo in accordance with Resolution 1244' (UPI, Suna News Agency, 2008). However a Russian spokesperson called for the removal of UNMIK's head, Joachim Ruecker, because of UNMIK's 'scandalous obstinacy' in curtailing UNMIK's mission (Agence France-Presse, 2008a). Despite Russian anger, on June 15 Kosovo's new Constitution came into force, drafted in accordance with the Ahtisaari Plan's proposals (XINHUA General News Service, 2008c).

In November 2008 a breakthrough occurred when the UN Security Council reached a consensus to support EU deployment under UN Resolution 1244 (XINHUA General News Service, 2008d). As an apparent concession to Russia, UNMIK's Head, Rucker had resigned from UNMIK in June 2008 (XINHUA General News Service, 2008e) and in November 2008, Ban Ki-moon emphasized that 'EULEX will fully respect Resolution 1244 and operate under the overall authority and within the status-neutral framework of the United Nations' (XINHUA General News Service, 2008e). The mention of 'status-neutral' appeared to allow for the new consensus. Thus, Serbia's government eventually supported it and its new and more moderate foreign minister Vuk Jeremić invited the Security Council to support the plan 'in the strongest possible terms' (Agence France-Presse, 2008b), stating that:

> What has always been a crucial condition for our acceptance of reconfiguration is a clear and binding commitment by the European Union – confirmed by the Security Council-to be fully status neutral, and completely anchor its presence in Kosovo under the authority of the United Nations, in conformity with resolution 1244.
>
> (BBC Monitoring Europe-Political, 2008)

However, attempts to stabilize Kosovo were threatened when on October 18, 2008, following Serbia's request, the UN General Assembly voted to refer Kosovo's declaration of independence to the ICJ (Phillips, 2012, p. 186). In July 2010, the ICJ declared that the declaration of independence did not violate international law (Phillips, 2012, p. 186).

The UN's policy to Kosovo underwent considerable shifts from the early 1990s to 2008. The absence of consensus on the Security Council undermined cohesion in its response to Kosovo's UDI. Similarly, the EU's policy to Kosovo altered since the 1990s and it too was faced with internal divisions about Kosovo's status, as the next section shows.

EU policy to Kosovo

As Chapter 3 showed, until the mid 1990s, the EU did not regard conflict resolution as its policy concern. However, the EU albeit reluctantly, became the lead actor in the Yugoslav crisis. In the next paragraphs, the evolution of EU policy to Kosovo is outlined, highlighting its deeper involvement in the region and the significance of the decision to deploy EULEX, as well as the significance of its response to the ICJ judgement on Kosovo's UDI.

In the early years of the Yugoslav crisis, the EU was the lead actor (Economides, 2013), establishing the EC Peace Conference on Yugoslavia. However, the failure of the EU to respond adequately to the outbreak of the conflict in Kosovo in the late 1990s was heavily criticized by many commentators (Belloni, 2009, p. 314) and highlighted various weaknesses in the EU's foreign policy machinery. The crisis in the ex-Yugoslavia in the early 1990s was one of the first foreign policy and humanitarian shocks to the EU that exposed its weakness and its failure to protect democracy and stability along its own borders (Tonra, 2007, p. 117).

From 2000, the EU's policy to the Balkans began to develop more firmly and as in the Cyprus case, EU foreign policy became intertwined with EU enlargement policy. Thus, in 2000 the EU offered the Western Balkans the prospect of EU membership if the region met EU conditions (Belloni, 2009, p. 317). However, the issue of Kosovo's status as a sovereign state with potential candidate status was sidestepped. The governing motivation for the EU and US at this time was not to threaten Serbia's democratic transition (Ker-Lindsay, 2009, p. 148). The 2004 riots led to a growing rejection of the standards before status policy approach (see above) and increased emphasis on the EU as the key actor in Kosovo (UN Secretary-General, 2006).

As the next section shows, from 2006 the EU was increasingly central in negotiations to resolve the Serbia–Kosovo conflict. The EU's own dissent with respect to Kosovo's status, the initial slowness of the Ahtisaari negotiations and their ultimate failure, implicitly heralded a return to a standards before status policy for the EU, whereby enlargement policy was used as a tool to encourage the development of democratic standards and dialogue and the issue of Kosovo's independence was side-stepped. It was hoped that through enlargement negotiations the EU's 'prevailing asymmetries of power' (Caplan, 2006, p. 185) would 'translate into greater influence for the EU' (Caplan, 2006, p. 185). In short, as the next paragraphs show, EU enlargement policy was the cornerstone of its policy to Serbia and to Kosovo and the Commission was central in devising and implementing that policy. A key condition set out by the Commission was that Serbia would cooperate with the ICTY in handing over suspected war criminals.

The first step in the enlargement negotiations was the decision to establish and then suspend a Stability Association Agreement (SAA). In March 2007, SAA negotiations were suspended amidst criticism from the ICTY Carla Del Ponte, that Serbia had not adequately cooperated with the ICTY, particularly as it had failed to capture Ratko Mladić (Tannam, 2013, p. 951) and the then Enlargement Commissioner, Oli Rehn reiterated her point (*European Voice*, 2007g). Despite this criticism, in June 2007, the SAA talks resumed, even though the key condition of handing over all war criminals to the ICTY had not been met. The then president of Serbia, Boris Tadić, lobbied EU states to resume the SAA, arguing that if the EU made no concession, extreme nationalists could win the forthcoming Serbian election negotiations (Tannam, 2013, p. 952). Following Tadic's election victory and despite the continued absence of cooperation with the ICTY, the SAA was agreed by the EU in April 2008 (*European Voice*, 2008a, cited in Tannam, 2013, p. 952).

The second key EU decision was the decision to deploy EULEX in 2008. As the previous section showed, the Ahtisaari Plan laid the way for EU supervision of Kosovo's independence. The core problem was how to reach agreement among EU states, not simply among the P-5 to establish an EU interim administration in Kosovo, EULEX, given that Cyprus, Slovenia, Slovakia and Spain did not support Kosovo's independence. The EU's solution was to reach agreement on EULEX's deployment by de-linking EULEX from the issue of recognizing Kosovo's independence (Tannam, 2013, p. 953). The strategy succeeded in that UN offices began transferring their assets and responsibilities to EULEX in August 2008.

The consensus on EULEX, despite initial opposition from the five EU states who supported Serbia was seen as a success in EU circles. Participants in the negotiations noticed a shift in Serbia's position from the start of the negotiations to the end, whereby it became more willing to compromise and has continued to do so to date. Serbia's support for EULEX marked the beginning of a more cooperative era in Serbia's general approach to the EU (Tannam, 2013, p. 953). In particular, the Progress Report for Serbia highlighted significant progress. Serbia's cooperation with the ICTY was particularly welcomed as was its implementation of a new constitutional framework (European Commission, 2010c, p. 12). However, progress in implementing anti-corruption measures, despite the creation of the anti-corruption agency in January 2010, was slow (European Commission, 2010c, p. 12). Similarly there were problems in implementing civil and political rights (European Commission 2010c, p. 13).

However, while Serbia was regarded as having made some significant improvements along the path to EU membership, there were various areas of concern listed in the 2010 progress report, particularly related to its relationship with Kosovo. The enlargement carrot continued to be used particularly vis-à-vis Serbia to increase Kosovo Serbia cooperation in 2010, when the ICJ ruled that Kosovo declaration of independence was not illegal. Moreover, the EU's political response was unanimous, despite its absence of consensus about Kosovo's status.

The ICJ's judgement in summer 2010 was greeted with surprise, not simply by Serbia, but by Kosovo, by the international community and by the European Council (Tannam, 2013, p. 946). Serbia responded relatively quickly, by proposing its own resolution to be put to the UN General Assembly, where it hoped to garner majority support. Again, despite different views among EU states, about Kosovo's status, the EU's reaction was unanimously opposed to Serbia's action and

Serbia was lobbied to propose a second UN resolution in September 2010, co-sponsored by the EU. This resolution was drafted by the PSC itself (Tannam, 2013, p. 955) and differed from the July resolution. Unlike the July resolution, the September text prioritized the readiness of the EU 'to facilitate a process of dialogue ... to promote cooperation, achieve progress on the path to the EU' (United Nations, 2010, cited in Tannam, 2013, p. 955). It did not mention Serbia's opposition to Kosovo's independence at all (United Nations, 2010, cited in Tannam, 2013, p. 955). Given the absence of consensus in the EU about Kosovo's status, the September Resolution was a landmark in EU history. In addition, it was the first time that the EU had drafted a UN resolution.

The above overview of UN and EU policy to Kosovo and the Serbia–Kosovo relationship highlights stark differences in their policy approaches and their procedures and processes. In the next section, an analysis of these procedures and processes is provided, highlighting the differences between both, as well as the ability of both organisations' secretariats to have relative autonomy from member state preferences.

The EU and UN policy process

The UN's policy process

Four key institutions dominated the UN's policy process to Kosovo and Serbia: the Security Council, the Secretariat, implying UN bureaucracy, senior secretariat officials, particularly Special Envoys and the UN, 'on the ground', that is UNMIK itself and also UNSOEK, established under the Ahtisaari process. The Security Council's role was relatively straightforward in that many authors have detailed how the absence of consensus among its members impeded various attempts to resolve the Kosovo–Serbia conflict. Most notably, as the above section showed, the Ahtisaari Plan was not supported by Russia and China. On the other hand, the Security Council did provide the mandate for various envoys to go to Kosovo, including Ahtisaari, and for UNMIK itself, as well as providing for the deployment of EULEX, albeit through the creative use of Resolution 1244. However, while many accounts of the UN and Kosovo focus on the Security Council, it is striking from the above overview that the Security Council's impediments did not prevent specific envoys from playing a relatively autonomous role and that sources of UN weaknesses in Kosovo did not always emanate from the Security Council, but were also derived from bureaucratic impediments. In the next section, the role of bureaucracy and of UN envoys in the UN's policy process to Kosovo and Serbia are examined in more depth.

The UN's policy process in the Balkans in 1992 met with criticism and many of the alleged weaknesses in the UN's policy process continued in UNMIK and under Kofi Annan as UNSG. The role of UN impartiality rules and also of senior UN Secretariat officials was highlighted by Traube's examination of the UN's role in the Balkans (Traube, 2007). For Traube, UNPROFOR was ill-equipped to deal with the scale of the violence in Bosnia in 1992. Despite the genocide at Srebenica, UNPROFOR felt constrained by its mandate to be impartial as a peacekeeping force and was fearful of siding openly with the Bosnian Muslims against Serbia. This constraint was particularly strong as Security Council members were also reluctant to intervene (Traube, 2007, p. 45): 'The Secretariat could not compel the Security Council to enforce its own mandate' (Traube, 2007, p. 45). However, in addition, the former chief political officer in UNPROFOR argued that the Security Council was not the only reason for UNPROFOR's weakness, but that the Secretariat was also to blame: 'they were hearing about the atrocities, they knew how bad it was, they knew there were alternatives, but they didn't bark' (Harland, quoted in Traube, 2007, pp. 45–46).

Similarly, Thant Myint-U, who was an assistant spokesman for UNPROFOR in 1994 'found himself fighting constantly with Yasushi Akashi, the Head of the UN mission and Sir Michael Rose, the force commander in Bosnia, both of whom, insisted on rigid impartiality' (Harland, quoted in Traube, 2007, pp. 45–46). For Thant:

> Akashi could have said something, but he chose not to . . . We used the authority of the UN to characterise the situation in such a way as to preserve an environment in which we could carry out the humanitarian mission. As long as the UN was viewed as impartial, Serbia would allow the UN to administer humanitarian aid, even though Serbia was primarily responsible for the humanitarian disaster in the first place.
>
> (Traube, 2007, pp. 45–46)

Iqbal Riza, a senior official in the DPA, 'took the position that UNPROFOR's commitment to neutrality had made it effectively an instrument of Serb war aims' (Traube, 2007, pp. 45–46). While deputizing for Annan, he wrote to Boutros-Ghali to ask him to lobby the Security Council to take stronger action under international law, but Boutros-Ghali 'curtly instructed him to cease communicating with him directly' (Traube, 2007, p. 46).

However, while Riza was not a UN-trained bureaucrat, Annan was a UN careerist, whose views were 'essentially what he understood the institutions' views to be' (Traube, 2007, p. 48) and 'his sense of what ought to be done was profoundly shaped by his understanding of what could..., or couldn't be done' (Traube, 2007, p. 48). Thus an unwillingness to jeopardize the UN's humanitarian mission by opposing Serbia became the cornerstone of UN policy to the Balkans in the early 1990s, so much so that after the Srebrenica massacre, Akashi asked Annan not to let the media know that 4,000 young men were missing (Traube, 2007, p. 48). In contrast, by 1998, as the atrocities orchestrated by Milošević grew ever more obvious, Annan, in a landmark speech written by aides (Traube, 2007, p. 92), argued that sovereignty could not be used an excuse for 'governments to trample on human rights' (Traube, 2007, p. 92). Annan reminded his audience of the UN's failure in Rwanda and in Bosnia and concluded that if violence in Kosovo exploded into ethnic cleansing, 'no one will be able to say that they were taken by surprise' (Traube, 2007, p. 92). Annan's efforts were initially impeded as under Clinton, US policy was to side-step the UN entirely in dealing with Kosovo, as Russia and China would veto any intervention (Traube, 2007, p. 94).

However, in March 1998, Annan began a strategy of 'sneaking' (Traube, 2007, p. 94) Kosovo onto the Security Council's agenda, through the back door of 'other business'. In addition, he ensured that Secretariat officials regularly briefed the Council on increased levels of violence in Kosovo, so as to 'keep the UN at the centre of decision-making over Kosovo' (Traube, 2007, p. 94), partly because his doctrine of humanitarian intervention (later termed responsibility to protect) needed Security Council support (Traube, 2007, p. 94). Annan's efforts met with resistance from the Security Council and, according to the then head of the DPA, Kieran Prendergast, 'was told more or less to mind his own business' (Traube, 2007, p. 94). In response, Annan appointed a retired diplomat, Pauline

Neville-Jones, to lobby for support in European capitals (Traube, 2007, p. 94). These efforts also met with resistance, particularly from the UK (Traube, 2007, p. 94). Despite this failure, Annan did succeed in 'upping' Kosovo on the Security Council's agenda and gradually to move from 'any other business' to be inscribed as a formal item on the agenda but for 'informal discussion' (Senior retired UN Secretariat official, interview with the author, July 3, 2013).

Despite Annan's entrepreneurialism, the 1999 NATO airstrike was not ratified by the UNSC. UN Secretariat staff were divided about the airstrike. For Kieran Prendergast, more careful diplomacy with respect to Russia could have prevented it (Traube, 2007, p. 97) and 'the war was a blunder that caused unnecessary suffering' (Traube, 2007, p. 97). However, for Annan, the fact that the UNSC did not ratify the airstrike did not make it illegitimate and he blamed 'Yugoslavs' for rejecting a political settlement' (Traube, 2007, p. 96). The following paragraphs show how divisions in the Secretariat influenced UN policy documents and rhetoric during this period, highlighting the autonomy of senior staff members.

Both camps in the Secretariat 'fought over the language' to appear in Annan's statements (Traube, 2007, p. 97). The DPA sent a draft statement to Riza, the *chef de cabinet*, who sent it to another official, Mousavizadeh, who edited the statement and sent it to a high-ranking DPA official (Traube, 2007, p. 98). However, the official, according to Riza argued that he had no evidence that the Serbian authorities used force against Kosovan civilians (Riza, cited in Traube, 2007, p. 98). In Annan's initial draft of a response to the airstrike, he expressed his regret for the failure of diplomacy (Traube, 2007, p. 97). Mousavizadeh and Edward Mortimer, Annan's key speech-writer advised heatedly that this mild statement would be seen as a defence of Serbia in taking violent action (Traube, 2007, p. 97) and rewrote the final version of Annan's statement which defined the airstrike as legitimate, 'the most difficult statement' Annan ever made as secretary-general (Annan, quoted in Traube, 2007, p. 98). The dilemma about whether a moral imperative to intervene complied with international law led to Prendergast suggesting that a Working Group on the Post-War Security Framework (for Kosovo) be established by Annan (Traube, 2007, p. 99).

The divisions of opinion that preceded Annan's statement continued in the senior Secretariat Lakhdar Brahimi, adviser to

Annan during the Iraq war (Traube, 2007, p. 99) argued that 'the more distance the Secretary General kept from this issue the better, at least for the moment' (Traube, 2007, p. 99), as the UN could be used to legitimize intervention (Traube, 2007, p. 99). Mortimer, in contrast argued that the UN's image was undermined by not intervening (Traube, 2007, p. 99). Annan spoke formally to the General Assembly about the need for humanitarian intervention where the state fails its people, that is, he espoused the concept of conditional sovereignty (Traube, 2007, p. 100). Thus the development R2P for Prendergast and other senior Secretariat staff was a direct reaction to the NATO airstrike (Senior retired UN Secretariat official, interview with the author, July 3, 2013), and for John Ruggie, one of Annan's advisers, Annan was an example of a 'norm entrepreneur' in launching the doctrine with his Secretariat colleagues (Traube, 2007, p. 100).

However, while the doctrine of R2P gained momentum, the version adopted by the Security Council was disappointing for some Secretariat staff (Senior retired UN Secretariat official, interview with the author, July 3, 2013) and was hindered by UN member state constraints. Many states in the developing world perceived R2P to imply neo-colonial intervention in domestic affairs (Senior retired UN Secretariat official, interview with the author, July 3, 2013). Moreover, while the first speech on R2P, drafted by Prendergast and his colleagues envisaged prevention and early intervention by the UN, the P-5 did not take it seriously and emphasized military intervention more strongly. The UN 'on the ground', UNMIK, also faced considerable obstacles, as the next section shows.

Although Secretariat staff in New York had significant autonomy, as the above section showed, UNMIK was constrained by bureaucratic procedures in New York and it also seemed to lack the expertise possessed by senior staff in New York. As regards Kouchner, it was observed that while he 'had a broad understanding of his responsibilities... UN lawyers interpreted the mandate narrowly, tying the hands of the SRSG' (Phillips, 2012, p. 122). Indeed, according to Phillips, 'UN headquarters were more a hindrance than a help' (Phillips, 2012, p. 122) and there were 'daily disagreements over UNMIK's mandate... between UNMIK in Pristina and UN headquarters in New York' (Phillips, 2012, p. 122). In response Kosovans, having initially welcomed UNMIK, increasingly resented and despised it (Phillips, 2012, p. 122) and complained about the slow process towards Kosovo independence (Phillips, 2012, p. 122) and about worsening economic conditions, with no clear economic strategy (Phillips, 2012, p. 122).

In addition to the UN's general bureaucratic procedures, there were also problems within UNMIK itself. Each pillar of UNMIK had its own procedures and corporate culture and the SRSG found it is difficult to control each unit (Phillips, 2012, p. 123). According to one British diplomat, UNMIK 'carried out its work in a completely arbitrary and unaccountable fashion. The supervisors were three desk-officers at DKPO . . .' (Ross, cited in Phillips, 2012, p. 123). Moreover, UNMIK staff 'shared a conviction that statehood for Kosovo was not a good thing' and UNMIK comprised 'second-rate staffers' who were at every level of Kosovo's administration, from central to local level (Ross, cited in Phillips, 2012, p. 123). Thus, Kouchner 'preferred consultation through his Transitions Council' (Perritt, 2010, p. 54), not directly with Thaci's interim government, as UNMIK stated that the interim government lacked legitimacy (Perritt, 2009, p. 54). The interim government in turn objected to UNMIK's adoption of Yugoslav laws from 1974, which they regarded as discriminatory, particularly with respect to property rights (Perritt, 2009, p. 57). UNMIK's policy process was also criticized for failing to engage with grass-roots society and business community, for example, 'senior UNMIK representatives simply did not show up for scheduled meetings about the cell phone procurement' (Perritt, 2009, p. 62). However, despite UNMIK's internal problems and the UN's procedural constraints, it is clear from the above section on UN policy to Kosovo that individual Secretariat staff had autonomy to alter UNMIK's approach and to influence UN policy in various ways.

In particular, Jessen-Peterson was proactive in circumventing UNMIK's negative aspects and attempting to improve its image and performance. He observed that when he arrived in Kosovo, some of UNMIK's staff acted imperiously, 'like colonial administrators' (Jessen-Petersen, cited in Phillips, 2012, p. 148). One of Jessen-Peterson's first tasks was to develop close relations with the US, so Jessen-Petersen appointed a well-connected US official, Lawrence Rossin, as Deputy Special Representative (Jessen-Petersen, cited in Phillips, 2012, p. 148). Another key task was to meet with Kosovo's leaders, but rather than meeting them in the SRSG's office, as was the usual protocol, he caused much 'bureaucratic handwringing' by visiting the leaders in their offices (Perritt, 2009, p. 82). UNMIK opposed such locations, as Thaci and Rasmush Haradinaj were not official government representatives, only party leaders and they feared that meeting in their offices implied recognition of Kosovo (Perritt, 2009, p. 82). UNMIK advisers were also 'wary of the continued KLA legacy in Kosovar politics' (Perritt, 2009, p. 82).

However, despite UNMIK staff opposition, Jessen-Petersen 'embarked on broad consultation' visiting Kosovo's government officials and party leaders (Jessen-Petersen, cited in Phillips, 2012, p. 148), Similarly, following the ICTY indictment of Kosovo's Rasmush Haradinaj for war crimes, Jessen-Petersen, much to the anger of the then Director of Prosecution of the ICTY, Carla Del Ponte (*Inner City Press*, 2007) issued a controversial press statement, without prior UNNY approval, expressing his condolences, in the attempt to stem any Kosovo Albanian anger (Jessen-Petersen, cited in Phillips, 2012, p. 153). Jessen-Petersen also made an official request that Haradinaj be released from detention until his trial started, as Haradinaj was helping to restore stability to Kosovo. The ICTY acquiesced (ICTY, 2005) and Haradinaj 'was restored as an active participant in Kosovo politics' (Perritt, 2010, p. 99). Similar initiative was evident in the Ahtisaari negotiations.

Ahtisaari's management of the 2007 negotiations demonstrated considerable autonomy and strategic planning on his part. According to Ahtisaari, his approach to the Contact group was to include every state, but not to pander to Russia (Ahtisaari, cited in Phillips, 2012, p. 163), a strategy that was criticized by some commentators for emphasizing only EU states, but ignoring Russia and Serbia itself (*European Voice*, 2007h). It also satisfied US preferences. Indeed, Russia increasingly opposed independence for Kosovo and according to one US official, Russia's representative to UNOSEK was instructed to delay the process by trying to exacerbate differences between the United States and Europe (Phillips, 2012, p. 163)... instead of playing a constructive role as the guarantor of Serbian rights in Kosovo' (Fried, cited in Phillips, 2012, p. 163).

Ahtisaari's twin strategy with respect to Serbs was to gain the confidence of Belgrade and Kosovo Serbs and to 'use the prospect of EU membership to entice Kosovo and Serbia to reach agreement' (Phillips, 2012, p. 164). Aware of the EU' s missed opportunity with respect to Cyprus, Ahtisaari impressed upon EU representatives that

Kosovo and Serbia must reach agreement before either could join the EU (Phillips, 2012, p. 164), an approach that continued to determine EU policy to Serbia and Kosovo.

Ahtisaari convinced the Contact group to adopt three guiding principles as a basis for talks: 'no return to the status quo; no partition of Kosovo; and no withdrawing of borders resulting in a "Greater Albania"' (Phillips, 2012, p. 162). Ahtisaari also got agreement at the Contact Group's meeting in Vienna in 2006, to coordinate messages from Contact Group states to Kosovo and Serbia, for example he transmitted a joint message of condolence when Rugova died (Phillips, 2012, p. 162). As in the Annan Plan negotiations, there was also no 'Plan B', if the plan failed (*European Voice*, 2007i). Having set the framework with 'strategic clarity and tactical flexibility' (Wisner, cited in Phillips, 2012, p. 162), Ahtisaari established the UN Office of the Special Envoy for Kosovo (UNOSEK) in Vienna (Wisner, cited in Phillips, 2012, p. 162): 'My goal was strategic leadership... When I started to organize my team, I always want people who know about the substance of the issues' (Ahtisaari, cited in Phillips, 2012, p. 162).

Ahtisaari, like de Soto in the Cypriot case, had an identifiable bargaining and mediating approach. One of his team in Kosovo observed that Ahtisaari did not 'leap at diplomatic opportunities until he is sure that there is some prospect of success' (Rohan, quoted in Perritt, 2010, p. 115). He was 'a master of knowing what and how much to say at meetings. He almost always knew more about the subject under discussion than anyone else in the room – at least at the strategic level... he could react in the course of discussion spontaneously' (Perritt, 2010, p. 115). Like the Cypriot case, Ahtisaari's team was also small: 'several... governments tried to get their people into UNSOEK' (Perritt, 2010, p. 115), but Ahtisaari resisted their efforts.

Ahtisaari's team was described by UNOSEK's legal adviser as being 'like a family' (Sauer, cited in Perritt, 2010, p. 116). The team comprised Albert Rohan as Deputy Envoy, Kauer Sauer, as Senior Adviser, legal advisers from Bulgaria and Ghana and Hua Jiang as UNOSEK's spokesperson (Sauer, cited in Perritt, 2010, p. 116) and it travelled intensively for initial consultations (Sauer, cited in Perritt, 2010, p. 116). Ahtisaari and Rohan were particularly close and often interchangeable at meetings (Perritt, 2010, p. 117). UNOSEK established liaison arrangements with the US State Department, the EU and NATO and these organizations had representatives embedded in UNOSEK (Perritt, 2010, p. 117). Stefan Lehne was Solana's

Special Envoy to represent the EU in UNSOEK. Oli Rehn, Commissioner for Enlargement was also involved, as was Pieter Fieth who had been designated by the EU as the Head of EULEX, once it was deployed (Perritt, 2010, pp. 136–37). Russia declined to be represented, so Ahtisaari appointed Peter Ivatsov, a senior Russian diplomat who had been head of UNMIK's Office for Political Affairs since 1999 (Perritt, 2010, pp. 136–7). Therefore there was 'a smooth flow of information... and political back-up for UNOSEK' (Perritt, 2010, pp. 136–37). In addition UNSOEK senior staff received regular intelligence briefings (Perritt, 2010, pp. 136–37).

Like de Soto, Ahtisaari and his team knew how to navigate UN processes (Perritt, 2010, p. 138). More specifically they were able to 'inoculate themselves from bureaucratic interference and process worship through their close relationship with Secretary General Annan' (Perritt, 2010, p. 138). Indeed, some general similarities between the Envoy's role in Cyprus and in Kosovo emerge from a comparison: both Envoys worked with small teams of advisers and officials, both operated relatively informally, outside formal committee systems, in planning and devising proposals and both Envoys knew the UN system and/or its senior officials so deeply that they could minimize its potential constraints and could carve out a degree of autonomy and creativity in their negotiating strategy. This relative autonomy extended to other senior officials in both teams. For example, Kieran Prendergast was a central figure in both the Kosovo and the Cypriot negotiations. While often de Soto and Ahtisaari drafted their own key briefing documents and reports, advisers often re-drafted significant UN reports to the secretary-general, or to the public and had the leeway to do so. Similarly, the above overview of Annan's response to the NATO airstrike illustrated the intense internal debate in the higher echelons of the Secretariat and at times, the ability of various senior staff to influence the secretary-general's stance. The EU's policy process to Kosovo and to Serbia also highlights relative Commission autonomy in reaching bargaining outcomes.

The EU's policy process

The key institutions of relevance in examining the EU's policy process to Kosovo and Serbia are the Commission and European Council and specifically, as explained in Chapter 2, the PSC. As regards the

SAA, various permutations occurred among EU states. The Commission lobbied for a rigorous application of conditionality, as did, Germany, the UK, the Netherlands, Belgium and Austria. However, France and Italy favoured relaxing conditionality. NO agreement was reached and the SAA negotiations were suspended (Tannam, 2013, p. 950).

The fear of destabilizing democracy Serbia and increasing support for extremists in the forthcoming election, led to the SAA talks resuming in June 2007 (Tannam, 2013, p. 953). By December 2007, Germany, France and Italy were in favour of relaxing conditionality. The Netherlands and Belgium were opposed, but faced with a majority in favour, they eventually agreed to resume the SAA (Tannam, 2013, p. 953). A new pro-European government was formed in July 2008 and one of the wanted war criminals, Mladic was arrested shortly after the government's formation. The role of state preferences in the above negotiation is obvious. However, the role of the Commission and the PSC is also highlighted.

The Commission's power to initiate a feasibility study about Kosovo and Serbia's ability to become candidates for EU membership and to submit annual progress reports to the PSC were its core sources of influence. The Commission's progress reports were essential tools in the enlargement process (European Commission DG1A, interview with the author, February 23, 2012,). The progress reports for Kosovo and Serbia were submitted to the PSC in November each year for discussion. The progress report and the informal information exchange that accompanied it were a vital source of information for the PSC in assessing how far a potential EU member had progressed on the path to democracy and economic sustainability. It was also important as an early–warning mechanism in itself, whereby seeds of conflict were evident. The Commission's field offices and diplomatic missions gave it a monopoly of information on the ground from states (Tannam, 2013, p. 963). Its desk officers based in Brussels were in frequent communication and travel frequently to Commission offices in the field and hence Commission expertise and information were heavily relied upon, as it generally had a wider network across EU states and non-states than that of national governments. For those on the PSC, the system was extremely consensual and informal (Irish Permanent Representation, interview with the author, February 23, 2012).

Thus, agenda-setting was highly important and permanent Secretariat staff in the Council, as well as the Commission had large influence, but subject to interests and views of member states. Similarly, the Western Balkan Group in the Council (comprising permanent Council staff and civil servants on secondment) and the Commission's enlargement staff closely overlap and it is difficult to define their roles, especially as an enlargement process with a particular state nears its fruition (Council Secretariat official, interview with the author December 12, 2010). In practice in preparing a progress report, there are often political and security aspects.

Therefore, in Kosovo and Serbia, as negotiations developed, the lines of demarcation between an enlargement technocratic issue and a political foreign policy were blurred. Clearly, the Commission's staff were in constant informal contact with their counterparts in the Council Secretariat (European Commission DG1A, interview with the author, February 23, 2012). Overall, the Council depended on Commission expertise when dealing with enlargement. Moreover, the Commission reached its own conclusions in its progress report and finally in its *avis* and these conclusions were passed to the PSC. It is noteworthy that while the PSC is not obliged to accept the Commission's *avis*, it normally does so (Nugent, 2001).

Overall, the process by which the EU agreed policy to Serbia and Kosovo unanimously, despite an absence of consensus about Kosovo's status, also highlights the role of the Council Secretariat and the PSC. The first stage of negotiations in response to the ICJ judgement involved a general round of reactions to the ICJ judgement. The aim of the Presidency and the Secretariat was to obtain a consensus view, regardless of each state's view of Kosovo's status. The consensus among states was to resolve the Serbia–Kosovo issue and also to support Serbia's membership of the EU, even if there were differences of opinion about timing. There was also an awareness that the task was an early test of EU foreign policy effectiveness, post-Lisbon Treaty.

Detailed negotiations occurred over various drafts proposed by the Council Secretariat, based on PSC discussions (Tannam, 2013, p. 955). The Secretariat played a strong mediating and problem-solving role, determining how far a state would compromise, identifying key areas of concern to individual states and on the basis of that information, presenting draft proposals (Tannam, 2013, p. 955). By the end of the negotiations in July, several drafts had been presented before agreement was reached unanimously (Tannam, 2013, p. 955).

The Council Secretariat, the Commission and the PSC were vital in the EU's ability to draft a UN resolution and to react coherently to Kosovo and Serbia. The absence of member state consensus about Kosovo's status highlighted the success of the PSC's problem-solving and consensual approach. The Council Secretariat's role has been highlighted by many PSC participants and while it does not undermine perceived state interests, its aim is to reach compromise and consensus. Its mediating role combined with its information about state preferences and problems enables it to shape proposals and set agendas.

The Commission's role in the timing of Ashton's initiative also cannot be underestimated: the essential information provided and the Commission's views about Serbia's readiness to join the EU were important in garnering PSC support and in devising the PSC's strategy. The provision of this information and the way in which it was framed were important components of the whole policy process to Kosovo and Serbia. Clear overlaps between enlargement policy and conflict resolution policy were highlighted by the above cases. Overall, the EU's policy process to Kosovo, despite internal disagreement about Kosovo's status and about the timing of Serbian candidacy and accession to the EU was:

> An important example of how the EU, by focusing on reaching unity on underlying principles and by working within the framework of constructive abstention, can in fact forge a unified position on major questions, even when there are deep divisions between the member states.
>
> (Economides and Ker-Lindsay, 2010, p. 509)

However, while the above cases highlight the hidden role of the Commission and the PSC, as with UN policy to Kosovo, the role of state preferences was fundamental. It is noteworthy that in December 2012, when the Commission's *avis* supported Serbia's candidacy, German preferences blocked it, despite French and British support for candidacy Tannam, 2013, p. 961). However, the delay to Serbia's candidacy was a rare example of the Commission's *avis* being ignored by the Council. The analysis of the EU and the UN's policy process to Kosovo and Serbia highlights the need for a nuanced explanation of policy outcomes. In the next section, the findings are summarized briefly before providing a fuller conclusion in Chapter 7.

Conclusion

As in the case of Cyprus, the above analysis of the EU and UN's policy process to Kosovo provides less obvious findings. Unlike the case of Cyprus, the Kosovo case indicates that the EU's bureaucratic committee system provided more bureaucratic autonomy in the Kosovo case than that enjoyed by UN Secretariat. The Commission had more autonomy to act and influence policy through enlargement policy and through its technical expertise and knowledge, as did the Council Secretariat. The PSC, while representing member states, as well as international bureaucrats, proved to be an effective forum for consensual decision-making, despite the absence of member state consensus about Kosovo's status. Indeed, the efficiency and coherence of EU policy between 2008 and 2012 is in stark contrast to its policy process towards Cyprus in 2004. Moreover, a striking feature of the EU's policy process to Kosovo is that EU officials and indeed Tadic himself, emphasized the need to avoid the mistakes made in 2004, when Cyprus was admitted to the EU in the absence of a political settlement. While a blunt measure of learning, this feature does seem to explain the Commission's key role in EU policy to Kosovo, the intensity of German and Dutch preferences against allowing Serbia into the EU unless EU conditions are met and the relative coherence of EU enlargement policy to Serbia and Kosovo since 2008.

In contrast, while the UN Secretariat demonstrated relative autonomy, it was far less able to carve out a constructive consensual policy in the midst of Russian and Chinese opposition on the Security Council. In contrast to the case of Cyprus, the flexibility and informality of Special Envoy processes and the less developed committee system had mixed implications for bureaucratic autonomy. On the one hand, the role of senior Secretariat staff in the Ahtisaari negotiations and in reporting on Kosovo (the Eide Report), as well as in managing UNMIK (Jessen-Peterson) demonstrated considerable autonomy from UN headquarters and the Security Council. The ability to carve out a more autonomous role rested on the skills and knowledge of the staff involved and also on the informality of the policy processes, as in the Cyprus case.

However, the above analysis of UN policy to Kosovo and Serbia also highlights the constraints of the UN Security Council and of headquarters in New York. Firstly, the above analysis highlighted how UN procedures and norms and the tight reign from UN headquarters undermined the ability of staff in UNMIK to deal with aggressors in the conflict, as the emphasis was on being non-partisan. Secondly, examples of Special Envoys having apparent autonomy, for example Jessen-Petersen and Ahtisaari himself, also reflect the importance of the Troika's mandate. While the Security Council was hindered by internal dissent, the Troika led the march in favour of Kosovo's independence post-2004. The above overview of UN policy highlighted how Jessen-Petersen accepted the role of Special Envoy on the condition that he should be free to put the status issue on the UN's agenda. However, as Kosovo's independence was also the US and troika's preference, such apparent autonomy may simply reflect an agreed mandate from key Security Council members (excluding Russia). Therefore, not surprisingly, in both the EU and UN, state preferences were key factors influencing policy processes and outcomes.

However, what is less obvious is that given the constraints of state preferences in both organizations, the Commission, the Council Secretariat and the UN Secretariat all had varying degrees of autonomy. Thus, in the analysis of the UN above, one senior official commented how Secretariat/UNMIK staff could have alerted the UN in New York to the gravity of the situation and could have concentrated resources on lobbying Security Council members, but chose not to do so. In a more positive vein, some Special Envoys and their staff did succeed in overcoming some of UNMIK's inherent weaknesses and also in lobbying the troika and other states for support. Choices of strategy, policy priorities and choices of implementation methods, within the constraints of the formal and informal mandates set by UN Security Council members, or the troika constituted a key example of autonomy.

Similarly, the above analysis highlighted how the Commission and Council influenced policy outcomes and how the PSC was a highly significant actor, producing outcomes that were consensual and coherent, despite the absence of consensus among EU states on Kosovo's status and on the timing of Serbian membership and candidacy of the EU. Indeed, this chapter has stressed that EU bureaucratic autonomy in the Kosovo case was higher than that in Cypriot case and was higher than that of the UN's in the Kosovo case. In the next chapter, an attempt is made to make sense of these findings, by summarizing and analysing the findings of the case study chapters and highlighting how the theoretical approaches examined in chapter can clarify the EU and UN's policy processes to conflict.

7
Conclusion

This book aimed to compare the role of EU and UN international bureaucracies in EU and UN policy approaches to specific conflict zones and to examine whether bureaucratic entrepreneurship or autonomy existed in the case studies examined. In this concluding chapter, it will be shown that a deeper analysis of the role of the UN Secretariat, the European Commission and EU committees reveals some findings about bureaucratic autonomy and changes in the EU and UN's institutional processes. Moreover, the theoretical approaches examined in Chapter 1 help make sense of the case study findings. In this chapter, a summary and analysis of the first part of the book are provided, followed by a synthesis and analysis of the case study findings.

The EU, UN and conflict resolution: Overview

EU and UN intervention in conflict increasingly became multifaceted, combining military, diplomatic and economic aspects. As Chapter 1 showed, the failures of both the EU and the UN in conflict resolution and the evolution of these organizations, particularly of the EU, led to the development of more sophisticated theoretical accounts of both organizations' policy determinants. This increased sophistication was especially true of accounts of the EU since the 1990s, coinciding with the mushrooming of ethnic conflict across the world.

The neo-realist view of EU and UN intervention was that policy outcomes were determined by the most powerful states in each organization. In the UN, the Security Council's P-5 dominated and in the EU, France and Germany were particularly dominant. The intergovernmental institutionalist approach also emphasized the role of more powerful states in the EU. According to Moravcsik, these states manipulated information and ideas to influence policy. However, unlike neo-realists, intergovernmental institutionalists argued that bureaucrats may be in a unique position to influence bargaining where there are information asymmetries. Moreover, EU enlargement was argued to be a policy area that has allowed for supranational entrepreneurship.

Rational institutionalists emphasized that international institutions and their bureaucracies were established to serve founding states' interests. However, unlike the neo-realist view, international institutions fostered cooperation, as the individual pursuit of national interests would impede long-term interests. In short, international institutions, including international bureaucracies, matter and states carefully consider their design and rules of behaviour for that reason. As new problems arose, institutions evolved. In engaging in new policy areas, there were unintended consequences that could further empower the institution. For constructivists, institutions also mattered and could be autonomous.

However, rather than emphasizing interests, constructivists examined norms and how norms became preferences. In common with institutionalists, constructivists argued that bureaucracies were often powerful because they had a monopoly of information and expertise. However, they served a cultural value, not interests and these values became internalized as preferences, or interests. Thus, in the case of Rwanda, the UN Secretariat's rules and norms dominated UN policy, culminating in a failure to prevent genocide.

The overview of theory in Chapter 1 led to a series of questions about the EU and UN's policy-making approaches to conflict zones – for example, what are the formal and informal rules that govern policy-making; how much communication exists between units in the EU and UN and between the EU and the UN; what are the role conceptions of bureaucrats in the EU and the UN. These questions led to the identification of indicators by which to compare the EU and UN bureaucracies (see Chapter 1).

In Chapters 2 and 3, some general comparisons were made of the EU and UN's policy environment by examining the overall policy-making processes and rules in each organization (Chapter 2) and by providing an historical overview of the EU and UN's involvement in conflict resolution (Chapter 3). Clearly, there were broad similarities between the EU and UN's historical development and policy processes. It was shown that both the EU and the UN's foundation were determined largely by key states and by the post-war international structure. The experience of the Second World War precipitated a general groundswell of opinion in support of organizations to foster international cooperation. The US, the UK and Russia were the key influences on the UN's foundation and Germany and France were the key influences on the EU's foundation, but American foreign policy also influenced its creation. In a general sense, the EU and UN's institutions reflected state interests and intergovernmental politics, and the case study chapters in this book have shown how state preferences continued to influence EU and UN policy to conflict resolution, as neo-realists and intergovernmentalists argued.

For example, as regards UN involvement in conflict resolution, there were many examples of cases where intervention was vetoed or ratified by the UN Security Council: the decision to ratify the Gulf War, or the difficulties faced in reaching Security Council agreement to intervene in Syria in 2012. The EU's reluctance to intervene in conflicts also reflected state preferences and its increased involvement in the 1990s reflected a shift in state preferences to support deeper engagement; for example, in Chad and in the Balkans. There were also other broad similarities in trends in EU and UN policy to conflict zones.

From the 1990s onwards, both the EU and the UN developed a more multifaceted approach to conflict resolution. The concepts of 'soft power' and responsibility to protect in the UN and 'normative power Europe' in the EU all included provisions for non-military intervention. Responsibility to Protect included provisions for conflict prevention and early warning procedures, by accessing information and communicating with NGOs. The enlargement era in the EU heralded emphasis on the EU using the incentive of EU membership to influence conflict zones and to enhance democracy. It was argued by some observers that ideas and norms could help resolve conflict, rather than reliance on military intervention. Again, in general terms the causes of this shift to strengthen 'soft' power were similar for the EU and the UN: the fall of the Berlin Wall and enlargement provided threats and opportunities to EU states and the crises of Rwanda and of Bosnia precipitated changes in state preferences in both the

EU and UN. However, these general trends and similarities masked many more complex factors at play and many differences between the EU and the UN's processes and evolution, as the next section shows.

Differences between the EU and the UN

There were many differences between the UN's and EU's foundation and institutional evolution, while both organizations were generally influenced by the same post-war intergovernmental forces. The centrality of sovereignty differed in importance in the EU and UN. The deep influence of the US, Russia and the UK on the UN's foundation meant that the Security Council's P-5 had a veto and the UN Charter enshrined sovereignty. Given the aim of the UN to preserve peace and security and the dominance of Russia and the US, the Cold War had an enormous impact on the UN's policy-making processes. The UN in the Cold War period was often frozen by the use of veto on the Security Council and many of its activities were used to score points in Cold War politics, for example the Conference on Disarmament. In contrast, because the EU focused more on common economic policy-making, it eschewed the idea of traditional sovereignty and allowed for the development of common policies and shared sovereignty in designated policy areas.

The EU's unique approach to sovereignty from the 1950s spawned a complex institutional system, where various committees worked together, representing the Commission and member state interests. The EU's committee system grew extensively as the EU's policy responsibilities increased and most substantial decisions were undertake on these interlinking committees. Chapter 2 highlighted how the power of these committees and of the Commission has increased unexpectedly (for some) through path-dependence. In other words, a perceived need for a new policy, or for deeper cooperation has led to institutional changes and these changes have at times empowered various actors, including the Commission, so that identifying rigidly which institution made a decision was less possible networks existed. Many institutional changes have been provided for under various EU Treaties since 1958, and these changes have altered rules about where decisions are made and who has authority to make decisions. In contrast, the UN has not been subject to reforms about the locus of decisions.

The UN system, by formally enshrining sovereignty as its founding principle, has been more rigid than the EU. Although trends have evolved, such as the use of informal groups of states to advise the Security Council, the increased use of the Secretary-General's Good Offices and the increased role of NGOs, the core rules governing who decides when to intervene in conflict, or how to respond to a conflict, have remained unchanged – the Security Council's membership and rules have not changed since the UN's foundation. Moreover, the committee system is less well developed and less complex.

The EU and UN also differ in their inclusion of NGOs and breadth. Chapter 2 showed how the EU's founders adopted an elitist approach to the EU's creation for fear of scuppering the project if the greater public was involved. Unlike the UN, NGOs were not invited to submit proposals, or consulted. Monnet did consult with trade union and business leaders, but the focus was clearly economic and technocratic. In contrast, the UN's founders explicitly stated the aim of preserving peace and security and engaged with NGOs and small states. Human Rights were part of the UN's policy agenda from the start, although human rights were legally enshrined as domestic issues. The UN's institutions evolved to allow consultation with NGOs and the number of human rights NGOs attending UN meetings and lobbying the UN mushroomed from the 1990s – the 'third UN'.

The salience of human rights and the role of NGOs in the UN distinguished it from the EU. The EU, by emphasizing economic policy was lobbied by businesses and economic interest groups and engagement with human rights, or political conflict issues was minimal until the 1990s. This different focus was reflected in the EU's less developed institutional engagement with conflict-based NGOs, compared to the UN. The UN's greater focus on human rights and conflict resolution issues from its creation contributed to the UN's identification with the dissemination of new norms and values, for example, the concept of global society, of international human rights, of gender equality and HIV/AIDS eradication. Thus, although the UN was often stifled by the role of the P-5 and blamed for its failure to resolve conflict, or to protect human rights, it was identified with new post-war norms.

Although rhetorically, the EU was often cited an example of a successful peace project, by the 1980s, it was identified strongly with economic policy-making and technocratic interests for its European members. In this way, the UN placed more emphasis on norms and values explicitly – peace, democracy and human rights. Unlike the UN, the EU's reluctance to engage politically led to minimal involvement in conflict resolution and to a perception that conflict resolution was UN's 'job' until the mid-1990s, as the case of Northern Ireland showed. Overall, the EU's evolution until the 1990s was more focussed on forging economic common policies.

Therefore, although both the EU and the UN were governed by similar intergovernmental logic and the context of the post-war period, their original frameworks and governing principles differed and their institutional evolution and reform processes have been markedly different. However, in the 1990s, the end of the Cold War and the mushrooming of ethnic conflict potentially altered the above comparison of the EU and UN. The case studies in this book examined how the EU and UN made policy towards conflict in the post-Cold War period and compared the role of their bureaucracies in conflict resolution. In the next section, a deeper institutional comparison of the EU and UN and an analysis of the case study findings are provided.

The EU, UN and conflict resolution: Case study findings

Northern Ireland

The second part of this book began with an analysis of Northern Ireland and the EU. The choice of Northern Ireland seemed counter-intuitive in that the UN was not involved in Northern Ireland at all. However, Northern Ireland was a vital case in demonstrating the changes that occurred in the EU and in EU–UN relations from the 1990s.

When violence erupted in the late 1960s in Northern Ireland, UN involvement was vetoed by the UK government, as it stated that Northern Ireland was a domestic and sovereign issue. UN involvement was limited to responses to submissions to its human rights agencies by NGOs and by the Irish government about various policies that undermined human rights – for example, the court system, the shoot-to-kill policy. Until the late 1980s, the EU was also only minimally involved and even in the 1990s, it limited its role to an economic one. However, as the next section shows, Northern Ireland was a benchmark by which to measure change in the international environment in the 1990s and change in the EU's policy-making approach to ethnic conflict.

The Commission's response to the conflict in Northern Ireland was relatively detached and it emphasized that Northern Ireland was an intergovernmental issue, not a European one. As Chapter 4 described, the Haagerup Report in 1984 encapsulated this approach and underpinned EU policy to Northern Ireland thereafter. The idea of the EU as a peace project, championed by John Hume and the SDLP, was not embraced as deeply by the EU itself. The Commission and the Council in the 1980s and early 1990s regarded their policy brief as economic, for example developing a single European market and developing a single currency.

The main reason why Northern Ireland received more attention from the EU over the 1990s was the lobbying efforts of John Hume and British and Irish governments. Hume successfully lobbied for Northern Ireland to be placed higher on the EU's agenda and his efforts and the evolving peace process itself, supported by successive British and Irish governments, led to increased EU involvement from the mid-1990s. The Peace Packages from 1995 heralded a more concentrated focus on Northern Ireland in the Commission. The perception that Northern Ireland was solely an intergovernmental issue was less dominant and there was evidence of greater interest in and engagement with the conflict. Moreover, in lobbying for EU aid, Hume also joined forces with Northern Irish unionist MEPs, namely Jim Nicholson and Ian Paisley. Commission officials at the time remarked on the close working relationship between the MEPS, when in Brussels. While the EU's committee system was less dominant in determining EU policy to Northern Ireland than in other cases in this book, the EU's general institutional framework did appear to facilitate cooperation between unionists and nationalists at EU level. However, while beneficial in itself, it did not signify that the Commission, or the EU played a supranational autonomous role in policy towards Northern Ireland.

Therefore, the policy process governing the EU's approach to Northern Ireland was very clearly intergovernmental. Until the late 1990s, the Commission implemented agreed policy, but it was not entrepreneurial. The decisions made with respect to Northern Ireland were determined by British and Irish governments and by John

Hume. The EU's committee system was not particularly relevant in EU policy to Northern Ireland. The Peace Packages were agreed at Council committee level, but they were not contentious. Financial aspects of the Peace Packages were agreed at financial committee level, but all the committees involved were intergovernmental.

Therefore, the EU's approach to Northern Ireland was intergovernmental, but a change occurred in the mid-1990s and its engagement with the conflict increased. This engagement did not signify a large increase in the Commission's autonomy, or entrepreneurialism and nor did it provide specific evidence of the importance of the EU's committee system and its institutional framework, but it did signify the beginning of a new era in the EU with respect to conflict.

From the late 1990s onwards, the EU became increasingly involved in conflict resolution through its enlargement policy. It is noteworthy from the Cypriot and Kosovo case studies that many of the guiding principles used in policy to Northern Ireland were adopted in enlargement policy to other conflict zones, specifically the use of economic aid and conditionality to influence conflict resolution in conflict zones. In the next section, the evolution of this policy and its implications for UN and EU bureaucratic autonomy are highlighted by analysing the findings from the Cypriot and Kosovo case studies.

Cyprus

Unlike the Northern Ireland case, both the EU and the UN were closely involved in the Cyprus case, particularly from 2002 to 2004, when Cyprus' accession process gained momentum. The examination of EU and UN policy to Cyprus in Chapter 5 illustrated the key role of the EU's enlargement strategy in the EU's approach to Cyprus, but the Commission's limited autonomy despite its primary role in the enlargement policy sphere. The end of the Cold War precipitated a Cypriot bid to join the EU, as it did in Eastern Europe. The EU became more engaged with Cyprus from 1990 and focused on attempting to improve the Greek–Turkish relationship and on providing incentives to Cyprus to resolve its conflict. The attraction of EU membership was the EU's key incentive. However, Chapter 5 showed that the Commission retained a relative detachment from a conflict resolution role, as it did in Northern Ireland. For example, it delayed its *avis* on Cypriot membership until 1993. On the other hand, its *avis* in 1993 did make Cypriot membership conditional on conflict resolution in Cyprus. The subsequent years saw a wave of policy reversals by the EU, crucially in 1999, 2003 and 2004. In 1999, the Helsinki Summit granted formal candidacy to Turkey, although in 1997, the EU stated that candidacy depended on a political settlement in Cyprus. In 2003, the Commission's *avis* formally supported membership of the EU, although no settlement had been reached in Cyprus and in 2004, Greek Cyprus was admitted to the EU, although it had rejected the Annan federal plan.

The policy process underpinning these reversals was predominantly an intergovernmental one. In particular, Greece supported Cypriot membership and lobbied other EU states to support it. Greek preferences were influential as in the 2004 European Council, Greece threatened to veto Swedish, Austrian and Finnish accession, if Greek Cyprus was not also allowed join the EU. EU states also (incorrectly) believed that Turkish Cyprus was the main obstacle to conflict resolution and that the possibility of Greek Cypriot accession, in the absence of Turkish Cyprus, would entice Turkish Cyprus to cooperate. There was also ambivalence among EU states about Turkish membership and this absence of consensus about Turkey increased Greece's lobbying influence about Cyprus. The Commission was subject to member state pressures in reversing its *avis*, and the main committees involved in the EU policy to Cyprus were not the PSC, but COREPER 11, and a special ad hoc intergovernmental group set up to deal with Cypriot issue and to attend the latter stages of the UN-sponsored talks. However, the Commission did provide vital information and had a considerable role in setting the tone of negotiations and in timing of when certain issues should be prioritized on the agenda Commissioner Verheugen was particularly commended for his political and strategic knowledge, but fundamental decisions were determined by state preferences. Moreover, as the next section shows, the UN dominated processes overall, and EU–UN cooperation was not extensive.

The UN's approach to Cyprus was strongly controlled by the Good Offices of the Secretary-General, and Kofi Annan's Special Envoy, Alvaro de Soto, enjoyed considerable autonomy in shaping the agenda and in negotiating agreement. An obvious difference between the EU's approach to Cyprus and that of the UN's is the lesser importance of formal committees in the UN system. Instead, the UN's key locus of decision-making was the mediation team sent to Cyprus.

Although the Security Council is the dominant institution in the UN's policy process generally and although in the end failure to gain acceptance from Russia on the Security Council for aspects of the Annan Plan contributed to the plan's rejection, the Cypriot case did highlight the autonomy of Secretariat officials. This autonomy was determined by whether officials had a general mandate from the Security Council and also whether the secretary-general tended to consult more widely with the Secretariat – 'some are more Secretary and some are more General' (Senior retired UN Secretariat official, interview with the author, July 3, 2013). In this way, the tripartite bargaining relationship between the Secretary-General, mediating teams and the Security Council could empower Special Envoys and their teams. Kofi Annan steadily extended Special Envoys' mandates and did so by diplomatically consulting with P-5 individually and then collectively. Annan, through this bargaining approach, managed to extend both his own mandate and that of Secretariat officials. Indeed, many crucial strategic negotiating decisions were made by de Soto in consultation with his team. For example, he devised and implemented the strategy of sidestepping the sensitive issue of whether the Annan Plan involved reunifying estranged units, or whether it involved creating a new unit. Many of the judgements made by the UN and the EU rested on information and perceptions from the UN mediating team.

The Cypriot case study also highlighted how informal was the UN's policy process. The core mediating group comprised a small team of UN officials who liaised with the EU's enlargement unit, but controlled decisions tightly. Formal processes comprised the Secretary-General's report (drafted by de Soto) to the Security Council and briefings by de Soto to UN New York, but core negotiating decisions were taken in relative isolation from UN headquarters and outside a formal committee system. This informality allowed for flexibility. The EU was also only minimally involved in the UN's mediation process. While it was kept informed, but EU and UN officials observed that the UN made it clear was not taking instructions from the EU for some participants in the final stages of the Annan negotiations, the EU was kept at arms length. Thus, informality and flexibility could also allow for the creation of 'insiders' and outsiders' in the mediation process. Ironically, however, the crucial decision of relaxing the condition that Cyprus could only join the EU if it resolved its conflict was purely an EU decision and one with which some participants in the UN team disagreed.

Thus there are various findings from the Cypriot case study. The policy processes of the EU and UN were very different. The Commission's level of autonomy was relatively small and EU states, particularly Greece, Germany, the UK and France, influenced policy decisions. EU processes were both formal informal, but COREPER 11 played a significant role and the and Cyprus working group established under the Irish Presidency in 2004. In contrast, the UN's mediating team enjoyed considerable autonomy, given its mandate from the Security Council. However, its reluctance to empower the EU was argued by some observers to reflect US influence. Indeed, the poverty of the EU–UN relationship was highlighted by Cypriot case. EU enlargement and the Annan Plan negotiations potentially created an ideal cocktail for success, but the absence of 'joined-up' thinking between the EU and UN severely undermined this potential.

Overall, the Cypriot case highlighted that explanations for the Annan Plan and even for the EU's decision to allow Greek Cyprus join the EU cannot be reduced purely to member states preferences in the EU and UN. While state preferences were dominant in the EU, other processes were also important and the weak EU–UN relationship is also an explanation for policy outcomes. As regards the UN, the mediating team, drawn from the Secretariat and under the aegis of the Secretary-General was significantly autonomous, implying that reducing the Annan Plan to a reflection of Security Council preferences provides an explanation that is, at best, incomplete and, at worst, inaccurate. Similar findings about bureaucratic autonomy in the EU and UN were also found in the Kosovo case, as the next section shows.

Kosovo and Serbia

Like Cyprus, both the UN and the EU became intertwined in the conflict in Kosovo and in the Serbia–Kosovo relationship. Similar to the case of Cyprus, the carrot of EU membership was used by the Commission and the EU to attempt to foster cooperation in Kosovo and in the Serbia–Kosovo relationship, and following the Cyprus case, a core team of Secretariat officials mediated between conflicting groups in Kosovo and Serbia. As the next section shows, also like Cyprus, initially the EU was detached from the conflict and the UN was the dominant actor, but by 2008 the EU was proactively involved.

An interim UN administration for Kosovo, UNMIK, was established in Kosovo in 1999, under UN Security Council Resolution 1244. Chapter 6 highlighted the significant discretion possessed by various envoys. In particular, Soren Jessen-Petersen and Ahtisaari showed significant autonomy. Jessen-Petersen accepted the post of envoy, on condition that he be given a mandate to put status talks back on the international agenda. He also altered the manner in which negotiations and communication took place between UNMIK and groups in Kosovo and Serbia, by including civil society actors more fully and by consulting more widely. He also made some decisions without consulting with New York headquarters, for example, the decision to condemn genocide in Srebenica. Ahtisaari was also noted for his creative and autonomous approach to mediation. He established a small team, UNSOEK, to advise him and to implement decisions and was noted for his inclusiveness in deciding on a strategic approach.

However, while Ahtisaari had a mandate from the Security Council, Russian and Chinese objections to Kosovo's independence meant that his Plan was not endorsed by the Security Council and negotiations moved from the UN to a troika comprising the US, EU and Russia. In November 2008, a breakthrough occurred when the Security Council agreed to support the deployment of EULEX, as long as it was clear that EULEX was deployed under Resolution 1244, so that EULEX's creation did not formally imply recognition of Kosovo's independent status and, from 2009, the EU began to subsume the UN's role.

The sensitivity of the status issue and the Russian veto over the Ahtisaari Plan implies that in the case of Kosovo, although UN teams did have autonomy and different envoys wielded their influence, the Security Council's dissent undermined success. Russia's veto over Kosovo's independence undermined UN mediation efforts. However, a distinction must be drawn between the success of the EU and UN in conflict resolution and the core question addressed by this book – the degree of Secretariat autonomy in the EU and UN's policy-making process. Security Council politics was an obvious factor in determining whether UN mediation efforts were successful, but that does not imply that UN Secretariat senior staff did not have autonomy in the policy process, or that they did not contribute to the final outcomes in Cyprus and Kosovo. Indeed, both cases studies have shown that the UN Secretariat often had leeway to set the agenda, manage information and choose a mediation strategy, regardless of the P-5's preferences. Overall, though this leeway appears to be stronger in the Cypriot case than in the Kosovo case, conversely the Commission's autonomy seemed stronger in the Kosovo case than its autonomy in the Cypriot case, as the next section shows.

The EU became increasingly involved in Kosovo and Serbia since 2000 and its involvement deepened since 2008 with EULEX's establishment and also through EU enlargement policy. The Commission became increasingly involved in various key decisions from 2006 to 2011. The enlargement directorate linked Serbia's accession to the EU to its efforts to resolve conflict in Kosovo. Unlike the Cypriot case, it pursued a relatively consistent approach to Serbia and to Kosovo during this period, but particularly from 2008 to 2011.

The Commission was a key actor in decisions to initiate SAA talks with Serbia, in securing agreement to deploy EULEX and in granting candidacy to Serbia in 2012. A source of its influence was the European Council's dependence on the Enlargement DG's information and expertise, reflected by its presence on the PSC and its survival as a separate DG, not subsumed under the EEAS. The Commission's agenda-setting role was regarded as significant in EU policy to Kosovo and Serbia. That is not to say that the Commission is the predominant influence over policy, but the Kosovo case study highlighted how policy emanated from a consensual framework involving Commission, member state and Council Secretariat influence. The PSC's agreement to draft a resolution on behalf of Serbia, in response to the ICJ's judgement on Kosovo in 2001 exemplified the strength of this consensual framework.

Critics of the argument that the EU's policy to Kosovo did not solely reflect state preferences point to the counter-argument that the Commission's consistency reflected German and Dutch preferences towards Serbia's membership and did not reflect Commission autonomy. However, Chapter 6 showed that in fact EU state preferences shifted through the negotiation process. The PSC was shown to be very influential in facilitating modifications of preferences and also in empowering the Commission's enlargement unit. Therefore, Commission preferences and EU policy were shown not purely to reflect key state preferences, but instead they reflected a cocktail of Commission and state preferences. Moreover, it was not the case that the same states, for example, Germany, continuously influenced policy. Therefore, overall, the Commission enjoyed considerable autonomy in the Kosovo case, more so than in the Cypriot case. In fact, the role of the Commission and UN secretariats in the Kosovo case is a mirror image of their role in the Cypriot case. In the Cypriot case, the UN Secretariat was found to have more autonomy than the Commission.

Overall, it is striking that the end of the Cold War brought the EU and the UN into overlapping policy areas, where they shared responsibility for conflict resolution, but that the EU and UN are remarkably distinctive in their policy approaches and relatively isolated from each other. The new post-Cold War policy agenda was particularly striking in the EU's case, where the Northern Ireland case highlighted the relative apathy of the European Commission to conflict issues in the late 1980s and early 1990s. By 1995, the Commission had altered from viewing conflict as not part of the EU's agenda to having a more informed role in conflict resolution. Northern Ireland represents the first case where the EU and the Commission specifically linked its economic role to conflict resolution, albeit modestly, by making economic aid conditional on cross-border and cross-community cooperation.

In 1999, the Copenhagen Council signified the EU and the Commission's coming of age with respect to conflict resolution when, as regards Cypriot and Turkish EU membership, it explicitly linked its enlargement strategy to conflict resolution in Cyprus. Yet, the Cyprus case study highlights the oft-criticized role of intergovernmentalism, especially Greek preferences in hindering a consistent and coherent strategy to Cyprus and the reversal of conditionality was viewed as a significant hindrance to the Annan Plan in 2004. Therefore, the Cyprus case not only highlighted the increased role of the Commission in conflict resolution and the potential of enlargement policy to garner conflict resolution, compared to the Northern Ireland case, but it also showed the flawed strategy adopted and the intrusion of state preferences. In contrast, the Kosovo case highlighted the ability of the Commission since 2008 to carve a coherent enlargement strategy and to use the carrot of EU membership to encourage conflict resolution and increased cooperation between Serbia and Kosovo, echoing its approach to Northern Ireland and more obviously to Cyprus, but deepening and embedding that approach so that it was very clearly a political long-term strategy. It was also clear that the Cyprus case in 2004 had provided lessons for Commission and Council officials involved in policy to Serbia and Kosovo.

Comparison of EU and UN policy processes

The case study chapters revealed underlying themes in analysing the role of the EU and the UN in conflict resolution. Like the EU case, the UN Secretariat did have some autonomy in both cases. However, there were also clear differences in the EU and UN's bureaucratic processes. Table 7.1 summarizes the main differences between the EU and UN's bureaucratic processes.

In the UN, small mediating teams, led by UN Special Envoys had discretion to set the agenda and to hammer out bargains. Clearly, the role of the Secretariat's teams differed from that of the Commission in three respects: there was a large distinction between the role of senior officials in the Secretariat – the secretary-general himself, his envoys and their teams and the role of other staff in the Secretariat. In the Commission, a desk officer could have significant influence, even in the Northern Ireland case (for example, Peace 11) and the Commission's influence seemed to be more evenly dispersed. Secondly, while the UN Secretariat displayed some autonomy, the level of autonomy enjoyed by the Commission's enlargement unit was higher.

Another difference between the EU and UN was that comitology was the hallmark of the EU's system and it was very much in evidence in its approach to Kosovo and Cyprus, but committees had lesser importance in the UN's policy process. Various committees were involved in the Kosovo and Cyprus cases. In the Cyprus case, COREPER 11, representing member states' ambassadors was central, but in the Kosovo case, the PSC was central, initially representing the Commission (enlargement and DG RELEX units), the Council Secretariat's and member states' diplomats and from 2010, also representing and chaired by the EEAS, but with DG1A still highly involved. The relative significance of COREPER 11 and of the PSC may in itself explain the differences between levels of Commission autonomy in the cases of Cyprus and Kosovo. However, intergovernmental politics and also consensual bargaining were features of both committees and also it is likely that the PSC's greater primacy reflected EU state preferences in the first place. Nevertheless, the PSC was commended for its role in agreeing a UN resolution in response to the ICJ's judgement on Kosovo's independence and the consensual process encompassing the Commission, member state and Council representatives on the PSC was highlighted by participants. The Commission was viewed to be a significant actor. The processes were formalized

Table 7.1 Comparison of the EU and UN's bureaucratic processes

Indicators	EU	UN
Flexibility of rules/formality	Formalized and also informal: more formalized than UN	Formalized and also informal: more informal than EU
Density of institutional framework	Denser institutionalization more committees Evolutionary processes over time	Fewer committees, less dense Less institutional evolution
Concentration of power	More widely dispersed influence across bureaucracy and across organization	Concentrated power in small group in Secretariat Power more concentrated in organization
Role conceptions	Less explicit political and normative focus Technocratic focus BUT Gradual evolution of political focus	Explicit normative and political focus
Policy Priorities	Technocratic but attached to political aims Elite-driven approach to conflict resolution	Explicitly political Elite-driven approach to conflict resolution
Issue uncertainty	Issue uncertainty exists but varies depending on case: greater for Cyprus than for Northern Ireland Kosovo and Serbia	Issue uncertainty exists for Kosovo, Serbia and Cyprus cases
Intensity of preferences	Commission: not known	Secretariat: not known
Autonomy	Higher institutionalized autonomy, but overall depends on case and existence of favourable conditions	Lower institutionalized autonomy, but overall depends on case and existence of favourable conditions

though committees, but often the negotiations were also informal and informal negotiations preceded committee meetings.

In contrast, the UN's policy processes in the case studies in this book have been relatively static and committees have been less prominent. The secretary-general is empowered to appoint a Special Envoy and mediating team, if there is a mandate from the Security Council and UN involvement in the case studies in this book was concentrated on this team and the Security Council. UN diplomats emphasized the relative insignificance of committees in the policy process and also the relative importance of consulting with a small tight-knit team of secretariat officials and of informality and flexibility. Paradoxically, this informality does not appear to have made the UN Secretariat more autonomous than the Commission. However, it did give envoys significant room to manoeuvre in mediating conflicts, so they were not simply beholden to Security Council preferences at all times.

Another key difference between the EU and the UN's policy process to conflicts has been the Commission and the UN's role perception, specifically DG1A in the Commission and specifically the DPA, in the UN. Differing role perceptions are also connected to the Commission and the Secretariat adopting different sets of policy priorities. A functional approach underpinned the Commission's approach to Northern Ireland, Cyprus and Kosovo: emphasis was on economic aid and the benefits of EU membership in stimulating conflict resolution. It was noteworthy that this linkage was deeply embedded in the case of Kosovo and Cyprus, compared to the case of Northern Ireland and the Commission was more autonomous and more proactive in the former two cases. In the UN, the DPA's role was explicitly political and economic aspects were part of a general negotiating package, but not dominant. However, the Commission used its economic technocratic underpinning to carve out a deeply political role. The UN's envoys and teams had autonomy, but there was no evidence of a deepening role through time, or of evolution.

However, there are also similarities between the UN and EU bureaucracies. Both bureaucracies adopted an elite-driven approach to conflict resolution. The emphasis was on garnering support from political parties in a conflict zone with the assumption that grass-roots followers would follow. In Cyprus, this approach failed in that the grass-roots members of Papadopoulos AKL party was divided, although it is likely with stronger support from Pap this grass-roots obstacle may have been overcome. In Kosovo–Serbia relations, the EU's elite-driven strategy has succeeded to date in enticing political parties to moderate their stance, but the UN's approach was heavily criticized, although, as in the Cypriot case, being elite driven was only factor in its policy approach and cannot be causally linked to its failure.

Another similarity is that there was issue uncertainty in EU and UN bureaucracies about conflict zones. This uncertainty was least in the case of the EU and Northern Ireland, where the EU's role was relatively small and British and Irish governments developed strategy. It was highest in the Cypriot case, where both EU and UN bureaucrats misperceived the intentions of Cypriot actors and the sources of Cypriot obstruction. Specifically, there was an inaccurate assumption that Turkish Cyprus would be the main obstacle to formulating and approving the federalizing Annan Plan. In the Kosovo case, from 2008, the Commission had relatively accurate information about Kosovo and Serbia and about political intentions and preferences in both places. However, the UN's issue certainty was less developed, even in the Ahtisaari negotiations and the absence of Russian support limited a rational policy process.

Finally, an obvious comparison between the EU and UN's approach to conflict zones is their mutual relative isolation from each other and the absence of joined up thinking when both organizations were dealing with the same conflict, or when one organization was handing over key responsibility to the other for a conflict zone. In the Northern Ireland case, the UN was not involved and the EU was only minimally involved compared to its role in Cyprus and Kosovo, so an absence of EU–UN communication was understandable.

However, in the Cyprus case, the EU's enlargement strategy and the deadline of May 1 for an agreement were deeply intertwined with the Annan Plan negotiations, but there appeared to be limited UN–EU consensual decision-making and although the Enlargement Commissioner, Verheugen was in constant contact with de Soto's team, the Commission and the Council were not involved in an ongoing manner. The EU was clearly influential in setting the deadline for negotiations, but in general, the UN dominated and there appeared to be very little evidence of sharing of ideas, or synergy. In the Kosovo case, levels of EU–UN cooperation were even lower. UNMIK's approach differed strongly from that of the Commission and for some observers UNMIK was very reluctant to share information and to hand over information to help EULEX's establishment. Although the ex-Yugoslav states sought EU membership, the UN's approach did not seek to build in the EU dimension to conflict resolution and according to some observers, it was far more influenced by US preferences. Thus, EU and UN involvement were very separate processes, both chronologically and also substantively. However, Ahtisaari did make frequent visits to Brussels and his efforts to communicate more fully with Council representatives were commended by various EU officials who were interviewed.

The comparison of the EU, UN and their policy approaches to Northern Ireland, Cyprus and Kosovo reveals a patchwork of findings, whereby neither the UN Secretariat nor the Commission were purely dominated by either EU or UN member states. The overriding conclusion from the case studies is that both the Commission and the UN Secretariat have more autonomy in conflict resolution than might be expected, but that the sources of autonomy differ and the degree of autonomy differs between cases, as Table 7.2 shows.

Table 7.2 summarizes the main sources of autonomy for bureaucratic autonomy in the EU and the UN and the conditions under which autonomy exists.

There are very few common sources of autonomy. Flexibility and informality are common features to a degree, but the EU is far more committee based. The condition that there is a UN mandate is similar to the need for the EU to have a long-term commitment to an aim, but it is not an identical condition, although given the EU and UN's different institutional frameworks and the role of the UNSC, that is to be expected. Personality factors are not irrelevant in the EU, but

Table 7.2   Sources of bureaucratic autonomy: EU and UN

EU	UN
Shared commitment to long-term aim	Mandate from the Security Council
Expertise and monopoly of information of Commission unit	Expertise and monopoly of information of Secretariat staff
EU applicant status of conflict zone: enlargement policy issue	Experience and personality of secretary-general – is s/he from Secretariat or not?
Committee system	Small size of team
EU's consensual framework	Informality and flexibility of UN team

given the UN's more shallow institutional development, personality factors seem to be more significant in the UN. The enlargement policy issue is major difference between the EU and UN, where the UN could not wield the carrot of membership. The only unequivocal common source of bureaucratic autonomy is bureaucrats' monopoly of information and expertise.

As regards the differences in levels of bureaucratic autonomy between cases, the core question is why were the Commission and Council Secretariat more empowered in the Kosovo case than in the Cyprus and Northern Ireland cases? In the Northern Ireland case, the EU and the Commission had a minimalist perception of their role in conflict resolution generally. The Commission's weaker autonomy reflected the Haagerup Report's conclusions that the conflict, while tragic, was an Irish–UK issue. By 1999, this perception had altered and the EU's agenda broadened to include conflict resolution because of enlargement.

In the Cyprus case, despite the EU's new focus on conflict resolution in the late 1990s, state preferences (Greece) dominated EU policy outcomes in Cyprus, but in contrast, in the Kosovo case, those states that opposed Kosovo's independence did not block EULEX's deployment, or the EU's draft resolution on behalf of Serbia to the UN Security Council. For participants in both processes, the difference between cases was that in the Kosovo case, there was a strong commitment among member states to the long-term aim of accepting Serbia as an EU member state. That commitment contributed to a commitment to resolve differences about EULEX and about Kosovo's UDI through the EU system. The consensual framework empowered the Commission, given its knowledge of both Serbia and Kosovo 'on the ground', its role in implementing enlargement policy and in deciding whether Serbia in particular was ready to be granted accession status. In addition, there is evidence that EU officials and state representatives wanted to avoid the mistakes made in the Cypriot case – a more coherent strategy to Kosovo and Serbia was prioritized.

In contrast, the sources of the UN Secretariat's autonomy in the case studies were whether Special Envoys and their team had a clear mandate from the Security Council. In the Cypriot case, there was a firm preference among Security Council members to resolve the Cypriot conflict. Once that mandate was provided, de Soto and his team had leeway about how they managed the negotiations and about crucial aspects of agenda-setting and timing. It was clear from the Cypriot case that not only the Security Council but also Kofi Annan allowed this relative freedom. Thus, the second source of autonomy, stressed by many participants, was the skills and experience of the secretary-general and his envoys and team. Kofi Annan was the first secretary-general to be drawn from the UN Secretariat and consequently consulted with senior staff often. He also knew the UN's rules and skilfully placed Kosovo on the Security Council's agenda, despite initial P-5 reluctance. In this way, the very mandate that empowered UN envoys in Kosovo was influenced by the secretary-general in the first place.

De Soto was also adept at managing the P-5 and weaving an independent path, while including the Security Council. Similarly, Ahtisaari was adept at informing the P-5 and the EU, but also displayed autonomy in decision-making and strategic planning. The informality and flexibility of the UN envoys' small teams were argued to contribute to increased autonomy. A flexible small team led to discretionary power and autonomy. In addition, Kieran Prendergast has noted that many senior UN Secretariat staff serve many years in New York and have expertise not shared by member states representatives, or Ambassadors, who have a faster turnover (Senior retired UN Secretariat official, July 3, 2013, interview with the author). Thus the UN Secretariat's senior staff has institutional memory and knowledge of conflict zones that member states may lack.

In contrast to the above examples, some UN envoys displayed less entrepreneurial skill, as the Kosovo case study also showed. Obviously, a proactive secretary-general, institutional memory, flexibility and knowledge in themselves were not sufficient conditions to increase the Secretariat's autonomy. Thus, the case studies show that personality factors are more significant in the UN than in the EU in explaining bureaucratic autonomy, but that the existence of a Security Council mandate is a necessary condition for this autonomy. The small flexible teams established by envoys can empower them, but whether this potential is maximized depends on the envoy and also on the secretary-general.

In short, the Commission's role in conflict resolution is institutionalized in the EU system, but the UN Secretariat's role is far less formal and is not as deeply embedded institutionally in the UN. This difference is related to another key difference between the role of the UN Secretariat and the Commission. The dispersal of influence across and within committees in the EU is mirrored by a dispersal of influence within the Commission and Council Secretariat. Thus a desk officer in DG1A has significant responsibility and expertise, whereas in the UN Secretariat, various sections are more responsible for secretarial and administrative functions. The question of autonomy is relevant to a small number of senior staff in the Secretariat, rather than to a wider group.

Another difference in examining sources of autonomy between the EU and UN bureaucracies is the technocratic functional basis of the EU and its unique institutional system devised under the Rome Treaty. The crucial role of the Commission's enlargement unit highlights the potential for a technocratic economics-based policy to gradually straddle political foreign policy. The EU's institutional framework both aided this evolution, but the role of DG1A also evolved in response to new policy challenges, such as the fall of the Berlin Wall and the mushrooming of ethnic conflict. The creation of the EEAS under the Lisbon Treaty is the EU's most recent institutional foreign policy evolution. However, it is noteworthy that DG1A was not subsumed under the EEAS and it is likely to remain a significant actor, as long as the enlargement process continues. Thus, although the Rome Treaty did not place peace and security to the fore, but instead emphasized economic policies, the Kosovo case highlights that by 2013, the EU had developed into a significant actor in conflict resolution and the Commission was not simply a tool of member states in policy formulation.

In contrast, it is striking that the UN Secretariat's autonomy rests on factors that have not evolved over time. Special Envoys and their teams showed autonomy in Cyprus and in Kosovo, but although the end of the Cold War did empower senior Secretariat staff, the other conditions necessary for autonomy have been relatively constant and not connected to institutional or policy evolution – a UN Security Council mandate, informality and flexibility, small teams, the Envoy's skill and the role of the Secretary-General.

The core importance of institutional factors in explaining different levels of autonomy also highlights the role of state sovereignty in the EU and UN's bureaucratic system. The 'elephant in the room' is the very starting point for this study, while the case studies show that

EU and UN state preferences are not the sole influences on EU and UN policy to conflict resolution, the primacy of sovereignty in UN Charter and of the P-5 in the Security Council has contributed to the array of institutional differences between the EU and the UN. In other words, it is not the case that UN bureaucracy differs from EU bureaucracy simply because of the use of veto and the primacy of sovereignty in the Security Council? The role of the Security Council oversimplifies an explanation of UN Secretariat autonomy. Firstly, EU foreign policy has also been constrained by state preferences. The Cypriot case showed how Greece exercised veto power, informally and formally over EU policy to Cyprus.

The case study findings highlight a more nuanced explanation of EU and UN bureaucratic autonomy than state preferences. The fundamental difference between the influence of state preferences on the UNSC and their influence on the EU is the more fluid nature by which states may use a veto or its threat in the EU and the larger number of states with bargaining power. For example, Greece is a peripheral member state of the EU, but it was able to wield influence with respect to the Cypriot issue, whereas the P-5 comprises more powerful states. Moreover, although the concentration of power in a small number of senior Secretariat officials may well reflect the UN's concentration of power in the UNSC, the case studies have shown that the UNSC and the primacy of sovereignty in the UN does not provide a blanket explanation for every level of Secretariat policy and that there are significant pockets where decisions were made by Secretariat officials in isolation from the UNSC and where senior Secretariat officials set the bargaining agenda. Overall, both the EU and UN bureaucracies can be relatively autonomous, but the different sources of autonomy are highly significant empirically and theoretically, as the next section shows.

The neo-realist emphasis on state preferences in explaining policy outcomes presents an incomplete picture of EU and UN policy to the specific conflict zones. Table 7.2 has highlighted that under conditions, bureaucracies played an independent role. The existence of a UN mandate does not imply that the Security Council delves into every decision and policy made by senior Secretariat staff. Indeed, there can be considerable room to manoeuvre. Similarly in the EU, even where there is a division of opinion among member states, the Commission can carve an independent and decisive path.

As regards the EU, the evolution of the EU's institutional system and the evolution of DG1A's role in foreign policy highlight the relevance of path-dependence and locked-in consequences. The manner in which the Commission's enlargement unit has extended its range and mission is similar to neo-functionalist logic, but the role of the PSC and the EU's committee system, as well as its consensual system imply that the supranational governance approach is a closer fit. The case studies highlighted that policy-making process is consensual and that in many cases power is shared. In the Cyprus case, member state preferences were dominant and the Commission was less autonomous. Therefore, intergovernmentalism is a strong feature of the EU policy-making process, but under certain conditions, the Commission, specifically the enlargement unit has more autonomy. Moreover, the contrast between the Commission role in Northern Ireland in the early 1990s and its role in both Cyprus and Kosovo is very stark and highlights the evolution of its foreign policy approach and the limits of neo-realism.

Although neo-realism does not present a complete picture of the UN's policy process, the role of path-dependence and locked-in consequences was less obvious in the UN case. The case studies highlighted that there is scope for senior Secretariat staff to be autonomous, but this scope is not related to institutional changes, or new policy directions. However, participants have noted that the increased burden of conflict resolution work has had implications for the Secretariat. Firstly, the Security Council relies on senior Secretariat staff more heavily for advice and expertise. Secondly, the new 'best-practice' unit established has been earmarked as an elite cadre within the Secretariat, to develop ideas and to provide advice to the Security Council. The need for information, expertise and problem-solving skills in conflict resolution may well empower the UN Secretariat, just as it does the Commission. The case studies have shown that there is scope for senior Secretariat staff to use their expertise to influence policy to conflict zones and that they have done so to varying degrees in Kosovo and in Cyprus. Thus, neo-realism does not fully capture the role of the UN and its Secretariat in Kosovo and Cyprus, but unlike the EU, path-dependence and comitology do not appear to fit the UN case. However, the general institutionalist logic of principal-agent theory does tie in with the case of UN Special Envoys and their teams. The Security Council needs senior Secretariat staff for their expertise and bargaining skills and delegates to them in conflict zones. The delegation process has empowered senior staff and they have enjoyed a degree of autonomy.

The distinction between the case studies in this book and the accounts of Rwanda and Srebenica is that the main UN actors in the case studies in this book were drawn from the DPA and were senior officials who were close to Kofi Annan. The Secretariat already had a mandate from the Security Council and it was not attempting to lobby the Security Council to give them a mandate, even if Kofi Annan was instrumental in gaining UNSC support to appoint a Special Envoy to Kosovo. In other words, the UN bureaucrats in Cyprus and Kosovo were insiders in the UN system and their insider status allowed them a degree of freedom from that system, once they played by certain general rules. In addition, the periods of conflict examined in the case study chapters were less intense than in the Rwanda and Srebenica cases.

Overall, the varying levels of autonomy enjoyed by the UN and EU bureaucracies are best explained by institutional factors, combined with member state preferences. Institutional changes themselves reflect some combination of normative factors and rational self-interest, as Chapter 1 explained, but the core aim in this book is not to identify whether norms are more important than values but to determine whether international bureaucracies have influence over policy outcomes, regardless of whether their preferences reflect norms, or interests. Moreover, the Secretariat's and Commission's rules and standard operating procedures may well be normative, or may well be normative *and* self-interested, but their basis is not relevant to assessing whether the Secretariat and Commission are free to pursue them and whether their rules and procedures advance, or inhibit their autonomy.

In short, this book has shown that under certain conditions the Commission and the UN Secretariat are not simply tools of EU and UN member states, but can have an independent impact on policy negotiations and outcomes. It also highlighted the role of the EU's unique institutional framework and technocratic focus in empowering the Commission and the Council Secretariat. The UN has been more static institutionally, but nevertheless, its senior Secretariat staff have a surprising level of autonomy, under certain conditions. While the aim of this book has not been to evaluate the success of EU and

UN policies to Northern Ireland, Cyprus and Kosovo, the findings do point towards practical ways of reforming the UN, that do not entail the thorny and sterile issue of reforming the Security Council. Specifically, the Secretariat has expertise, institutional memory and resources that can be usefully deployed and the development of a high calibre unit within the Secretariat to advise on conflict resolution is a way of integrating this expertise. The UN's relative advantage is its deeper focus on normative issues (not necessarily for normative reasons), such as human rights and civil society, as opposed to the EU's more functional and pragmatic focus.

Thus, the EU and UN could work constructively together to maximize the benefits of their expertise, although this book has also shown the poverty of the EU–UN relationship to date. Therefore, a second possible avenue of reform is improvement of the EU–UN relationship, institutionally and informally. A third aspect of UN reform derived from this book is the relative insulation of Special Envoys and their teams. While this was empowering, it also may contribute to misperceptions and judgement errors. The EU's deeper institutionalization of policy processes, combined with its consensual and informal procedures implies that ideas are exchanged more freely and more frequently than was the case in UN mediation efforts. This book also provides lessons about EU reform.

While the Kosovo–Serbia case showed the success of the EU's system in providing a coherent strategy despite division among EU member states, the Cyprus case showed the influence of state preferences on the Commission and the absence of a clear EU strategy. The creation of the EEAS may not necessarily overcome the problems that emerged in the Cypriot case. The success of the Kosovo case is noteworthy, but its success was based on certain conditions, for example a commitment among all states that Serbia should join the EU at some stage. The absence of these conditions in a future case could imply that the EU has not necessarily learnt from the Cypriot case and that a future conflict could also meet with policy failure. In other words, it is too soon to tell if the EU's policy process to conflict zones has improved and that a learning process has occurred.

Secondly, the comparison of the three cases highlighted the extent to which the EU's strategic approach relied on its enlargement policy and the role of DG1A. The Kosovo case highlighted the relative benefits of this technocratic focus. However, the emphasis on enlargement as a tool to facilitate conflict resolution implies that if current EU members are subject to conflict, albeit frozen conflict, the EU's conflict resolution machinery is less effective. Therefore, while this book highlighted the differences between the EU's approach to Northern Ireland and its approach to Cyprus and Kosovo – namely its deeper involvement in Cyprus and Kosovo – a comparison of the EU's approach to Northern Ireland in the early 1990s and its approach to Cyprus in 2012 shows fewer differences. As EU members, the leverage of enlargement policy is not possible and the EU has not developed an alternative strategy. In other words, the book not only revealed the deepening political role of the EU in conflict zones seeking to join the EU, but also highlighted the continuation of gaps in its approach and the absence of a deeper political strategy to deal with frozen or post-conflict situations among its own members.

There are not many comparisons of the EU and the UN systematically and even fewer comparative studies of their bureaucracies. However, both organizations were established in the shadow of the Second World War and both have increasingly dealt with similar problems. It is hoped that this book has shown that there are grounds for optimism in many aspects of the EU and UN's bureaucratic processes and also avenues for reform that are not merely prescriptive or aspirational. It is also clear from this book that further comparative research on international organizations is necessary to provide a deeper and more complete understanding of international intervention in ethnic conflict and of the causal links between specific actors' decisions and policy outcomes.

Notes

1 International Intervention, Ethnic Conflict and Theory

1. The EU agreed to call Greek Cyprus 'Cyprus' when it entered the EU in 2004.

2 The EU and UN: Institutional Frameworks and Conflict Resolution

1. Monnet's version of this account is that he had written to Bidault to ask him to meet to discuss an enclosed proposal, but Bidault 'had not taken the time to read the letter' (Monnet, 1978, p. 299).

Bibliography

Agence France-Presse (2004a) 'Bush Urges Greece to Push for Reunification of Cyprus', January 2.

Agence France-Presse (2004b) 'Turkey Prepares to Ask Annan to Relaunch Cyprus Peace Talks', January 22.

Agence France-Presse (2004c) 'UN Rush for Peace Draws Scant Enthusiasm from Cyprus', February 6.

Agence France-Presse (2004d) 'UN Cyprus Envoy Due in Brussels Ahead of New Peace Talks', February 16.

Agence France-Presse (2004e) 'Second Week of UN Talks on Cyprus Ends with Nothing Concrete', March 5.

Agence France-Presse (2004g) 'UN Envoy Rules out Extending Cyprus Reunification Talks', March 11.

Agence France-Presse (2004f) 'UN to Change Tactics as Cyprus Peace Talks Falter', March 12.

Agence France-Presse (2004h) 'UN Shifts Gear as Deadline for Cyprus Reunification Deal Looms', March 15.

Agence France-Presse (2004i) 'UN Envoy Bemoans Lack of – Give-and-Take in Cyprus Talks, but Upbeat', March 22.

Agence France-Presse (2004j) 'Turkey Claims Victory in Cyprus', April 1.

Agence France-Presse (2004k) 'Greece FM Warns of Repercussions of a "No" Vote on Cyprus', April 4.

Agence France-Presse (2004l) 'Russia Defends Stunning Veto of Cyprus Resolution', April 22.

Agence France-Presse (2004m) 'EU Plans Office in Northern Cyprus after Greek Vote Snub', April 27.

Agence France-Presse (2004n) 'EU's Solana Regrets Cyprus Vote, Praises "Courageous" Turkish Cypriots', April 24.

Agence France-Presse (2004o) 'EU Urges Cyprus Not to Throw Away "Remarkable Progress" ', April 1.

Agence France-Presse (2004p) 'Turkish PM, Dentkash try to Smooth over Differences over Cyprus', January 11.

Agence France-Presse (2004q) 'UN Chief and Greek Foreign Minister Discuss Cyprus Problem', February 2.

Agence France-Presse (2004r) 'Turkey Unhappy with UN Give-and-Take Document for Cyprus Talks', March 17.

Agence France-Presse (2007) 'Mediator Open to "Additional Proposal", as Kosovo Talks Begin', November 5.

Agence France-Presse (2008a) 'Russia Demands Removal of UN Kosovo Mission Chief', June 12.

Agence France-Presse (2008b) 'UN Backs Plan for EU Rule of Law Mission in Kosovo', November 26.

Ajello A. and Wittmann P. (2004) 'Mozambique', in Malone D. ed., *The UN Security Council: From the Cold War to the 21st Century*, Boulder, London, Lynne Rienner, pp. 437–51.

Allen D. and Smith M. (2010) 'Relations with the Rest of the World', *Journal of Common Market Studies*, Vol. 48, Annual Review, pp. 205–23.

Allen D. and Smith M. (2012) 'Relations with the Rest of the World', *Journal of Common Market Studies*, Vol. 50, Annual Review, pp. 162–77.

Anglo-Irish Agreement (1985) Dublin, Department of Foreign Affairs.

Antonini B. (2004) 'El Salvador', in Malone ed., *The UN Security Council: From the Cold War to the 21st Century*, Boulder, London, Lynne Rienner, pp. 423–37.

Arthur, P., (2000) *Special Relationships: Britain, Ireland and the Northern Ireland Problem*, Belfast, Blackstaff.

Arthur P. and Jeffrey K. (1996) *Northern Ireland Since 1968*, 2nd edition, Oxford, Blackwell.

Associated Press Worldstream (2004a) 'Turkish Cypriot Leader Says Solution to Cyprus "Difficult" by May', January 26.

Associated Press Worldstream (2004b) 'Cyprus Reunification will be Negotiated', February 13.

Associated Press Worldstream (2004c) 'Foreign Envoys, Local Leaders Disagree Over Progress in Cyprus Talks', March 1.

Associated Press Worldstream (2004d) 'Top UN Official Joins Reunification Talks in Cyprus that Appear to be Stalling', March 2.

Associated Press Worldstream (2004e) 'UN Envoy: Participation of Greece and Turkey in Cyprus Talks is Inevitable', March 15.

Associated Press Worldstream (2004f) 'UN Envoy Says Agreement Still Possible as Cyprus Talks Enter Last Phase in Switzerland', March 22.

Associated Press Worldstream (2004g) 'Annan Hands Over Cyprus Plan, Promising "Win-Win" Changes; Greek Delegation Expresses Reservations', March 29.

Associated Press Worldstream (2004h) 'Negotiators Reach the Final Hours in Deciding the Future of Cyprus', March 30.

Associated Press Worldstream (2004i) 'EU Approves 311m for Part of Cyprus', April 29.

Associated Press Worldstream (2004j) 'EU Official Says Cyprus Results "tragic", No Better Reunification Deal Likely', April 24.

Associated Press Worldstream (2004k) 'EU Excludes Permanent Exemptions for Unified Cyprus', March 31.

Associated Press Worldstream (2004l) 'European Union Says Relations with Cyprus Will Change if One Side Rejects Reunifcation in Referendum', April 22.

Associated Press Worldstream (2007a) 'Deputy UN Special Envoy: "Nobody can Prevent Kosovo's Independence"', December 6.

Associated Press Worldstream (2007b) 'UN Chief Gets Report from Envoys Who Failed to Resolve Impasse Over Kosovo's Future Status', December 7.

Associated Press Worldstream (2007c) 'Russia Urges Security Council to Support New Talks on Kosovo, but US and Europe Say No', December 13.

Associated Press Worldstream (2007d) 'UN Chief Warns Kosovo Progress at "serious risk", Political Solution Needed Soon', December 31.

Associated Press Worldstream (2008) 'UN Gives Green Light for EU in Kosovo', November 26.

Balkan Insight (2011) 'UN Calls for More Belgrade-Pristina Dialogue', August 31.

Barkey H. (2003) 'Cyprus: Between Ankara and a Hard Place', *The Brown Journal of World Affairs*, Summer/Fall, Vol. 10, no. 1, pp. 229–40.

Barnett M.N. (2003) 'Bureaucratizing the Duty to Aid: The United Nations and Rwandan Genocide', in Lang A., ed., *Just Intervention*, Georgetown, Georgetown University Press, pp. 174–91.

Barnett M.N. and Finnemore M. (1999) 'The Politics, Power and Pathologies of International Organizations', *International Organization*, Vol. 53, no. 4, pp. 699–732.

BBC Monitoring Europe-Political (2008) 'Serbia Will "Never ever Accept" Kosovo Independence' – Foreign Minister', November 27.

BBC Summary of World Broadcasts (2004a) 'Turkish-Cypriot Leader-Turkish Premier Crisis Averted in Cyprus Talks', February 12.

BBC Summary of World Broadcasts (2004b) 'Turkish Sources: Deficiencies Found in Document on Cyprus Conveyed to UN Envoy', March 17.

BBC Summary of World Broadcasts (2004c) 'EU Commissioner Says Cyprus President "Cheated" Him', April 21.

Beach D. (2008) 'The Facilitator of Efficient Negotiations in the Council: The Impact of the Council Secretariat', in Naurin D. and Wallace H. eds., *Unveiling the Council of the European Union: Games Governments Play*, Brussels, Basingstoke, Palgrave Macmillan, pp. 219–38.

Bellamy A. (2005) 'Responsibility to Protect, or Trojan Horse? The Crisis in Darfur and Humanitarian Intervention after Iraq', *Ethics and International Affairs*, Vol. 219, no. 2, pp. 31–53.

Bellamy A. (2009) *Responsibility to Protect: The Global Effort to End Mass Atrocities*, Cambridge, Polity.

Bellamy A. (2010) 'Responsibility to Protect – Five Years On', *Ethics and International Affairs*, Vol. 24, no. 2, pp. 143–69.

Belloni R. (2009) 'European Integration and the Western Balkans: Lessons, Prospects and Obstacles', *Journal of Balkan and Near Eastern Studies*, Vol 11, no. 3, pp. 313–31.

Berdal M and Leifer M. (2007) 'Cambodia', in Berdal M. and Economides S. eds., *United Nations Interventionism 1991–2004*, Cambridge, Cambridge University Press, pp. 32–65.

Birnie E. and Bradley J. (2001) *Can the Celtic Tiger the Irish Border?* Cork, Cork University Press.

Blair T. (1998) Address to the General Assembly, September 21.

Blockmans S. (2012) 'The EEAS one year on: First Signs of Strengths and Weaknesses', Centre for the Law of EU External Relations, The Hague, *Working Papers 2012/2*.

Borzel T. and Risse T. (2006) 'Conceptualising the Domestic Impact of Europe', in Featherstone K. and Radaelli C., eds., *The Politics of Europeanisation*, Oxford, Oxford University Press.

Brammertz S. (2011) 'Address to the Security Council' June 6, 2011, available at: http://www.icty.org/sid/10691

Bulley D. (2010) 'The Politics of Ethical Foreign Policy: A Responsibility to Protect Whom?' *European Journal of International Relations*, Vol. 16, no. 3, pp. 441–61.

Caplan R. (2005) *International Governance of War-Torn Territories: Rule and Reconstruction*, Oxford, Oxford University Press.

Caplan R. (2006) *Europe and the Recognition of New States in Yugoslavia*, Oxford, Oxford University Press.

Carr E.H. (1981) *Twenty Years' Crisis, 1919–1939: An Introduction to the Study of International Relations*, Basingstoke, Palgrave Macmillan.

Chandler D. (2010) 'The Un-Critical Critique of 'Liberal Peace', *Review of International Studies*, Vol. 36, pp. 137–57.

Channel News Asia (2004) Annan to Carry Cyprus Talks into Third Day, February 11.

Checkel J. (2003) 'Going Native in Europe?: Theorizing Social Interaction in European Institutions', *Comparative Political Studies*, Vol. 36, no.1/2, pp. 209–31.

Checkel J. (2005) 'International Institutions and Socialization in Europe: Introduction and Framework', *International Organization*, Vol. 59, pp. 801–26.

Checkel J. (2013) 'Theoretical Pluralism in IR: Possibilities and Limits', in Carlnaes W., Risse T. and Simmons B. eds., *Handbook of International Relations*, 2nd edition, London/California, Sage, pp. 220–43.

Chowdury A. (2011) 'Ban's Second Term: The Case for a Woman Secretary-General', available at: http://www.ifor.org/WPP/June, June 20

Christiansen T. and Larsson T. (2007) *The Role of Committees in the Policy-Process of the European Union*. Cheltenham, Edgar Elgar.

Coakley J. (2002) 'The North-South Institutions: From Blueprint to Reality', Institute for British-Irish Studies (IBIS), *Working Paper* no. 22, Dublin, IBIS/University College Dublin.

Copenhagen European Council, Presidency Conclusion (2002) Council of the European Union, Brussels, January 29, 2003, 15917/02.

Cordell K. and Wolff S. (2010) *Ethnic Conflict*, Cambridge, Polity.

Cordell K. and Wolff S. (2011) 'The Study of Ethnic Conflict' in Cordell K. and Wolff S. eds., *Handbook of Ethnic Conflict*, London/New York, Routledge, pp. 1–15.

Cortright D. Lopez G. Gerber-Stellingwerf L. (2008) 'Sanctions', in Weiss T. and Daws S. eds., *The Oxford Handbook on the United Nations*, Oxford, Oxford University Press, pp. 349–70.

Council of the European Communities, Brussels (1986) *Single European Act*, Council of the European Communities, Brussels.

Cyprus News Agency (2004) 'EU Officials Sees Points of Approach in Cyprus Talks', March 30.

Daily Telegraph (2004) 'UN Brokers Quit Cyprus as Greeks Reject Peace Deal', April 26.

Daily Telegraph (2008) 'Radovan Karadzic Arrest: Serbia Reconciles with West', July 24.

Defense and Foreign Affairs Daily (2004) 'Cyprus Talks Move Ahead at UN Behest, but Deadline Tight and No Evidence of Turkish Commitment', February 6.

Demetriou O. (2004) 'The EU and the Cyprus Conflict: The View of Political Actors in Cyprus', Paper Presented to ECPR Joint Workshops, Uppsala, April 2.

Deutsch K. (1957) *Political Community and the North Atlantic Area*, Princeton, Princeton University Press.

Deutsche Presse-Agentur (2007) 'No More Delays in Kosovo Status Process, says German Official', November 1.

Diehl P. (2008) Peacekeeping Operations, Cambridge, Polity Press.

Diez T. and Pace M. (2011) 'Normative Power Europe and Conflict Transformation', in Whitman R., ed., *Normative Power Europe: Theoretical and Empirical Perspectives*, Basingstoke, Palgrave Macmillan, pp. 210–25.

Diez T. Stetter S. and Albert M. (2006) 'The European Union and Border Conflicts: The Transformative Power of Integration', *International Organization*, Vol. 60, no. 3, pp. 563–93.

Dinan D. (2004) *Europe Recast: A History of the European Union*, Basingstoke, Palgrave Macmillan.

Doyle M. and Sambanis N. (2008) 'Peacekeeping Operations', in Weiss T. and Daws S. eds., *The Oxford Handbook on the United Nations*, Oxford, Oxford University Press, pp. 323–49.

Duchêne, F. (1972) 'Europe's Role in World Peace', in Mayne, R. (ed.) *Europe Tomorrow: Sixteen Europeans Look Ahead* London, Fontana), pp. 32–47.

Duke S. (2007) 'The Role of Committees and Working Groups in the CFSP area', in Christiansen T. and Larsson T., eds., *The Role of Committees in the Policy-Process of the European Union*, Cheltenham, Edward Elgar, pp. 120–52.

Economides S. (2012) 'The European Pull in the Balkans', in Mayall J. and Soares R. de Oliveira eds., *The New Protectorates: International Tutelage and the Making of Liberal States*, Colombia, Colombia University Press.

Economides S. (2013) 'Kosovo, Self-Determination and the International Order', *Europe-Asia Studies*, Vol. 65, no. 5, pp. 823–36.

Economides S. and Ker-Lindsay J. (2010) 'Forging EU Foreign Policy Unity from Diversity: The "Unique" Case of the Kosovo Status Talks', *European Foreign Affairs Review*, Vol. 15, pp. 495–510.

EUbusiness.com (2010) 'Tadic Absent as Balkan Leaders meet on EU Integration', March 20.

EUbusiness.com (2011) 'Serbia-Kosovo Tackle Border Tension at Talks', December 2.

EUObserver.com (2004) 'Deadline Looms for Solution on Cyprus', March 12.

Eurolink Supplement (1995) no. 9, Belfast, European Commission.

Europa (2008) Available at: http://ec.europa.eu/enlargement/potential-candidates/kosovo/financial-assistance/index_en.htm

European Commission (1990) *Notice Laying Down Guidelines for Operational Programmes Which Member States Are Invited to Establish in the Framework of a Community Initiative Concerning Border Areas* (Interreg), OJ, no. C215/4, 30.8.90.

European Commission (1995) *Special Support Programme for Peace and Reconciliation in Northern Ireland and the Border Counties of Ireland 1995–1999*, Brussels, European Commission.

European Commission (2000) *Reforming the Commission – A White Paper* Brussels, European Commission.

European Commission (2009) ICJ Hearings on Kosovo's Declaration of Independence, European Commission ELARG C3, Reg 108043, December 1, 2009.

European Commission (2010) EU Enlargement Strategy, 2010–11, November 2010, Brussels, DG for Enlargement Information and Communication Unit.

European Commission (2010a) EU Enlargement Strategy, 2010–11, November 2010, Brussels, DG for Enlargement Information and Communication Unit.

European Commission (2010b) Progress Report: Kosovo, 2010, SEC (2010) 1329, Brussels, November 9, 2010 SEC(2010)132, available at: http://ec.europa.eu/enlargement/pdf/key_documents/2010/package/ks_rapport_2010_en.pdf

European Commission (2010c) Progress Report: Serbia, Brussels, November 9, 2010 SEC(2010) 1330, available at: http://ec.europa.eu/enlargement/pdf/key_documents/2010/package/sr_rapport_2010_en.pdf

European Commission (2010d) Commission of the European Community, available at: http://ec.europa.eu/enlargement/potential-candidates/serbia/financial-assistance/index_en.htm

European Commission (2010e) Available at: http://ec.europa.eu/enlargement/potential-candidates/kosovo/financial-assistance/index_en.htm

European Commission (2011a) *A New Response to a Changing Neighbourhood*, Brussels, Commission of the European: A review of European Neighbourhood Policy Joint Communication by the High Representative of The Union For Foreign Affairs And Security Policy and the European Commission, Brussels, 25 May 2011.

European Commission (2011b) Commission Staff Working Paper, Kosovo (under UNSCR 1244/1999) 2011 Progress Report, Brussels, 12.10.2011 SEC(2011) 1207 final.

European Council (1997) Luxembourg Presidency Conclusions, (1997) Brussels, European Council.

European Council (2002) Copenhagen, Presidency Conclusion, Brussels, European Council.

European Council Joint Action 2008/124/CFSP of February 4, 2008 on the European Union Rule of Law Mission in Kosovo, EULEX KOSOVO, Official Journal of the European Union, EN L 42/92, 16.02.2008.

European External Action Service (EEAS) (2011) Annual Activity Report, available at: http://eeas.europa.eu/background/docs/20121017_eeas_aar_2011_en.pdf, accessed January 22, 2014

European External Action Service (EEAS) (2013) Available at: http://www.eeas.europa.eu/csdp/missions-and-operations/completed/index_en.htm, accessed November 22, 2013

European Report (2004) 'EU/Cyprus: Four-way Talks on Cypriot Reunification Set to Resume', March 20.

European Voice (2002) 'Paying Homage to Joshka, the Man Who Saved the Copenhagen Summit', December 19.

European Voice (2002a) 'What Next for Turkey and the Cyprus Conflict?', December 19.

European Voice (2002b) 'Pressure Set to Pay Off for Turkey', December 12.

European Voice (2006a) 'Serbs Told to Do Their Own Homework', June 29.

European Voice (2006b) 'Member States Split on Kosovo "Viceroy" role', July 6.

European Voice (2006b) 'EU to Launch Serbian Charm Offensive', December 15.

European Voice (2007a) 'Ahtisaari to Propose Partial Independence for Kosovo', January 18.

European Voice (2007a) 'Balkan Peace Still Needs EU Enlargement', October 31.

European Voice (2007b) 'Foreign Ministers Plot a New Course for Serbia', January 25.

European Voice (2007b) 'Rumbles over Kosovo', February 8.

European Voice (2007c) 'Leaders Fail to Reach Settlement on Kosovo Status', March 8.

European Voice (2007d) 'Kosovo's Future Haunts the UN,' July 19.

European Voice (2007e) 'Russia and West Must Find Kosovo Solution', July 26.

European Voice (2007f) 'EU's Kosovo Envoy Calls for Unity', September 6.

European Voice (2007g) 'Kosovo-the End-Game', December 6.

European Voice (2007h) 'A Long Hot Summer Awaits in the Balkans', February 22.

European Voice (2007i) 'Ahtisaari Plan Is Only Solution for Kosovo', February 2.

European Voice (2008a) 'Serbia to Sign SAA with EU Today', April 29.

European Voice (2008b) 'Times Changing Fast in Serbia', July 22.

European Voice (2011) 'Serbia, Kosovo, Agree Border Deal', December 3.

European Voice (2012a) 'Tadic Excludes Serb-controlled Parts of Kosovo from Elections', March 15.

European Voice (2012b) 'The EU Must Call Serbia's Bluff – And Kosovo's Too', February 23.

Evans, G. (2011) 'Ethnoconflict: When Is It Right to Intervene?, *Ethnopolitics*, Vol. 10, no. 1, pp. 115–23.

Evrivades M. 2003, 'Europe in Cyprus; the Broader Security Implications', *The Brown Journal of World Affairs*, Summer/Fall, Vol. 10, no. 1, pp. 241–56.

Farer T.J. and Gaer F. (1993) 'The UN and Human Rights: At the End of the Beginning', in Roberts A. and Kingsbury B., eds., *United Nations, Divided World: The UN's Roles in International Relations*, Oxford, Oxford University Press, pp. 243–54.

Farrell M. (1977) *The Orange State*, London, Pluto Press.

Faustmann H. (2001) 'The UN and the Internationalization of the Cyprus Conflict, 1949–1958', in Richmond O. and Ker-Lindsay J., eds., *The Work of the UN in Cyprus*, Basingstoke, Palgrave Macmillan, pp. 3–35.

Fearon J. (1995) 'Rationalist Explanations for War', *International Organization*, Vol. 49, no. 3, pp. 379–414.

Fearon J. and Wendt A. (2002) 'Rationalism v. Constructivism: A Skeptical View', in Carlsnaes W., Risse T. and Simmons B., eds., *Handbook of International Relations*, Thousand Oaks, CA, Sage Publications, pp. 52–72.

Federal News Service (2004) 'UN, Prepared Text of Press Conference with UN Secretary-General Kofi Annan on the Subject of Cyprus', United Nations, New York, February 13, 14.

Fitzgerald G. (1968) *Planning in Ireland*, Institute of Public Administration/Political and Economic Planning, Dublin/London.

Fligstein N. and McNichol J. (1998) 'The Institutional Terrain of the European Union', in Sandholtz W. and Stone Sweet A. eds., *European Integration and Supranational Governance*, Oxford, Oxford University Press, pp. 59–92.

Fortna, V. (2004) 'Does Peacekeeping Keep Peace? International Intervention and the Duration of Peace after Civil War', in *International Studies Quarterly*, Vol. 48, pp. 202–269.

Frohlich M. (2007) 'The Ironies of UN Secretariat Reform', *Global Governance*, Vol. 13, pp. 151–59.

Garfield R. (1999) *Morbidity and Mortality Among Iraqi Children from 1990 to 1998: Assessing the Impact of Economic Sanctions*, Goshen Ind. John B. Kroc Institute for International Peace Studies, Fourth freedom Forum, March.

Good Friday Agreement (GFA) (1998) Dublin, Department of Foreign Affairs.

Goulding M. (2002) *Peacemonger*, London, John Murray.

Grieg M. and Diehl P. (2005) The Peacekeeping, Peace-making Dilemma', *International Studies Quarterly*, Vol. 49, no. 4, pp. 621–46.

Guelke A. (1988) *Northern Ireland: The International Perspective*, Dublin, Gill and Macmillan.

Haagerup Report (1984) 'Report Drawn up on Behalf of the Political Affairs Committee on the Situation in Northern Ireland', *European Parliament Working Document 1–1526/83*, March 9, 1984.

Haas E. (1958) *The Uniting of Europe*, Stanford, Stanford University Press.

Hadfield A. and Fiott D. (2013) 'Europe and the Rest of the World', *Journal of Common Market Studies,* Vol. 51, Annual Review, pp. 168–82.

Hainsworth P. (1979) 'The European Election of 1979 in Northern Ireland: Linkage Politics', *Parliamentary Affairs*, Vol. 32, no. 4, pp. 470–81.

Hannay D. (2006) 'Cyprus, Turkey and the EU: Time for a Sense of Proportion and Compromise', *Policy Brief*, London, Centre for European Reform.

Hayward K. (2006) 'Reiterating National; Identities: The European Union Conception of Conflict Resolution in Northern Ireland', *Cooperation and Conflict*, Vol. 41, no. 10, pp. 261–84.

Hooghe L. (2005) 'International Norms and the European Commission', *International Organization*, Vol. 59, pp. 862–98.

Hooghe L. (2013) 'What Officials Believe', in Hooghe L., Kassim H., Peterson J., Bauer M., Dehousse R., Connolly S. and Thompson A. eds., *The European Commission in Question,* Oxford, Oxford University Press.

Horowitz D. (2007) 'The Many Uses of Federalism', *Drake Law Review,* Vol. 55, pp. 953–66.

Howorth J. (2007) *Security and Defence Policy in the European Union,* Basingstoke, Palgrave Macmillan.

Huber J.D. and Shipan C.R. (2002) *Delegate Discretion? The Institutional Foundations of Bureaucratic Autonomy,* Cambridge, Cambridge University Press.

Hulton S. (2004) 'Council Working Methods and Procedure', in Malone D.M. ed. *The Security Council: From the Cold War to the 21st Century,* Boulder, Lynne Reiner, pp. 237–53.

ICTY (International Criminal Tribunal for Yugoslavia) (2005) Prosecutor V Haradinaj, case No. IT-04-84-PT, decision granting provisional release, June 6.

ICTY (International Criminal Tribunal for Yugoslavia) (2007) *Prosecutor's Statement on Serbia's Cooperation with her Office,* October 3, available at: http://www. icty.org/sid/8838

Independent (2004a) 'Dentkash Willing to Discuss UN Plan to Reunite Cyprus', January 13.

Independent (2004b) 'EU Throws North Cyprus a Lifeline', April 29.

Independent Inquiry Committee into the United Nations Oil-for-Food Programme, Manipulation of the Oil- for- Food Programme by the Iraqi Regime (2005) October 27, available at: http://www.iic-offp.org/story27oct05.htm

Inner City Press (2007) 'At the UN, Del Ponte "Stupified" by UNMIK's Support for Rasmush Haradinaj, Dodges UN's, Srebrenica's Role', December 10.

International Court of Justice (2010) *Accordance with International Law of the Unilateral Declaration of Independence in Respect of Kosovo,* available at: http://www.icj-cij.org/docket/files/141/15987.pdf

Irish Times (2004a) 'Cyprus EU Entry in Balance as Talks Continue', February 12.

Irish Times (2004b) 'Cyprus Set to Remain Divided as UN Plan Effort Fails', April 1.

Jenne E. (2011) 'The Causes and Consequences of Ethnic Cleansing', in Cordell K., and Wolff S., eds., *Routledge Handbook of Ethnic Conflict,* London/New York, Routledge, pp. 112–21.

Jolly R., Emmerij L. and Weiss T.J. (2009) *UN Ideas that Changed the World,* Bloomington, Indiana, Indian University Press.

Jones B.D. (2004) 'The Middle East Peace Process', in Malone ed., *The UN Security Council: From the Cold War to the 21st Century,* Boulder, London, Lynne Rienner, pp. 391–407.

Jonah J. (2008) 'Secretariat: Independence and Reform', in Weiss T. and Daws S., eds., *The Oxford Handbook on the United Nations,* Oxford, Oxford University Press, pp. 160–75.

Jupille J., Caporaso J. and Checkel J. (2003) 'Integrating Institutions: Rationalism, Constructivism and the Study of the European Union', *Comparative Political Studies,* Vol. 36, no. 1/2, pp. 7–41.

Karatas E. (2011) 'The Politics of Accession', in Ker-Lindsay J., Faustmann, H. and Mullen F., eds., *An Island in Europe: The EU and the Transformation of Cyprus*, Basingstoke, Palgrave Macmillan, pp. 13–42.

Keatinge P. (1986) 'Un-Equal Sovereigns: The Diplomatic Dimension of Anglo-Irish Relations', in Drudy P.J. ed., *Irish Studies 5: Ireland and Britain since 1922*, Cambridge, Cambridge University Press, pp. 139–61.

Keohane R. (1984) *After Hegemony: Cooperation and Discord in the World Political Economy*, Princeton, Princeton University Press.

Keohane R. and Martin L. (2001) 'The Promise of Institutionalist Theory', *International Security*, Vol. 20, no. 1, pp. 39–51.

Keohane R. and Nye J. (1977) *Power and Interdependence: World Politics in Transition*, Boston, Little Brown.

Ker-Lindsay J. (2005) *EU Accession and UN Peace-Making in Cyprus*, Basingstoke, Palgrave Macmillan.

Ker-Lindsay J. (2009) 'From Autonomy to Independence: The Evolution of International Thinking on Kosovo, 1998–2005', *Journal of Balkan and Near Eastern Studies*, Vol. 11, no. 2, pp. 141–56.

Ker-Lindsay J. (2009) 'United Nations Peace-Making in Cyprus: From Mediation to Arbitration and Beyond', in Diez T. and Tocci N., eds., *Cyprus: A Conflict at the Crossroads*, Manchester, Manchester University Press, pp. 147–65.

Kerr M. (2009) 'A Culture of Power-Sharing', in Taylor R. ed. *Consociational Theory: McGarry and O'Leary and the Northern Ireland Conflict*, London, Routledge, pp. 206–20.

Keukeleire S. and McNaughton J. (2008) *The Foreign Policy of the European Union*, Basingstoke, Palgrave Macmillan.

King I. and Mason W. (2006) *Peace at Price: How the World Failed Kosovo*, London, Hurst & Co.

Knoll B. (2005) 'From Bench-Marking to Final Status? Kosovo and the Problem of an International Administration's Open-Ended Mandate', *European Journal of International Law*, Vol. 16, no. 4, pp. 637–60.

Koremenos B., Lipson C. and Snidal D. (2001) 'The Rational Design of International Institutions', *International Organization*, Vol. 55, Autumn, pp. 761–99.

Krasner S. (1983) *International Regimes*, Princeton, Princeton University Press.

Kuperman A. (2008) 'The Moral Hazard of Humanitarian Intervention: Lessons from the Balkans', *International Studies Quarterly*, Vol. 52, no. 1, pp. 49–80.

Laffan B. (2003) *Ireland, Britain, Northern Ireland and the European Dimension*, Institute for British-Irish Studies, *Working Paper*, no. 27.

Laffan B. and O'Mahony J. (2008) *Ireland and the European Union*, Manchester, Manchester University Press.

Laffan B. and O'Mahony J. (2008) *Ireland and the European Union*, Manchester, Manchester University Press.

Laffan B. and Payne D. (2001) *Creating Living Institutions: EU Cross-Border Co-operation after the Good Friday Agreement*, Dublin, Institute for British-Irish Studies, University College Dublin.

Laffan B., Smith M. and O'Donnell R. (1999) *Europe's Experimental Union. Rethinking Integration*, London, Routledge.

Lake D. and Rothchild D. (1996) 'Containing Fear: The Origins and Management of Ethnic Conflict', *International Security*, Vol. 21, no. 2, pp. 41–75.

Lederach J.P. (1997) *Building Peace: Sustainable Reconciliation in Divided Societies*, Washington DC, United States Institute of Peace.

Le Roy Bennett A. and Oliver J.K. (2001) *International Organizations: Principles and Issues*, New Jersey, Prentice-Hall.

Lewis J. (2013) 'The Council of the European Union and the European Council', in Cini M. and Borragan P.S., eds., *European Union Politics*, Oxford, Oxford University Press, pp. 142–59.

Lindberg S. and Scheingold L. (1970) *Europe's Would-be Polity: Patterns of the Change in the European Community*, Englewood, Prentice-Hall.

Luck E. (2003) 'Reforming the UN: lessons from a history in progress', *International Relations Studies and the United Nations Occasional Papers* 2003 No. 1.

Malone D.M. (2008) 'Security Council', in Weiss T. and Daws S., eds., *The Oxford Handbook on the United Nations*, Oxford, Oxford University Press, pp. 117–36.

Mani R. (2008) 'Peaceful Settlement of Disputes and Conflict Prevention', in Weiss T. and Daws S., eds., *The Oxford Handbook on the United Nations*, Oxford, Oxford University Press, pp.300–323.

Manners I. (2006) 'Normative Power Europe Reconsidered: Beyond the Crossroads', *Journal of European Public Policy*, Vol. 13, no. 2, pp. 182–99.

Mansergh M. (2002) 'Cross-Border Bodies and the North-South Relationship-Laying the Groundwork', Institute for British-Irish Studies', (IBIS) *Working Paper*, no. 12, Dublin, IBIS, University College Dublin.

Marsh S. and Mackenstein H. (2005) *The International Relations of the European Union*, Harlow Essex, Pearson and Longman.

Martins L. (1992) *Coercive Cooperation: Explaining Multiateral Economic Sanctions*, Princeton, Princeton University Press.

Martins L. and Simmon B. (2013) 'International Organisations and Institutions', in Carlnaes W., Risse T. and Simmons B., eds., *Handbook of International Relations*, 2nd edition, London/California, Sage, pp. 326–52.

McGarry J. and O'Leary B. (2003) *Consociational Engagements*, Oxford, Oxford University Press.

Mearsheimer J. (1994) 'The False Promise of International Institutions' *International Security*, Vol. 19, no. 3 (Winter 1994/1995), pp. 5–49.

Meehan E. (2000) 'Britain's Irish Question: Britain's European Question: British-Irish Relations in the Context of the European Union and the Belfast Agreement', *Review of International Studies*, Vol. 26, no. 1, pp. 83–97.

Merlingen M. and Ostrauskaite (2006) *European Union Peacebuilding and Policing*, London, Routledge.

Mingst K. and Karns M. (2007) *The United Nations in the 21st Century*, Colorado, Westview.

Monnet J. (1978) *Memoirs*, London, Methuen.

Moravcsik A. (1999) 'A New Statecraft? Supranational Entrepreneurs and International Cooperation', *International Organization*, Vol. 53, no. 2, Spring, pp. 267–306.

Moravcsik A. (2009) 'Europe: The Quiet Superpower', *French Politics*, Vol. 7, no. 3–4, pp. 403–22.

Muller P. (2012) *EU Foreign Policymaking and the Middle East Conflict*, London, Routledge.

Murray G. (1998) *John Hume and the SDLP*, Dublin, Irish Academic Press.

Newman E. (2001) 'The Most Impossible Job in the World: The Secretary-General and Cyprus', in Richmond O. and Ker-Lindsay J., eds., *The Work of the UN in Cyprus*, Basingstoke, Palgrave Macmillan, pp. 127–44.

Newman E. (2008) 'Secretary-General', in Malone D.M., ed. *The Security Council: From the Cold War to the 21st Century*, Boulder, Lynne Reiner, pp. 175–93.

Niemann A. and Schmitter P. (2009) 'Neo-functionalism', in Diez T. and Wiener A. *European Integration Theory*, Oxford, Oxford University Press, pp. 45–67.

Nugent N. (2002) *The European Commission*, Basingstoke, Palgrave Macmillan.

O'Duffy B. (2007) *British-Irish Relations and Northern Ireland: From Violent Politics to Conflict Regulation*, Dublin and Portland OR, Irish Academic Press.

Official Journal of the European Union (2003) Vol. 46, September 23, L236.

O'Leary B. and McGarry J. (1993) *The Politics of Antagonism*, London, Athlone Press.

O'Leary B. (2004) 'The Limits to Coercive Consociationalism in Northern Ireland', in O'Leary B. and McGarry J. eds., *Consociational Engagements*, Oxford, OUP, pp. 97–132.

Pace M. (2005) 'EU Policy-Making Towards Border Conflict' *Working Papers Series in EU Border Conflicts Studies*, June 15.

Painter M. and Yee W-H (2011) 'Task Matters: A Structural-Instrumental Analysis of the Autonomy of Hong Kong Government Bodies', *The American Review of Public Administration*, Vol. 41, no. 4, pp. 395–414.

Paris R. (2004) *At Wars End: Building Peace after Civil Conflict*, Cambridge, Cambridge University Press.

Paul S.V. (2005) 'Soft-Balancing in the Age of U.S. Primacy', *International Security*, Vol. 30, no. 1, pp. 46–71.

Peck C. (2004) 'Special Representatives and the Secretary General', in Malone D.M. ed. *The Security Council: From the Cold War to the 21st Century*, Boulder, Lynne Reiner, pp. 325–41.

Perritt H.L. (2009) *The Road to Independence of Kosovo: A Chronicle of the Ahtisaari Plan*, Cambridge, Cambridge University Press.

Peterson J. and Shackleton M. (2002) *The Institutions of the European Union*, Oxford, Oxford University Press.

Phillips D.L. (2012) *Liberating Kosovo: Coercive Diplomacy and US Intervention*, Cambridge, Massachusetts/London.

Pierson P. (1998) 'The Path to European Integration: A Historical Institutionalist Analysis', in Sandholtz W. and Stone-Sweet A., eds., *European*

Integration and Supranational Governance, Oxford, Oxford University Press, pp. 27–59.

Piiparinen T. (2008) 'The Rise and Fall of Bureaucratic Rationalization: Exploring the Possibilities and Limitations of the UN Secretariat in Conflict Prevention', in *European Journal of International Relations*, Vol. 14, no. 4, p. 697–724.

Pitt D. (1986) 'Power in the UN Super-Bureaucracy: A Modern Byzantium', in Pitt D. and Weiss T., eds., *The Nature of United Nations Bureaucracies*, London/Sydney, Croom Helm.

Pollack M. (2003) *The Engines of European Integration: Delegation, Agency and Agenda Setting in the European Union*, New York, Oxford University Press.

Prantl J. (2005) 'Informal States and the UN', *International Organization*, Vol. 59, no. 3, pp. 559–92.

Pugh M. (2008) 'Peace Enforcement', in Weiss T. and Daws S. *The Oxford Handbook on the United Nations*, Oxford, Oxford University Press, pp. 370–87.

Ramsbotham O.H. Miall T. Woodhouse T. (2009) *Contemporary Conflict Resolution*, Cambridge, Polity, 2nd edition.

RFERL.org (2011) 'EU Postpones Serbia Candidacy Decision', December 11.

Reilly B. (2001) *Democracy in Divided Societies: Electoral Engineering for Conflict Management*, Cambridge, Cambridge University Press.

RIA Novosti (2008) 'Serbia Announces Results of May 11 Parliamentary Polls', May 21.

RIA Novosti (2008a) 'UN Should Restrain States Pushing Kosovo to Independence-Russia', February 15.

Rice C. (2008) *US Secretary of State, Condoleezza Rice, Statement Recognising Kosovo's Independence*, February 18, Available at: www.cbc.ca?...?story/2008/02/18/kosovo-independence.html).

Richmond O. (1998) *Mediating in Cyprus: The Cypriot Communities and the United Nations*, London, Frank Cass.

Richmond O. (2012) 'Beyond Local Ownership in the Architecture of International Peacebuilding', *Ethnopolitics*, Vol. 11, no. 4, pp. 354–76.

Rosamund B. (2013) 'Theorizing the European Union after Integration Theory', in Cini M. and Borragan P.S., eds., *European Union Politics*, Oxford, Oxford University Press, pp. 85–102.

Ruane J. and Todd J. (2011) 'Ethnicity and Religion', in Cordell K. and Wolff S., eds., *Routledge Handbook of Ethnic Conflict*, London/New York, Routledge, pp.68–78.

Rubin B.R. and Jones B.D. (2007) 'Prevention of Violent Conflict: Tasks and Challenges for the United Nations', *Global Governance*, Vol. 13, pp. 391–408.

Russia and CIS Diplomatic Panoroma (2010) 'Serbia will not Recognise Kosovo', September 14.

SET Times.com (2012) 'Agreement Reached on Kosovo's Regional Representation', February 25.

Schimmelfennig F. (2006) *International Socialization in Europe: European Organizations, Political Conditionality and Democratic Change*, Basingstoke, Palgrave Macmillan.

SEUPB (2003) *Building on Peace: Supporting Peace and Reconciliation after 2006*, Monaghan, ADM/CPA.

Shala B. (2000) 'Because Kosovars are Western, There Can Be No Homeland Without a State', in Buckley J., ed., *Kosovo: Contending Voices on Balkans Interventions*, Edrermans, Cambridge.

Simmon B and Martins L. (2001) 'International Organizations and Institutions', in Carlsnaes W., Risse T. and Simmons B., eds., *Handbook of International Relations*, Oxford, Oxford University Press.

Smith K. (2008) *European Union Foreign Policy in a Changing World*, Cambridge, Policy, 2nd edition.

Smith M.E. (1998) 'Rules, Transgovernmentalism and the Expansion of European Political Cooperation', in Sandholtz W. and Stone-Sweet A., eds., *European Integration and Supranational Governance*, Oxford, Oxford University Press, pp. 304–34.

Smith M.E. (2001) 'The Quest for Coherence: Institutional Dilemmas of External Action from Maastricht to Amsterdam', in Stone-Sweet A., Sandholtz W. and Fligstein N., eds., *The Institutionalization of Europe*, Oxford, OUP, pp. 171–94.

Stephenson, C. (2000) 'NGOs and the Principal Organs of the United Nations', in Taylor, P. and Groom. A.J. ed., *The UN*, Paul Taylor and A.J.R. Groom (eds.), *The United Nations at the Millennium: The Principal Organs* London, Continuum, pp. 271–293.

Stivachtis S. (2002) 'Greece and the Eastern Mediterranean Region: Security Considerations, the Cyprus Imperative and the EU option', in Thomas D., ed., *The European Union and the Cyprus Conflict: Modern Conflict, Postmodern Union*, Manchester, MUP, pp. 34–54.

Stone A. (1994) 'What Is a Supranational Constitution? An Essay in International Relations Theory', in *The Review of Politics*, Vol. 56, no. 3, pp. 441–474.

Stone Sweet A. and Sandholtz W. (1998) 'Integration, Supranational Governance and the Institutionalization of the European Polity', in Sandholtz W. and Stone-Sweet A., eds., *European Integration and Supranational Governance*, Oxford, Oxford University Press, pp. 1–27.

Stone Sweet A. and Sandholtz W. (2011) 'Neo-Functionalism and Supranational Governance', available at: http://scienzepolitiche.unical. it/bacheca/archivio/materiale/1821/OPE%202010-2011/neofunction alim%20and%20suprnational%20governance.pdf, November 12, 2013

Tannam E. (1997) 'The European Commission and the Conflict in Northern Ireland: A Supranational role?' *Cambridge Review of International Affairs*, Vol. 11, no. 1, pp. 8–27.

Tannam E. (1999) *Cross-Border Co-operation in the Republic of Ireland and Northern Ireland*, Basingstoke/New York, Macmillan/St Martin's Press.

Tannam E. (2001) 'Explaining the Good Friday Agreement: A Learning Process', *Government and Opposition*, Vol. 36, no. 4, pp. 493–518.

Tannam E. (2006) 'Cross-Border Co-operation between Northern Ireland and the Republic of Ireland: Neo-Functionalism Re-visited', *British Journal of Politics and International Relations*, Vol. 8, no. 2, pp. 256–76.

Tannam E. (2011) 'Explaining British-Irish Cooperation: A Rational Institutionalist Approach', *Review of International Studies*, Vol. 37, no. 3, pp. 1191–214.

Tannam E. (2012) "The European Union and Conflict Resolution: Northern Ireland, Cyprus and Bilateral Cooperation, *Government and Opposition*, Vol. 47, no. 1, pp. 47–71.

Tannam E. (2013) 'The EU's Response to the International Court of Justice's Judgement on Kosovo's Declaration of Independence', *Europe – Asia Studies*, Vol. 65, no. 5, pp. 946–64.

Thakur R. (2006) 'Humanitarian Intervention', in Weiss T. and Daws S. eds., *The Oxford Handbook on the United Nations*, Oxford, Oxford University Press, pp. 387–404.

The Australian (2004) 'Cyprus Reunion "Almost Certain" ', February 17.

Tocci N. (2008) *The EU and Conflict Resolution: Promoting Peace in the Backyard*, London, Routledge.

Tonra B. (2007) 'Conceptualizing the EU's Global Role', in Cini M. and Bourne A., eds., *Advances in European Studies*, Basingstoke, Palgrave Macmillan, pp. 117–30.

Traube J. (2007) *The Best Intentions: Kofi Annan and the UN in the Era of American World Power*, London, Bloomsbury.

Trondal J. (2010) *An Emergent European Executive Order*, Oxford, Oxford University Press.

UN (United Nations) (1992) *An Agenda for Peace, Preventive Diplomacy, Peacemaking and Peace-Keeping, Report of the Secretary-General Pursuant to the Statement Adopted by the Summit Meeting of the Security Council on January 31, 1992*, A/47/277 - S/241111 June 7, 1992.

UN (United Nations) (2006) Report of Secretary General to General Assembly, *Comprehensive Review of Governance and Oversight within the UN and Its Funds, Programmes and Specialised Agencies*, New York, UN A/60/883, July 10.

UN (United Nations) (2006) *Annan Proposes Overhaul of UN to Realign Operations from Headquarters to Field*, New York, UN News Centre, March 7.

UN (United Nations) (2013) Available at: http://www.un.org/en/peacekeeping/operations/current.shtml, accessed November 22, 2013

UN Press Release (2007) S/A, 927, 'Secretary-General Appoints Kai Eide as His Special Envoy to Undertake Comprehensive of Kosovo', June 6.

UN Report of Secretary General to General Assembly (2006) *Investing in the United Nations for a Stronger Organisation Worldwide*, New York, UN, available at: http://www.un.org/ga/president/62/issues/resolutions/a-60-692.pdf, March 7

United Nations General Assembly (2010) *Resolution to General Assembly on Request for an Advisory Opinion of the International Court of Justice on Whether the Unilateral Declaration of Independence of Kosovo Is in Accordance with International law* A/64/L.65?Rev.1, September 8.

United Nations General Assembly (2011) *Report of the Secretary-General on the Work of the Organization*, General Assembly Official Records, Sixty-Sixth session, supplement no. 1, New York, A/66/1.

UNSC (UN Security Council) (1996) Letter Dated September 24, 1996 from Chairman of the UNSC Committee Established Pursuant to Resolution 724 (1991) Concerning Yugoslavia Addressed to the President of the Security Council, Report of the Copenhagen Roundtable on UN Sanctions in the Former Yugoslavia, held at Copenhagen on June 24 and 25, 1996, UN document S/1996/776, September 24.

UNSC (UN Security Council) (1999) *Resolution 1250 (1999) Adopted by the Security Council at its 4018th Meeting, on June 29, 1999*, June 29, 1999, S/RES/1250 (1999).

UNSC (UN Security Council) (1999) *Resolution 1244*, S/RES/1244, (1999) June 10, 1999.

UNSC (UN Security Council) (2001) *UN Regulation no. 2000/9 on Constitutional Framework to Establish Provisional Institutions of Self-Government in Kosovo*, available at: http://www.assembly-kosova.org/common/docs/FrameworkPocket_ENG_Dec2002.pdf

UNSC (UN Security Council) Secretary-General (2006) *Progress Report on the Prevention of Armed Conflict: Report of the Secretary-General* (A/60/891), July 1.

UNSC (UN Security Council) (2006) Secretary-General, Letter from the UN Secretary-General Addressed to the President of the Security Council, UN Security Council Document, S/2005, 635, October 7.

UNSC (UN Security Council) (2007) S/2007/168, Letter Dated March 26, 2007 from the Secretary-General addressed to the President of the Security Council, The Comprehensive Proposal for Kosovo Status Settlement. Report of the Special Envoy of the Secretary-General on Kosovo's Future Status, March 27.

UNSC (2007) Letter Dated March 26, 2007 from the Secretary-General Addressed to the President of the Security Council Addendum Comprehensive Proposal for the Kosovo Status Settlement, available at: http://www.unosek.org/docref/Comprehensive_proposal-english.pdf

UPI Suna News Agency (2008) Letter from Ban Ki-moon to Kosovo President Fatmir Sejdiu, June 12.

Urwin D. (1995) *The Community of Europe*, London, Longman.

Urwin D. (2013) 'The European Community: From 1945 to 1985', in Cini M. and Borragan P.S., eds., *European Union Politics*, Oxford, Oxford University Press, pp. 11–26.

Vassiliou G. (2003) 'Cypriot Accession to the EU and the Solution to the Cyprus Problem', *The Brown Journal of World Affairs*, Summer/Fall, Vol. 10, no. 1, pp. 213–21.

Verhoest K., Peters G.B. Bouckaert G. and Verschuere B. (2004). 'The Study of Organizational Autonomy: A Conceptual Review', *Public Administration and Development*, Vol. 24, no. 2, pp. 101–18.

Verney S. (2009) 'From Consensus to Conflict: Changing Perceptions of the Cyprus Issue in the European Parliament 1995–2006', in Diez T. and Tocci N., eds., *Cyprus: A Conflict at the Crossroads*, Manchester, Manchester University Press, pp. 124–47.

Viemont P. (2013) 'Unrevised Transcript of Evidence Taken before Select Committee on EU External Affairs, Sub-Committee C, Inquiry on European External Action Service (EEAS)', evidence session no. 9, questions 158–179, January 22.

Waldheim K. (1985) *In the Eye of the Storm: The Memoirs of Kurt Waldheim.* London: Weidenfeld and Nicolson.

Weiss T. (2010) 'The John W. Holmes Lecture: Reinvigorating the International Civil Service', *Global Governance*, Vol. 16, pp. 39–57.

Weiss T.J. (2011) 'RtoP Alive and Well after Libya', *Ethics and International Affairs* Vol. 25, no. 3, pp. 282–97.

Weiss T.J. (2012) 'Lessons from Libya', *America, the National Catholic Review*, March 19.

Weiss T.J., Forsyth D. and Coate R. (2007) *The United Nations and Changing World Politics*, Colorado, Westview.

Whitman R. and Wolff S. (2010) 'Much Ado about Nothing? The European Neighbourhood Policy in Context', in Whitman R. and Wolff S., eds., *The European Neighbourhood Policy in Perspective: Context, Implementation and Impact*, Basingstoke, Palgrave, pp. 29–51.

Whitman R. and Juncos A. (2012) 'The Arab Spring, the Eurozone Crisis and the Neighbourhood: A Region in Flux', *Journal of Common Market Studies*, Vol. 50, Annual Review, pp. 147–61.

Williams A. (2010) 'Strategic Planning in the Executive Office of the UN Secretary-General', *Global Governance*, Vol. 16, pp. 435–49.

World Markets Research Centre (2004) 'European Commission President Visits Turkey, Urges Cyprus Settlement', January 15.

XINHUA General News Service (2004a) 'UN Special Representative Says No Plan 'B', February 17.

XINHUA General News Service (2004b) 'Britain, US Seek Quick Endorsement of Cyprus Unification Plan', April 20.

XINHUA General News Service (2007) 'Negotiations on Kosovo Status Fail after 120 days: UN Report' December 7.

XINHUA General News Service (2008a) 'UN Security Council to Meet on Kosovo, Thursday', February 13.

XINHUA General News Service (2008b) 'UN Security Council Debates Kosovo Emergency Session', February 19.

XINHUA General News Service (2008c) 'Kosovo Constitution Enters into Force', June 15.

XINHUA General News Service (2008d) 'UN Security Council Backs EU Deployment in Kosovo', November 27.

XINHUA General News Service (2008e) 'Kosovo UN Mission Chief to Leave Post This Week', June 16.

Zaum M. (2008) 'The Security Council, the General Assembly, and War: The Uniting for Peace Resolution', in Lowe V., Roberts A., Welsh, J. and Zaum D., eds., *The United Nations Security Council and War*, Oxford, Oxford University Press, pp. 154–75.

Index

Printed and bound by CPI Group (UK) Ltd, Croydon, CR0 4YY